A Moth on the Fence

A Moth on the Fence

Memoirs of Russia, Estonia, Czechoslovakia
and Western Europe

by

Nikolay Andreyev

With an Introduction, Notes and Afterword
by Catherine Andreyev

Translated by Patrick Miles

Hodgson Press

First published in Great Britain by Hodgson Press 2009

Hodgson Press
PO Box 903A
Kingston-upon-Thames
Surrey
KT1 9LY
United Kingdom

enquiries@hodgsonpress.co.uk

www.hodgsonpress.co.uk

ISBN: 978-1-906164-02-7

First published in Russian in 1996.
Second edition in Russian 2008.

Printed in Great Britain by Lightning Source Ltd.

Dedication

For Nikolay Andreyev's grandchildren:
Laura, Joe, Danny, Ben, Anna and Celia.

1.   Nikolay Yefremovich Andreyev (1908–1982).

Contents

List of Illustrations

List of Maps

Introduction

When helping Nikolay Andreyev to get the documents he needed to survive in occupied Berlin Colonel Bibikov in the French Administration likened his position to "a moth on a fence", emphasizing the extreme fragility of an individual. This phrase has been adapted as the title of these memoirs with the idea that the fence is a metaphor for history or time and that survival depends on camouflage. Nikolay Andreyev used the idea of being blown about by the winds of history a number of times. His life and those of the people around him were profoundly altered by the upheavals and cataclysms of the twentieth century: war, revolution, epidemic, economic collapse and yet the individuals concerned were powerless to affect the situation in which they were caught.

When my father was composing his memoirs, he once said to me: "It is very odd but there seems to be a pattern in events. It isn't one I understand or can explain but so many times I remained alive when others who were in a similar position and with similar abilities perished. There must be a reason why I have survived." My mother's explanation for this was that my father was never lost for words. He could always find some way of getting out of a difficulty. Even when arrested by SMERSH, the Soviet counter-espionage organization, he was able to invent a quotation from Lenin which made his interrogator stop and think and which had an impact on his subsequent fate. When I repeated what my father had said to Patrick Miles in the very last stages of polishing the translation, Patrick said much the same. "Your father was able to engage with everyone he met. He was interested in them all, even his warders and sentries in the prison, and found the good in them. The bad things were in some sense irrelevant as they will become subsumed in a greater purpose." This sense of engagement with the everyday as well as with the lofty or profound, is why these memoirs are of interest.

Nikolay Andreyev was Russian and even though he only spent the first eleven years of his life in Russia throughout his life he continued to think of himself as Russian and remained loyal to the best traditions of his country and his culture. Yet although coming from a very specific place and seeming to describe a particular era, his experience has a wider application in which many can share. He combined an excellent memory with the ability of a historian to place his experience in a wider context and of a teacher who could make things clear. Throughout his account, he retained a strong sense of the comic and ridiculous, as in his description of his arrest. The reader is well aware that this is no laughing matter and could lead to tragedy but the details of his first night in detention are both absurd and amusing. Later in life, Nikolay Andreyev was to say that good could come out of anything. When I asked if this applied to his arrest, he replied: "Yes in that too. At that time there were three women in Prague who hoped that I would marry them, I had no intention of marrying any of them and my arrest dealt neatly with what could have been a complicated situation!" This sense of amusement was also combined with an acute sense of realism. My father emerged from prison psychologically unscathed. He explained this by the fact that he only needed to worry about his mother, and he knew that she was intelligent and resourceful. If he had had to worry about a wife and small children, he thought that this might have destroyed him. As it was he could concentrate on his own situation and that helped in keeping some sense of sanity.

The richness and variety of the Russian is one of the striking features of the original. This text was dictated, never composed sitting at a desk. Those who knew him will testify that this was the way in which my father spoke and lectured.[1] He never wrote out his lectures but would deliver them in complete sentences. Digressions abounded but would in the end be seen to have a bearing on a strong analytical argument. Nikolay Andreyev was a master stylist. He had great oratorical gifts which would frequently be combined with parody and the sense of the comic in order both to deflate himself and to convey atmosphere. This is all very apparent in the memoirs. He spoke in complete sentences of high literary Russian. This could change into the vernacular or combine with mimicry to convey essential characteristics of those with whom he was conversing or whom he was describing. All of this contrasts clearly and strikingly with his written style, particularly of serious pieces of research, where the spoken digressions are condensed into a clear analytical framework. The fact that the memoirs are the spoken word creates a sense of immediacy. Those who knew him can hear him speaking and it is very fortunate that Patrick Miles knew my father and could appreciate this aspect of the text. Patrick has also been most successful in reproducing the richness and variety of the language.

The process of creating this text has been long and unusual. In 1978, my father had an operation for cataract which was unsuccessful. The retina was diseased, and combined with glaucoma this meant he was unable to read for a time and even when things improved he continued to have difficulty reading footnotes – which for a scholar who hoped to write in his retirement was a tragedy. However, when blindness prevented him from reading, my mother took my younger brother's tape recorder and my father recorded his memoirs of childhood in Russia, youth in Estonia, university and academic career in Prague, his imprisonment for two years by the Soviet authorities, his release and

1   Memoir by Dr Tony Stokes in the author's archive and G. Hosking, A. Pyman and
    C. Brancovan, 'Record of a Testimonial Evening to the memory of N. Andreyev' in
    Transactions of the Association of Russian American Scholars in the USA, vol XVI (1983),
    pp.361-373.

eventual departure for Britain. In the first instance my father began recording his memoirs for his family. However, quite quickly the recording of the memoirs progressed from simply a family reminiscence for his children to something more complex. It was a record of the time as he experienced it by someone who was aware that certain episodes might not be known or that the record had been altered. As he recorded his memories so he would elaborate and change things as he recalled other details or episodes.

All of this was shaped by his scholarly experience and understanding. He was a historian of medieval Russia and the chapters of his memoirs detailing his research at the Pskov-Pechery monastery show the thought processes, methods and problems of his research. He was also deeply interested in Russian literature, was one of the earliest critics of Vladimir Nabokov for example, and was deeply interested in the debate about the development of Russian literature in emigration and its interaction with literature in the Soviet Union. He published widely on these subjects. His interests in the culture of the Russian emigration meant that he was well placed to become a historian and chronicler of the emigration long before it was recognized as an important subject for scholarly discussion. Most of his life, moreover, took place when the USSR was a very dominant power. His childhood and youth were all determined by what was happening in the Soviet Union. When he came to Cambridge, he found very few people who understood his views or sympathized with him. During the Second World War, British public opinion had been sympathetic to the USSR as a war-time ally. With the onset of the Cold War, these attitudes shifted and polarized but had little room for émigrés who continued to love their country even though they abhorred the government. Throughout his account there is a sense that he is explaining the nature of Russian culture to those who are not fully aware of its richness and complexity. At the same time, he is not an apologist, it is simply that he knows about aspects which have been ignored and forgotten and which amplify the picture.

After his death in 1982, the tapes were transcribed and then transferred to computer. None of this was straightforward as this was still in the early days of such technology when computing in Cyrillic was far from the norm. My mother's determination had much to do with the resulting success. Grateful thanks are also due to the late Catherine Cooke for the loan of a computer and to Aleksei whose understanding of software is unparalleled. The resultant text was voluminous and my mother, with advice from the late Dr Militsa Greene who had known my father in the Baltic States and who taught at Edinburgh University, carried out the first stage of editing, removing hesitations, repetitions, interpolations from the family and the like. After my mother's death, I was extremely fortunate to meet Dr Irina Belobrovtseva of Tallinn University, who was on a Soros scholarship to Oxford University and who was interested in the history of the Russian emigration. Her husband ran a Russian publishing company and they took on the job of publishing the memoirs in a two-volume edition which appeared in 1996. This was greeted by reviewers as a valuable contribution to our understanding of Russian émigré life in Estonia and Czechoslovakia in the inter-war period as well as a personal story.

For the English reader something a little different was required. Patrick Miles has done an excellent job translating the memoirs and his advice in the cutting and editing of the text was invaluable. The human story had to stay, with a strong story line and at the same time the impact of political events in this period and the historical dimension needed to be conveyed to the reader. A considerable amount had to be cut, particularly details of life in Estonia and Czechoslovakia. Those wishing to know more about this will have to learn Russian and return to the original! Some of the detail of my father's youthful romances, for example, has also been cut. Such detail although charming did not necessarily add to the overall story. This has meant that the resulting text has fewer digressions than the original. It is not easy to analyse how far this changes the text and certainly I can imagine my father laughing and expostulating about the way in which his image has changed in the process, but the essence of him and his story has not been altered. One of the striking qualities of the translation is how often there is a religious element. My father was religious, if frequently quite anti-clerical, and this religious belief was very important at all critical points of his life. In the original, some of the spiritual dimension tends to be hidden in the detail and is thus seemingly less dominant in the Russian text.

The memoirs were composed from memory and the detail of what Nikolay Andreyev remembered is striking. I was recently sent a long letter which my father had written from Prague to his grandparents in Torzhok in 1928. What he said to them there does not differ substantially from what he remembered fifty years later. He said that his mother's insistence that as a child he learn large quantities of poetry by heart helped to develop his memory. He also read very widely from a very early age and this also may well have had a similar function. His later experience must have had an effect on how his powers of concentration developed. My grandparents were very badly off in Tallinn and lived in one room. A large wardrobe divided the sleeping area and living area. Here there was a large table at which my grandmother gave private lessons. My father used to do his homework on the other side of the table. This must have helped him to learn how to concentrate despite all kinds of distractions, which was a notable feature of the way in which he worked in later life. When in prison, one of the things he did to remain mentally alert was to recite to himself all the poetry he knew. On his arrest, the Soviet authorities asked him about the life of the emigration in Prague. He had to write down all he knew and this writing and rewriting must have helped him to recall details in a fairly orderly way. Until he married, he never had a large personal library. He read books and then gave them away, just as in his younger days he may have borrowed books but not been able to keep them. He had the kind of mind which systematized his knowledge and experience. When the Iron Curtain fell, it was possible to consult archives which had been closed for many years. Nikolay Andreyev's memories of the Kondakov Institute were corroborated by what could be found in the archives. In this respect, therefore, the memoirs are a useful historical source.

The decision to finish his account when he left for Cambridge University in 1948 was a conscious one. Nikolay Andreyev said that his early life in Russia, Estonia and Czechoslovakia was in the past and he could, to some extent, be objective about it. His life in England was not over. Many of the people whom he would need to discuss were still alive and he did not feel he could be objective about this. He was grateful for what had happened in Britain, his personal life had been happy. Professionally he was more equivocal. His appointment to Cambridge University had extracted him from Europe and a very problematic future. Yet at the same time, he was never allowed to have the position in Britain in which his abilities and interests could be properly developed. Overall, his view was that discretion was probably wiser, otherwise he and his heirs would be involved in a great many libel suits.

Catherine Andreyev, Oxford 2009

Translator's Note

As explained, this translation has been made from a transcription of tape recordings of Nikolay Andreyev speaking spontaneously; but as those who heard him lecture without a script can vouch, he was able to extemporize perfectly formed literary Russian sentences that could have gone straight into print. Much of the original text of these memoirs reads like that. However, much of it is also manifestly *viva voce* and colloquial. I have tried to retain this mixture of the 'written' and the oral through my choice of vocabulary and punctuation.

I am extremely grateful to Dr Peter Squire for his advice concerning certain Soviet prison terms, and to Richard Davies and *Baedeker's Russia 1914* for repeated consultation.

A simplified form of the BGN/PCGN system has been used to transliterate Russian words, except where there are already accepted English versions (e.g. Tchaikovsky, Beria), or the owners of names used particular forms in emigration, or the context requires a more phonetic rendering (e.g. 'Peetyer', 'Droog'). Some essentially Russian concepts (e.g. *mama, papa, povoynik, etap*) have been kept in transliterated form, but where necessary English explanations are given the first time they occur. The form 'Pechery' has been used in references to the monastery, as that is how it is spelt in Nikolay Andreyev's well-known articles on the subject. Academic citations are transliterated according to the Library of Congress System.

Dates before February 1918 are given 'Old Style' with western equivalents in square brackets; all dates from February 1918 are western style.

Patrick Miles

Map 1. Europe covering most of the places mentioned in the book.

A Moth on the Fence

Part I: Russia

Map 2. Russia.

20ᵒ Іюля 1905года.

В. Соловьевъ   Торжокъ.

2.   Yefrem Andreyev (standing) with some of his brothers
and a friend in 1905.

1

Early Childhood

Whenever I asked my mother why she and my father got married, she replied: 'What strange questions you ask! We loved each other, that's all. We loved each other with a great love which, as you can see, has lasted all these years.'

There were two things, she explained, that had struck her about my father. The first was his gentleness. He wished ill to no-one. She said this was unusual amongst the young people she knew at the time, who were more self-centred and go-getting. Yefrem Nikolayevich was simply a good man with a very human soul. The second thing was his truthfulness and modesty. For instance, she had been deeply moved by his account of taking part in 'Bloody Sunday' in St Petersburg on 9 [22] January 1905.

My father was not a political activist, but he lived amongst people who were interested in politics and Russia's future. When the priest Father Gapon started his movement, it was welcomed by many working people. My father, who knew the movement well, always denied that it had any hidden political agenda. He believed that Gapon really did want to organize the workers in a way that would encourage government circles to satisfy some of the workers' needs, such as their children's education and raising their living standards – things that any government should be addressing. Gapon thought that since he could not achieve this by writing to ministers, perhaps he should try a 'people's petition' to the Emperor. This would get into the newspapers and the government would have to do something about it.

Various mass meetings were held and my father was twice elected chairman of them. He said he was chosen precisely for his political innocence: he was simply a young man with a pleasant face, who obviously did not understand what this was all about. Consequently, he chaired the meetings but the comrades sitting next to him told him what to say and do. It was decided that it would be a peaceful demonstration, but they had to attempt to reach the Winter Palace where, singing 'O Lord Save Thy People' and 'God Save the Tsar', they would deliver the petition, someone would accept it, and then they would all go home.

On the day itself he was processing with a column of people seven or nine across from the islands to the Winter Palace. They were carrying a portrait of the Tsar, were walking along in a very orderly fashion, there were no incidents, and the mood was totally peaceful. As they passed one of the ministries close to Palace Square, they saw a fat door-keeper standing in the porchway. In Russia door-keepers were usually retired NCOs and naval petty officers. This door-keeper berated the demonstrators for roaming the streets instead of being at church and shouted: 'You wait! You'll cop it now!' However, as instructed the demonstrators did not react, and marched on.

Very soon the column halted, as it had reached the entrance to the square, which was blocked by rows of soldiers. To right and left were detachments of Cossacks. An officer ordered the crowd to disperse, but it linked arms in a solid front and kept moving forwards. Then a battle-alarm sounded, the officer again shouted something, but the procession inched forwards. The soldiers took aim, and when the officer ordered 'Fire!' the crowd lay down as the organizers had directed it to.

Of course, the soldiers fired over the heads of the demonstrators and ironically the door-keeper was killed outright. The second volley was aimed at their feet. There were wounded, and the crowd broke up. My father ran with them and jumped over the wall of a church to escape the Cossacks, who were lashing out at people with whips. At this moment, he realized he had lost one of his galoshes. It was a new pair, he was sorry to lose one, so he did something mad: he jumped back over the wall to look for it! He found it, put it on, and went home.

He personally was not hurt, but nearly 70 people died and about 150 were wounded. *Why* was it perpetrated? All it did was stoke the passions; it solved nothing. Goodness knows who the administrative clot was who ordered it. Afterwards the whole of Russia, Europe and the world was disgusted with the Tsarist government for firing on its own people. Whenever my father recounted it, he stressed that the procession was peaceful and did not have the slightest intention of causing political or any other harm. But he added that he considered himself then and afterwards a politically immature person, and regretted that when he chaired these meetings he did not understand that he was exposing people to mortal danger. He criticized and condemned himself as much as others.

And it was this self-criticism, the way he told the story without the least self-advertisement, that appealed to my future mother. She felt he had an amazingly pure heart. He was indeed a man of absolute spiritual clarity and honesty, he was completely devoid of egotism, and he never allowed himself to offend people, although other people took advantage of him terribly.

Both of my parents were born at Torzhok in Tver province. My mother knew all the members of the large Andreyev family (there were a total of eleven children) before she met my father, but as soon as she did meet him their fate was decided. They married in 1906.

By common consent, my mother was good-looking. Curiously enough, she had a rather Greek profile. She always dressed with taste, very simply, and did not believe in wearing jewellery. She had some jewels – she was given a lot in her time – but she didn't wear them, because she believed that a teacher should not display a liking for such fripperies to other people. She was obsessed with cleanliness. We children were washed all over once a day, she herself had a bath twice a day, and she believed that women should wash three times a day. In this respect she was extremely demanding towards her family and anyone who lived with us.

My father was also pretty good-looking, and at one time reminded you of the writer Leonid Andreyev (no relation), who was a literary idol of the times. This was partly because they wore similar outfits: summer capes and white boaters were very fashionable then, and my father was always dressed like that, very elegantly. Once as he was leaving a theatre he was mobbed by a group of girl students demanding his autograph!

My father had graduated from a technical college in Tver and got a fairly well-paid job in St Petersburg in charge of the ventilation plant at some enormous distillery warehouses. Count Witte had just introduced the state monopoly on spirits and new warehouses had been built incorporating the latest technology. According to my father, this ventilation system was so well constructed that he had very few problems. In 1906, however, he paid an extended visit to Torzhok because his favourite brother, Platon, was killed by the police when they broke up a peaceful traditional celebration of May by young people, with picnics, singing and courting, which someone had denounced to the police as a political demonstration.

My mother's family were called Kvasheninnikov and her father had been a 'merchant of the first guild' carrying grain and flour. He was suddenly bankrupted in the 1880s when his brothers' IOUs, for which he stood surety, were all called in at once. As a child I used to play in his derelict coach-houses, which still had one or two old coaches in them, and I loved doing this because they smelt of leather and somehow even of horses, although by then he had not had horses for many years.

As a girl, my mother was the apple of my grandfather's eye. She was very clever. When she graduated from the local secondary school in 1900 at the age of seventeen, she caused a sensation by announcing that she was going to leave Torzhok to work as a teacher in a village school belonging to the *zemstvo*.[1]

The school was a simple peasant hut with a large, light classroom and behind the partition her living-quarters. She taught three classes at once. The children were generally well-behaved, not at all hostile to their teacher, but listened to her at first with amazement and then increasing excitement – my *mama* always spoke very clearly and knew how to hold their attention. But for some time she was not sure what their parents thought of her. When she passed the peasant women in the street, they would bow, but the peasant men would just look at her sullenly and walk on.

One day during lessons a dozen male peasants turned up in the break and asked to speak to her. They had very long faces.

'How can I help you?' she asked.

'We want you to tell us what you're a-teaching our children.'

'I am teaching them what I'm supposed to teach them, what is in the school curriculum, what they have to learn by the spring when they take their exams.'

'Ah but what – that's what we want to know.'

This put my mother on the spot. So she said to them:

'Well, if you want to find out, come into the classroom, sit at the back, and listen!'

The peasants came in, and my mother started teaching. One class was doing Russian grammar, another sums, and the third something in geography. The peasants listened with rapt attention. At the end, they said: 'Please miss, schoolmarm, can we come here again?' 'Certainly,' she replied.

They came for the rest of the week. On one occasion a peasant smashed his son's face into the top of his desk because his son could not answer a question, and my mother had to reason with him and explain that he could not do that, she was in charge here, and the child was simply tired. The peasants were delighted by the lessons and the 'dissolving view' shows she gave in the evenings.[2] When

---

1   A *zemstvo* was a local assembly which was a body of provincial self-government in Russia 1864-1917. Many developed a liberal character and their members became an important part of the Constitutional Democratic Party (Cadet) formed in 1905 (see page 20). Tver province, where N.E. Andreyev (senior) had been secretary to the *zemstvo* (see page 15), was particularly known for its liberal policies and attitudes.

2   Pictures projected onto a screen and fading one into another.

my mother left after three years, they had a farewell service said for her by the local priest – who had spent all his time denouncing her to the authorities.

When my father got married, he decided to give up his job and become a teacher like my mother. The particular reason was that since he worked on site and could buy alcohol at a discount, he was drinking a lot whether he wanted to or not, especially on Saturdays, when the workers got their pay and invited him for a tipple, which for various reasons he could not refuse. So every Saturday he came home tight! After a year's hard work as an external student, my father got his teaching certificate. My parents then accepted an offer to work as a couple in a totally new area of education: the fight against juvenile delinquency.

Before the First World War, as a result of the growth of the towns and the proletariat, every year 10-12,000 children in Russia ended up on the streets and turned to crime. The new way of dealing with this was not to submit these young criminals to the usual punishments of the penal system, but to find ways of influencing them that would prevent them from reoffending. By the early nineteen-hundreds, as part of the growing movement among Russian lawyers towards 'humane solutions' in sentencing, a group of them had decided to concentrate on fighting child crime through what was known as 'work education'.

The leading lights were the 'three Nikolays' (Kagantsev, Shmeman, and Okunev) backed up by famous psychologists like Bekhterev and Lesgaft. The psychologists showed that most crimes occurred not because the children were 'bad', but because they did not have enough to do and turned to stealing for the thrill of it, or were exploited by adult criminals. It was decided, then, that if a young offender reoffended within a couple of years a juvenile court would send him to an institution – a colony – where he would be taught the standard primary or secondary subjects, but also learn a trade. The main such institution was the agricultural colony and training school at Rzhevka, just outside St Petersburg. It was headed by Mikhail Bekleshov, whose name is synonymous with the whole 'work-education' movement. Bekleshov was keen to get young teachers who were not stuck in their ways and my parents started there in February 1907.

It was as little like a prison as possible. The boys lived in groups of about thirty. They were not dressed like prisoners, but wore a school uniform consisting of dark-blue smock, long trousers, high boots, and a cap with a badge. There were no barred windows or guard-dogs. Each group had an 'usher', who slept in the same dormitory. He was usually an ex-soldier. His role was a passive one – he was there basically to ensure things did not get out of hand. At the head of each group was a trained teacher, an educator.

The day began with reveille, followed by prayers, breakfast, lessons, after lunch there would be an hour of games, then they would work in the workshops for several hours. The principle was on no account to give a boy time to daydream and plan crime. He was forever occupied in varied and interesting ways: in the evening there was choral singing, they rehearsed plays, they made things with their hands, there were 'dissolving view' shows, everything was very carefully thought out. Gymnastic displays were also very popular.

The family into which I was born shared a fundamental feature of the morality of the Russian intelligentsia. They were innately well-meaning towards people and treated everyone the same regardless of rank. It was assumed that people are basically good. If people did things that were bad, you should not respond by annihilating them, but try to put them right. In this sense, we belonged to the working intelligentsia that served not governments, or systems, but what one might call national unity. We tried to find good everywhere. 'Ideologically' this took the following form. Whenever I asked my mother what I should be, what she would like to see me become, she answered simply and persuasively: 'A human being – a human being in the good sense in which we have always understood this high calling. What career you choose, how you earn your living, is a different matter. But you must try to be a human being, by which I mean express those kind feelings found in Christian teaching, which tells us that man is made in the image of God.' Whenever she elaborated on this, it was to show that a human being should be moral, kind, honest, and not only enjoy life himself but 'live and let live'. My mother's idea of a 'human being' was compounded of simple truths like that.

I was born in my parents' flat at the colony on 28 February [13 March] 1908. The boys were very kind to me, but I had another friend as well: a St Bernard called Polkan, who belonged to the Principal, Bekleshov. Polkan was gigantic and very clever. When I was left with him he was instructed not to let me crawl off my rug, so when I reached the edge he would grab the bottom of my woolly and very carefully pull me back. My parents said it was so amazing it could have become a circus-act!

Once, when my parents were away in St Petersburg for the day, there was a fire in a workshop next door. The houses were wooden, so there was always a danger of fire spreading quickly and the firemen ordered everything to be taken out of our flat. Who would do it? The boys from my father's group jumped to and carried me out as well, and the most touching thing was that they even brought out my special sweet rusks without eating a single one. My nanny was particularly impressed by this. 'They are only boys,' she said. 'They too like rusks, don't they?' So she baked them a really tasty pie. I mention this incident to show how good the human relations were there, in the colony.

I can remember things more or less continuously from my fourth birthday. I was given a toy hussar's uniform, which I had been wanting for ages and later adapted for my teddy bear and then for my sister Tanya. It consisted of a wonderful hat, a cardboard breastplate that did up round the neck, and a shiny sabre in a scabbard. I was happy. It was a frosty but sunny day at the end of February Old Style, I was sitting by the window next to my father's desk, the whole room had been polished as usual, everything was gleaming. Outside it was cold, despite the sun, but here there was such heavenly warmth from the tiled stove that heated all four rooms. I looked out of the window, I saw the snowdrifts sparkling in the sun, and some sparrows hopping about making a commotion. They had eaten everything on the tray fixed to the window, but a sparrow suddenly flew up and started drinking water from one of the jars, throwing his head back and looking about him. The garden outside was deep in snow, but the main pathway had been cleared and the wooden sidewalk to the house was sprinkled with sand.

My parents used to say that I developed my passion for reading whilst I was still in my pram. Apparently what I most liked doing there was taking a newspaper and tearing it into small pieces. All my childminders used this to keep me quiet, although my mother disapproved because I got covered in printer's ink. I think I thought: *mama, papa,* and Nanny, and all my uncles when they visit, read things, so why shouldn't I? I wanted to read very much. I started at five and by the age of six I was reading everything I could get my hands on. I read newspapers. I didn't understand everything, but I could certainly make out the headlines and find what was where. My father used to say: 'He's going to be an editor!'

I do not remember the brother who died in the summer of 1910 aged less than one. I don't really remember my grandfather Aleksandr Yefimovich Kvasheninnikov either, although I can feel his tickly beard on my cheek and lips when I look at his photograph. He died in 1910 when I was two and my sister had not yet been born. I was aware that I was my parents' only child. And I loved them very much and my Nanny, and I prayed very hard for almighty God to make them live for ever and let them stay with me for ever.

Strangely, then, my very first intelligent memory is associated with a 'metaphysical problem' – immortality. Only now, as I am dictating these memoirs, have I realized that God heard my prayer and granted it, but in a slightly different sense. I asked Him to make them live for ever, but He has made my memories of them live for ever. I see my parents as young as they

were, smiling, full of concern for me, their firstborn, and I can see my dear
Nanny, who told me wonderful stories and looked after me so well. All of these
memories I have kept intact all my long life, they are always with me. Sceptics,
of course, will say that it is make-believe, but for me this is the actual feeling
of immortality. I am never alone in the world, because my parents and Nanny
never leave me – my child's prayer was answered.

2

Torzhok, Town of my Forefathers

In 1914, when I was six and my sister Tanya two, we all went to visit our
relations in Torzhok for two months, Nanny included.

For reasons of economy, we travelled third class. But it was the famous
Nikolayevsky railway, so the carriages were clean and spacious, everything
was shining, and the attendants were very polite. Because our group included
children, we were given a whole compartment to ourselves. We caught an
early train from St Petersburg, arrived in Likhoslavl five or six hours later, and
changed there for Torzhok.

To begin with we stayed with my mother's mother. As we rolled up to her
houses in two barouches with rubber tyres, she came running out streaming
tears of joy, followed by the servants, and everyone kissed each other, took us
indoors and set about wiping the dirt off us and washing us, after which we had
a splendid tea with doughnuts, Tver spiced cakes, and all sorts of things that I
did not generally see at home in Petersburg. It was interesting, pleasant, and
scrumptious.

We were to stay in the stone house, which my grandmother had set aside
for us. For tea-drinking and meals we went to my grandmother in her wooden
house, since she had servants; but Nanny, who had previously worked for my
grandmother, naturally helped with everything too.

I ran through the courtyards and checked out the coach-houses. Yes, they
still smelt of leather, and all the buildings were so solidly built you could tell my
grandfather had been a merchant 'of the first guild'! But they were all empty…

Between the stables was a path into the garden, which was wonderful: huge,
long, with a tall fence on two sides and a sheer drop at the open far end. It had
everything. There was an arbour, a bath-house (*de rigueur* in these country
towns), and rows of bushes planted by my grandfather and now taller than me:
currants, raspberries, gooseberries, superb cucumbers, hot-frames everywhere,
all maintained by my grandmother and a man who came in two or three times
a week.

The next day we went to visit my grandfather Nikolay Yefremovich and grandmother Yevdokiya Platonovna. They lived in a house with a mezzanine on the other side of the river Tvertsa. As at my other grandmother's, everything was sparkling. It was amazing how clean they managed to keep these houses, despite the fact that they had no expensive parquet flooring, only painted boards. There were druggets all over the place, mind you, which they were always changing, washing, or beating out. As was then the custom, the sitting-room was full of flowers. Everything was on a more modest scale than at my other grandmother's, but I was amazed by the number of books in my grandfather's study and the piles of newspapers everywhere: the Constitutional Democrat paper *Rech* ('Speech'), *Moskovskiye vedomosti* ('Moscow News'), and *Russkoye slovo* ('The Russian Word'). My grandfather read a lot and was deeply immersed in politics. He had retired from the *zemstvo* that year, but still worked for it as a consultant, and was therefore up to date with everything.

My grandfather had a reputation for plain speaking. After lunch, which was very talkative, we went onto the veranda to drink our coffee. Grandfather then started looking me up and down. He had looked me over earlier, of course, but had just kissed me and expressed his pleasure that we had the same Christian name and patronymic. I was dressed à la Petersburg in a sailor suit, short trousers, short socks, and sandals.

'Yevdokiya Platonovna,' he now said to his wife, 'don't you think our son Yefrem's finances must be in a bad way?'

Everyone was startled. Obviously, if the entire family had come to Torzhok for our holidays, it couldn't be true. Grandmother looked at him anxiously, because she knew that such statements always presaged an outburst of some sort. So she said:

'Nikolay Yefremovich, stop counting your sons' money for them. How do you know? Leave them alone!'

'I am leaving them alone,' he replied. 'But look at their son: what on earth is he wearing? Slippers with holes in (i.e. sandals), and they didn't have enough money to buy him proper stockings. Look at those socks: cut off in their prime!'

My father kept quiet, but my mother spoke up:

'But they are the latest St Petersburg fashion, Nikolay Yefremovich, and we wanted you to see it…'

'Ridiculous nonsense! Either go barefoot or, if you have to buy slippers, buy ones without holes in. And either wear stockings that protect your legs, or wear none at all!'

This was all he said, but when we went to see him after that I always wore stockings. And I never turned up again in sandals! I think my grandfather noticed this, and appreciated it. It pleased him that his criticism had been heeded.

That summer we were invited everywhere in the town and countryside. We began, of course, with our town calls. The first was to my late grandfather's sister, Auntie Anya. She lived in her own house, wore deep mourning, and turned out to be a delightful little old lady. She had granddaughters, but no grandson, and took a liking to me as a 'serious-minded young man'. She asked my opinion about all sorts of things, and that pleased me. She had lots of icons in her rooms, some of them dark with age and showing the saints full-length. These were of Old Believer origin.[3] Unfortunately, of course, I didn't know anything about icons then, but I would give a lot to see them now.

As I was leaving Auntie Anya's, she gave me a sealed envelope. 'This is for you, dear boy,' she said. 'Make sure you don't lose it. Grow up tall and clever!' When we got home, I gave the envelope to my mother. It contained 300 roubles in three *katenka*'s as they were called, because each note had Catherine the Great's head on it. This was an enormous sum for those days.[4] 'It's quite impossible,' said my mother, and rushed back to my aunt to tell her so. 'No, it's perfectly possible, my dear, perfectly possible,' said my aunt. 'I am old, I won't live much longer, and you have this wonderful son, so this can give him a start in life.' My parents were very touched, and put most of the money in a savings account for me.

We also called on my grandfather's brother, Vasily Yefremovich Andreyev. He was a widower and a different type altogether from his brother. My grandfather liked a drink, but he made a noble ritual out of it, whereas Vasily Yefremovich did it with a lot of fuss. He had a nose of crimson hue which could be seen from a distance. 'I drink no more than other men,' he complained, 'but to look at my nose you'd think I was an alcoholic.' As soon as we arrived, he shouted: 'Malanya (the name of his half-blind old cook), what you've got there, bring it here!' And we started with some delicious pickled fungi. Even my mother, who hated men drinking, had to admit that my great-uncle had charm.

---

3   Old Believers rejected the reforms brought into the Russian Orthodox Church by Patriarch Nikon in 1652. Most of the differences were a matter of church practice and ritual. The Old Believers were heavily persecuted and not tolerated until 1905. Old Believers were often associated with more culturally conservative trends and many members of the merchant class were Old Believers.

4   According to Baedeker, 300 Roubles was worth just over £30, which would be approximately £1800 at today's prices.

What was particularly amusing about him, however, was that he was a staunch conservative, whereas my grandfather was a radical. He thundered: 'I can't stand journalists! They're all liars! They get paid to be! The only paper I read is *Novoye vremya* ('New Times')! Suvorin's got a head on him, he knows what he's writing about!' Since my father could not stand Suvorin or his newspaper, this was a delicate subject.

I only met Vasily Yefremovich once, but I have remembered him all my life. He was captivating. He kept trying to give my father a gold watch, as he owned a lot of clocks. My father kept refusing, so my uncle said to him: 'Yefrem, would you mind going out and standing in the passage?' My father was bemused, but went out and my uncle immediately grabbed the watch and put it in my pocket. 'Don't tell *papa*. It's a present from me.' So I suddenly became the possessor of a fine gold watch, which remained with me up to the Civil War. In fact for all his shouting my uncle was extremely kind, he gave alms to widows and orphans out of his pension, and actually he subscribed to other papers as well as *Novoye vremya*.

Another event of that summer which I clearly remember is when we went to see Nanny's daughter Masha. She was beautiful, had married a prosperous peasant, and the two of them wanted Nanny to go and live with them; but my nanny resisted. Possibly she did not like the peasant way of life, had grown away from it, and thought that her son-in-law just wanted her to mind the children, cook, and take the pressure off Masha. Nanny said that they had enough money to pay for home-helps from the village. 'I don't wish to be there,' she said, and would not compromise.

We travelled by train and were met by Masha with a pair of horses and a smart, sprung cart full of scented hay and with carpet on its floor – proof that as peasants they were well-off. It was a warm summer's evening. We arrived at a large village and went to a hut that seemed enormous. One third, which no-one lived in, was furnished like a town house and given to us. We ate with the peasant family in the middle area, which had a large stove and always smelt deliciously of food and freshly baked bread. We visited the third part, where they all lived, only once.

We stayed about thirty-six hours. So that Masha should not have to waste half a day driving there and back, my father hired a troika and driver for us all. This was my first experience of a troika. The horses were fabulous! There was a lead-horse and two out-runners, a proper tarantass mounted on poles, rather than a sprung cart, and we covered the eight miles to the station at top speed in high spirits.[5] In the train, Nanny repeated that she wanted to stay in the town. 'I feel at home there,' she said.

Jumping ahead, when in 1916 she had been working for us for ten years, my father said: 'we must have a word with Nanny, she can't stay with us forever, can she? We must let her go, I'm prepared to give her a monthly pension, and she can go and live with her daughter.' When he told Nanny this, she did not reply, she just walked away, and after a while my mother ran in and said: 'Nanny is weeping her eyes out in the kitchen and saying "Yefrem Nikolayevich is throwing me out, what wrong have I done him, why is he sending me packing?"' Well, we all rushed to comfort her and my father was stunned, because the last thing he wanted was to 'throw her out'. He convinced her of that and she said: 'I am not going to the country, I'll stay with you.' Then my father said: 'Very well, but what can we do to mark your anniversary? You've worked for us for ten years, and even before that you worked for the Kvasheninnikovs!' So Nanny said: 'I would like to change my name to Andreyev.' And that is what they did. My father made it all official and she actually became Olga Mikhaylovna Andreyeva.

She was a person of the old school. She had spent all her life outside her own family. She was born a peasant in 1849, but she found herself at a very early age in the 'big house'. She played with the landowner's little daughter and learned with her to read, write and count. When the serfs were emancipated, she carried on living for a while at her former master's. Then she returned to the village, but did not like it. As soon as she could, she went to look for work in Torzhok, and found it with the Kvasheninnikovs. She married, had Masha, but her husband soon died. Masha grew up and married, without particularly asking her mother's permission, so Nanny went back to the Kvasheninnikovs, where she was nanny to my mother, then to me.

She took a very strict line on the peasant question. She believed that they were better off under serfdom, because they were more frightened – not of the landowner, who was hardly ever there, but of his steward. Consequently they got drunk only four times a year: at Christmas, Easter, Whitsun and on the local saint's day. But when they were freed they started celebrating and drinking more often, every Sunday, and then even on weekdays. This theory of hers terribly offended some people, and not just my radical uncles but various historians I mentioned it to later, for instance Mark Szeftel, who commented waspishly: 'That's a completely impossible explanation of social processes.' I agree that it is not an exhaustive explanation, but it does explain my Nanny. She always

5   A tarantass was a four-wheeled, horse-drawn Russian vehicle mounted on poles.

fought off my uncles' objections with: 'You, my dear men, judge everything by books, but my knowledge comes from life, from life!'

She was always dressed neatly, very cleanly and with taste. She always wore a *povoynik*, a cloth wound round her head. When I asked her why, she said it was because she had been married but was now a widow, and in such cases women should always cover their hair. She wore glasses to read, but not when she was working in the kitchen – and she did not like people coming into the kitchen. She was a master-cook and made the most amazing dishes, especially pies and so-called *pirozhony*, which were small pies made with special dough, and the secrets of how to make them and their filling were known virtually only to the Kvasheninnikovs. The kitchen was truly her 'domain'. My mother gave her a completely free hand there and the only thing Nanny asked was that she be told two days in advance if people were coming for a meal, so that she could work out how much to buy.

She was particularly caring and respectful towards my father and considered him, as she put it, 'a man of true soul'. When I asked her what this meant, she said: 'It means, my dear boy, that he is a man whose soul talks with God.' I was puzzled: how could my father's soul talk with God? Later I understood what she meant: she considered my father a just man who tried to live in accordance with God's law, which he might not always succeed in doing, but he still tried to. All her life she treated my mother – a prominent, cultured woman, an educator and an amazing speaker – like a little girl who needed her loving Nanny's advice. My father's student brothers she treated with an almost motherly solicitude, even darning and cleaning their clothes when they came to visit, so that they could go out into the world again looking respectable!

Returning to that summer, the fateful time of mobilization was approaching. The newspapers were full of arguments about it. My grandfather got very worked up and at every meal or tea-taking he would deliver at least one speech about the political situation. I understood that most people were definitely against a war. All the *zemstvo* officials, including my grandfather, and teachers like my parents, understood what a terrible blow the war would be to the normalization of life in Russia, which it seemed was proceeding quite well. Military collapse would send convulsions through the whole of Russian society. All hopes were pinned on the wisdom of the Ministry of Foreign Affairs.

At the same time, I remember people suddenly started discussing the Emperor, Nicholas II. The only believer in absolute monarchy in our family was Nanny. She always wept whenever she talked about Alexander II's assassination, and looked with awe at portraits of the Most August Family.[6] My grandmother Liza was also a strong supporter of the monarchy, as she had grown up in a similar environment where the Tsar was venerated. But my parents were essentially members of the liberal intelligentsia and could hardly feel any devotion to the monarchy. My father always openly supported the Constitutional Democrats ('Cadets'), whom he considered the strongest intellectual force in Russia. My mother put moral truths above politics and was very doubtful about the things going on around the royal family, although she recognized that the tsarevich's haemophilia excused a lot. For me as a six-year-old who already knew a lot about Russian history, Nicholas II was the embodiment of Russia. On the other hand, my grandfather's friends openly criticized the tsar's ministers and his policies in my presence, and I once made an unusual contribution to their discussion.

Someone asked why the Tsar was hesitating so much, why didn't he just declare peace, or if he couldn't do that, declare war?

'I know why!' I exclaimed.

Everyone looked at me intrigued, and my grandmother Liza asked: 'You? What can you know?'

'I know *why*,' I said. 'It's because he has a hole in his head!'

This was an echo of the story about a samurai attacking the tsar and wounding him. Everyone was taken aback by my directness. My grandmother smoothed it over by saying:

'A hole, my dear boy, what can you mean?! If he had a hole in his head he would be ill, but he's perfectly well: he rides a horse and is smiling on all his portraits.'

Suddenly one morning I was woken by the rumbling of carts, getting closer and closer. I rushed to the window and saw long lines of them coming down the street, with peasant men and women on them weeping, wailing and shouting. The street filled with people and their noise was deafening. There was an army office on the corner and mobilization had begun.

A few hours later my father received a telegram telling him to return to Petersburg. He and I went to a service at the monastery for the last time. There was a very kind monk and a lay-brother there in charge of the communion bread,

---

6   Alexander II was assassinated in 1881 by members of Narodnaya Volya on the day that
    he signed the Loris-Melikov constitution which was a plan for a consultative assembly.
    Alexander III rescinded this plan but the question as to whether it might have evolved into
    a legislative assembly is still discussed as one of the great lost opportunities in Russian
    history.

and they always gave me a piece. The monk said: 'You are leaving? You're returning to Petersburg... Well, may God grant that you come back to us, that this war will soon be over. We don't need war, all they that take the sword shall perish with the sword...'[7]

He gave me a piece of communion bread. I did not know then that it symbolized I was leaving Torzhok for ever, saying farewell to this town of my forefathers and the diverse life that had gone on around me so peacefully and happily there.

3
The First World War Years

My father was not called up, firstly because he had poor eyesight, secondly because Bekleshov managed to bring the St Petersburg Agricultural Colony and Training School under the aegis of the central prison service, which meant that his teachers were exempt from conscription except in emergency.

The fortunes of the war fluctuated wildly, of course. There were great victories in Galicia, followed by major setbacks in Poland. We were having lunch one day when Sergey Pirozhnikov, *mama*'s brother-in-law, who also taught at the Colony, walked in unannounced and very worked up. He stopped in the middle of the room and spoke three words: 'Warsaw has fallen...' There was a terrible silence, my father stood up and left the room, he was so overcome. I must emphasize that once the war began, criticism of the Tsar subsided – everyone was yearning for a speedy, victorious conclusion. But events such as the capture of Samsonov's army at Tannenberg had a devastating impact.[8]

In the summer of 1915 my father was given a fortnight's leave and he and my mother decided to visit the monasteries on the islands of Lake Ladoga. My sister Tanya stayed behind with Nanny, but they took me with them.

The steamship along the Neva was large, with high sides and paddle-wheels. All the crew were monks. There were about 400 passengers, many of them from St Petersburg high society with parasols and fashionable clothes. Approaching where the Neva issues from Lake Ladoga, we passed Schlüsselburg. I had heard all about this town captured from the Swedes by Peter the Great, now I saw its low walls and bastions and the forbidding fortress in which, I knew, particularly dangerous state criminals were incarcerated. Then we emerged into the lake. It

---

7   The Gospel according to St Matthew 26:52.

8   General Samsonov's 2nd Army was encircled and destroyed in late August 1914 in the area of the Tannenberg Lakes in East Prussia. Samsonov committed suicide following this defeat.

amazed me: you couldn't see any shoreline, it was like being at sea. We sailed on for three or four hours, I suppose, until we reached Konevetsky monastery, and that evening I went down with tonsillitis.

I was prone to throat infections and in those days there was no way of killing a bug at source, so I often suffered. Several times I had an almost diphtheria-like quinsy and could hardly breathe.

My parents were horrified: I had a high temperature and was very ill. I was taken below. There were no cabins, so I was given a corner where I could lie down, *mama* sat beside me, and my father ran to the monastery to see if they had a doctor. They hadn't, but there was a monk who knew about pharmacy. He examined me, confirmed that it was tonsillitis, my mother knew by heart what pills I should take, so he supplied them.

'You must stay on the steamer,' he said. 'Early tomorrow morning it will set sail for Valaam. Spend the night on board whilst everyone else goes to the hotel. At Valaam there is a doctor, and a hospital if you need it.'

I had a raging temperature during the night and was fighting for breath. We sailed on. The captain had been informed, so everyone else was let off first. The monks gave us a separate room for three. This was against the rules, because usually the men were kept separate from the women. My father fetched the monk who was their doctor, he examined me, and gave me more medicine.

'O Lord, let him live,' prayed my mother as she sat beside me. 'Usually he needs a special regimen, and this is just a hotel in the middle of nowhere.'

My father was a very religious man: not only did his soul talk to God, as Nanny put it, but he was always praising God in his church singing. He went to the shrine of Saints Sergius and German at the monastery and prayed fervently. He later told me that he had prayed so hard for me to get better that his face was drenched in tears. Whilst he was there and my mother was sitting terrified beside me, she noticed what seemed like an improvement. She took my temperature and it had dropped. This was miraculous, because it was less than forty-eight hours since I fell ill and had never happened before.

My father maintained that I had got better thanks to the intercession of Sergius and German, and my parents knelt by my bed and thanked God. The next day, when the doctor came, he too was surprised, but said: 'It's the Valaam miracle-workers who helped the boy! It means he is a good child, and God wants him to stay in the world, there's something he still has to do here.'

We stayed another three days. Steamers left every other day, so we had to miss our turn and go back on a different one. By this time I could walk about on deck as though nothing had happened.

At the end of 1915 it was decided to move the colony out of St Petersburg. The gunpowder factory next to it needed more space and the decision was hastened by a colossal explosion there around seven one summer evening. How many people were killed, I don't know; hundreds if not thousands, it was said, but the details were a military secret. At ten o'clock the same evening we still saw workmen running around in total shock trying to hide. A special commission decided that the colony should move to the estate of Izvary near Volosovo station about forty-five miles south-west of Petersburg. In June 1916 we left Rzhevka for good.

The estate consisted of a fine manor house with 3000 acres of land, of which over 700 were arable. Around the house was a huge garden that blended into a park, which itself was said to merge into the forest, although I never got far enough to find out. Izvary had originally been one of the rewards Peter the Great handed out to generals who distinguished themselves, and it had changed hands many times. The house had a tower which was said to be haunted by an evil landowneress who had been murdered by her serfs. On autumn nights when the wind howled round it, you could believe this.

There were wonderful flower-beds in the garden, and coachmen often drove young horses round the park to break them in. My particular friend, Abram, once took me round it in a charabanc with a team he was training. On autumn and winter nights the park was full of mysterious and frightening sounds. It had lots of ponds in it, which had elegant bridges across them. Some ponds were as big as lakes, and trout were bred in them and the ditches connecting them. The estate sold these fish commercially and one of its main customers was the famous delicatessen store Yeliseyev's in Petersburg.

The estate produced a huge amount of milk and butter. It had over 120 head of cattle, which were kept in palatial stalls. There were large stables with dozens of excellent working horses, and a superb manorial stable for the Orlov Trotters which came with the estate.[9] I simply worshipped these horses. One of them was called Orlik, a very intelligent horse. If we went out with him in a droshky or charabanc, the coachman would even give me the reins, and then I was in seventh heaven.

Christmas 1916 was very special for us children, as we were celebrating it in our new home built specially for us on the Izvary estate.

---

9   A breed of horse originated by Count Orlov in 1777 and famous for its trotting speed.

The snowdrifts were huge. We played at being Jules Verne's Captain Hatteras on his extraordinary journey. We skied quite a long way from home over the fields. We built snow fortresses.

The Christmas tree was put up in my father's study. As was the custom, it was unveiled only on Christmas Day; Christmas Eve was kept for religious observance. I was just as determined to fast until the first star appeared as everyone else, but I remember it being agony. I managed it, however, and was the first to shout 'The star's appeared!', and ran to Nanny, who gave me some delicious rice kasha with raisins in. I was not allowed into my father's study, although I knew very well that there was nothing 'miraculous' about the arrival of the Christmas tree, that it was put up by *mama* and *papa* who hung it with all kinds of decorations that we ourselves had made. But Tanechka, who was four years younger, believed in it utterly, and the whole 'mystery' of the approaching festival only became clear to her on Christmas Day, when Grandfather Frost visited us and brought us presents in a stocking.

We were completely taken over by the spirit of Christmas. But then so were the boys in the boarding houses which my father was in charge of (he was now assistant principal to Bekleshov). They too had enormous Christmas trees, and there was a massive programme of preparations for Christmas, because like many other teachers my parents believed Christmas should be celebrated in a special way.

Within the 'families' A, B, C etc the boys were divided into age groups of ten to fourteen, fourteen to sixteen, and sixteen to eighteen, and the teachers tried to show them that the great Orthodox festival of Christmas was very important for those who called themselves Christians, because the Christian era of civilization began with Christ's birth. From the darkness of paganism mankind was climbing towards the heights of idealism; with Christianity came the concept of sin, the desire to make oneself better, and a finer sense of morality. These values were taught in R.E. at the school and formed the background to its educational work, but at Christmas everyone tried to convey that it was first and foremost a festival of joy, of childlike joy, and that all the children should be happy.

For many weeks in advance, the recreation hall of the colony was given over to making decorations in the shape of birds, animals, chains and so forth, and cribs with pictures painted on their walls and the stable, Mary, the newborn babe in a manger, and the magi, lit up with candle-stubs. Using paper of different colours, they also made large murals, often illustrating Russian fairytales. The groups vied with each other in their inventiveness.

In addition, it was decided to stage an evening of entertainment which anyone could come to, not just the boys and their teachers. This meant, for instance, the farm-workers and the many people who worked on the power station that supplied the farm with electricity. There was a hospital for wounded soldiers close by and many of them wanted to attend. The commanding officer of a company of bicyclists – trained for intelligence-gathering on bikes and skis – also came to see my father and asked if eighty-five of them could be let in. Finally, there were young people from the villages around. So it was decided to hold the evening twice, on 23 December [5 January] and Christmas Day [7 January] itself; theatrical presentations were banned by law on Christmas Eve, because of the solemn all-night vigil.

The entertainment consisted of *tableaux vivants*, dramatic dialogues, poetry, choral pieces, stage adaptations of fables, and even a mime of the fairytale in which a little boy is freezing to death in the forest and is rescued by Grandfather Frost. It was all vivid, unpretentious and endearing because everyone put such enthusiasm into it. The school had an excellent Russian choir, thanks largely to my father, but also to other musically gifted teachers, including the string-player Konstantin Verezhnikov, who subsequently became famous in the emigration. I myself, although only eight, was coached by my mother to declaim an historical poem by Yakov Polonsky about King Kazimir of Poland.

Everything that was done for this show was done quite consciously to offset the martial mood which by December 1916 was weighing heavily. Nevertheless, I remember how united everyone was in singing 'God Save the Tsar'. True, my father was very good at training his choirs to sing it sensitively, but everyone present sang it as though they believed it, from the boys themselves and the bicyclists standing at attention, to the wounded, the village lads, and the Polish doctor from the hospital. My poem, describing how Kazimir's eyes were opened to the misery of his subjects and he then did something about it, also went down very well. The school chaplain approved of it, the peasants in uniform approved of it, even the local police officer approved of it. Yet it was hardly revolutionary: it praised an absolute monarch who responded in an enlightened way to his people. I think this aspect of my simple memories of the last big Christmas celebration that I experienced under tsarism is interesting.

Immediately after Christmas, my father had to go to 'Petrograd' for extensive dental treatment. Petrograd was the official name of the city after 1914, but it was not popular and everyone still called it Petersburg or 'Peetyer'.

By the middle of January 1917 my father's treatment was coming to an end and he suggested that my mother and I go and visit him for a few days and we all come home together. I wanted to do this, because I had not been to Petrograd for some time. But the weather was extremely cold and snowy, so before we set off we had to make sure we would stay warm. I wore what I considered my smartest clothes: a long-waisted coat lined with fox fur, which suited me very well, a red sash like a coachman's, and a white, shaggy Caucasian hat of the kind that someone told me was worn by His Majesty's bodyguard. But because it was so cold I had to wear ear-muffs under this hat and a *bashlyk* (cowl) over the lot. As well as my ordinary stockings I had to don thick woollen ones knitted by Nanny that reached above my knees. Over these I wore some rather flashy Russian jack-boots of which I was very proud.

However, even this was not all. When the pair of horses were brought round, they turned out to be harnessed not to the usual heavy sledge used by the upper classes, but a big, low, open sleigh filled with hay. We sat back in the hay and were then covered not just with rugs but with special loose Siberian fur coats. Before we set off it all seemed terribly overdone. But there were soon so many drifts across the road that the horses could only walk. A distance of seven miles that our Orlov Trotters would cover in forty-five minutes in summer pulling a rubber-tyred barouche, took us several hours. My mother was glad, then, that on top of her elegant winter coat, warm costume and fur boots, she was wearing my father's fur coat. This was a polecat coat of prodigious dimensions and weight, which he had been given on his wedding-day by his father-in-law; a 'relic of my former glory', as Aleksandr Yefimych put it. My father called it his 'Boyar coat' and never wore it because he said it was for performances of *Boris Godunov*, not life in twentieth-century Russia. But it served my mother well.

Volosovo was a large military, commercial and agricultural centre but when we got there it was practically invisible in the driving snow. As always, however, the station was ablaze with light. Inside it was almost too hot, and full of all kinds of smells: it was packed with people, because the heavy snowfalls had delayed the trains so much that one wit said they were exactly twenty-four hours late. Although we were travelling second class, we walked straight through to the first-class waiting-room because it had a buffet that was famous all along the Baltic line. We found a place and after a while the waiter, who knew my mother, brought coffee for her and the lady travelling with us, and fried eggs in a pan for me.

When the train eventually pulled in, it was crammed with soldiers. The corridor of the carriage was a solid wall of them. They were extremely polite, however, and two officers came out of a compartment and offered us their seats. We then settled down to what was to be an extremely interesting journey.

Generally these trains travelled very fast, but because of the snowdrifts we literally crept along. This was conducive to conversation, especially after my mother produced a box of candied fruits and handed them round. Some of the officers had been wounded and had bandages on their head, or their arm in a sling, others were going home on leave, others were on missions and had briefcases which they kept a close eye on.

They consisted of captains, staff captains and lieutenant-colonels – middle-ranking officers, not very young, but experienced and fairly well-informed. It was the first time I had heard such frank criticism of the Empress. Because of the school's ethos and the fact that my parents were teachers, people simply could not have such conversations there or repeat such gossip about the Court. Here it came to the fore. The officers did not mention the Emperor by name, but I understood that most of them blamed the Empress and her circle for the fact that the war was being conducted so lethargically. Who her 'circle' were, was not spelt out, but I got the impression everyone was supposed to know. The officers said we had the troops, we had the weapons, but we weren't doing anything to tighten our front, we had withdrawn behind our natural frontiers such as the Dvina. Dragging out the war was a bad thing, it was bad for the soldiers because it dragged out their military service; they all wanted to get on with it. The Empress's influence was baleful in that respect. I subsequently asked my mother about these conversations, and she confirmed that I had understood them correctly.[10]

With an enormous delay, we crawled into Petrograd's Baltic Station. My uncle Kolya, with whom my father was staying, had a telephone and my mother rang him to say we were taking a taxi. This was a novelty for me, because taxis and cars generally were still rare in the provinces.

The city seemed in fine form. Many of the streets had hardly any snow on them. It had been cleared away and the famous wood-block highways gleamed as though they had just been polished; in fact it was a veneer of ice. Petersburg looked festive, there was electricity, the squares were floodlit, the shops were all open, their windows full... Altogether, contrary to reminiscences I read later, in January 1917 'Petrograd' gave the impression – at least to me, a boy from outside – not of a city in need, but of one that had everything.

---

10 The views of the Andreyev brothers spanned the whole political spectrum. Although no one was a Bolshevik, Nikolay Nikolayevich Andreyev (Uncle Kolya) was a Menshevik. Apparently, he had a disagreement with Lenin in 1912 and also spent six months or so in jail during Stalin's terror in 1937 as a result.

4

The Abdication and Our New Masters

On 28 February [13 March] 1917, my own birthday, my parents celebrated a decade of working in the school of the Agricultural Colony. This was quite an event, because the work was hard and usually teachers did not stay long. The staff held a reception, at which my father was presented with a super ten-stringed guitar and silver plectrum, and my mother with a gramophone and records. Then there was a banquet with a lot of people, many of whom had come from Petersburg.

These people were full of the fact that the guards companies sent out to put down demonstrations in the days before had started fraternizing with the workers, a more revolutionary mood had suddenly sprung up, everyone was going around wearing red armbands, and the police were not shooting at anyone. However, the impression I had as a child was that no-one was expecting serious changes. They thought that a compromise would be reached between the demonstrators and Petersburg's military commanders who had threatened to use bullets, that the Duma and ministers would step in, and nothing much would happen because everyone knew there was a war on. 'This isn't a time to change horses,' someone at the banquet said. No-one imagined that we were at the very end of the Russian monarchy and empire.

After the celebrations Bekleshov left for Petersburg. On the evening of 2 [15] March he rang my father and told him that the Emperor had abdicated. It produced a furore. My father rang round his colleagues, and about twenty of them gathered in our flat. Many of them were excellent musicians, so at my father's suggestion they got hold of various instruments and played the Marseillaise. Everyone was in a state of high excitement and astonished by the speed of events. No-one had expected the Emperor to abdicate, they thought he would make big concessions and *de facto* become something like the King of England. Now he had abdicated and there might not be a monarchy at all: would Grand Duke Michael take over, or what would happen?

Although I was only nine, I was stunned. For whatever people said about him, the person of His Imperial Majesty had a certain romantic aura, he was still 'Our Sovereign Emperor'. Only recently in our establishment 'God Save the Tsar' had been sung with enthusiasm. Now I myself was gripped by the euphoria and kept saying: 'Don't things happen fast in Russia!'

The only person who did not share our enthusiasm was Nanny. She sat on a stool and wept bitterly. When people finally asked her what the matter was, she sobbed the same thing over and over again: 'Woe unto you all, woe! You have raised your hand against the Tsar, God's Anointed! You will all live to regret it!'

This warning, although sincere, seemed somewhat unjustified. At least, those present were not going to revise their opinion about the Tsar's abdication. It was impossible to stop her crying, however, so in the end my mother said to her very sternly: 'Nanny, you are spoiling it for everyone. Go to your room!' And, covering her face with her handkerchief, she went. This made a strong impression on me. What Nanny had said did not seem very convincing, because everyone else – *mama*, *papa* and all their friends-cum-colleagues – was so pleased. Everyone seemed happy, so why was my Nanny crying?

Much later, in 1918, when the Bolsheviks had unleashed their terror and one evening my father was warned not to sleep at home in case he was arrested, he suddenly looked at my mother and in my presence said: 'You know, when the Emperor abdicated the only person in our room with any sense was Nanny.' Of course, neither he nor his friends ever suspected what the Russian Revolution would turn into. By the 1920s, after the Civil War, when we were in Estonia, my father looked upon 1917 up to the October coup as a period of extreme immature excitability. On several occasions he even mocked himself and his colleagues, calling them all 'political ignoramuses' for spouting clichés from the French Revolution.

Although this hypothesis about the French prototype has not featured in serious historical studies of the Russian Revolution, I think it is right, because mentally everyone was aping the model of the French Revolution. It was as true of Kerensky as it was later of Lenin, particularly when he set up a system of terror. My father felt that one of the most disgraceful speeches he personally had ever made was soon after the abdication, at a large gathering of teaching staff and personnel at the school. As he put it later, he had 'talked a load of political claptrap' about the 'three hundred years violence' of the Romanov dynasty and how the Romanovs had 'drunk the people's blood' all that time. He was terribly ashamed to recall it. But that is how people saw events at the time.

My own attitude to the revolution became highly negative, because a gang of drunken deserters rampaged through the estate and with a few grenades tossed into the ponds and hatchery ditches they put an end to its fishing industry. Only the thousands of dead trout floating on the surfaces of the ponds and lakes were left to remind us how fragile everything created by man's unremitting labour is, and how easily it is destroyed by stupidity. Another thing that repelled me about the revolution was that our universally respected principal, Bekleshov, was soon declared an undesirable element by some Committee of the Poor. It shocked me that such a good man, well-known for his kindness and political liberalism, could be virtually condemned to death by completely unknown persons from the neighbouring *volost* (rural sub-district) which had nothing to do with us. I was even more shocked when stories started circulating about attacks on army officers, and yesterday's heroes were trampled in the dirt by the nameless 'masses'.

From the start of the Russian Revolution to the very end of that period, i.e. until the elections to the Constituent Assembly, which I remember well, my world was a blend of vivid childhood impressions and political events that were constantly invading our lives.

The first big change was that open meetings were always being held. My parents participated in these as we lived next door to the recreation room of section A, where the meetings often took place. They were elected to the top table of these meetings and my mother was often secretary as she was very good at keeping minutes. My father started to get involved with the cooperative movement and joined the Central Administration of the Volosovo-Kikerino Union. He also arranged the opening of the local Russian Consumer Society, a cooperative of which he was elected chairman.

In this capacity he had an interesting experience. He had to set up a cooperative based in a new building between the estate and Izvary station, but there was no suitable manager. My father found someone called Zilberman. He was of indeterminate occupation and poor health, so he was exempt from military service. Nanny described him as 'a ne'er-do-well boozer'. But in my father's opinion Zilberman was businesslike. He introduced proper book-keeping and was a good salesman. He knew what people wanted and always put sensible proposals to the Administration about orders of goods.

My father thought that the cooperative should sell books of interest to the peasants. The main task facing Russia's population was to elect a Constituent Assembly. Lots of parties had sprung up, which nobody knew anything about, and my father believed that the cooperative should sell these parties' programmes and pamphlets so as to disseminate them among the masses. I was involved in this myself, because I used to go to the cooperative with him and he was given a special bookcase with a glass front, in which we displayed the pamphlets. It wasn't political propaganda, just information about the parties. He and other teachers were keen to buy this literature and discuss it.

Zilberman was very sceptical about this stall. He said that the peasants wouldn't buy any of it. He was right. Very few of the pamphlets went, and in the end my father bought some himself and took them to the peasants in order to inform them about the forthcoming election. Obviously Zilberman had been more realistic. 'The peasants aren't interested,' he said. 'All that stuff is for townies. There's only one thing the peasants want – land. And the SRs and Bolsheviks are promising them it. So the peasants will vote for one of them. You don't need any party programmes here.'

My father replied that even if that was true, the peasants should still be informed about other political views. The episode has stuck in my memory, because I was amazed that whatever my father said Zilberman was convinced the peasants did not want any information and had their own, well-formed interests which came down to 'the land must be ours'.

The exceptional snowfalls that winter contributed to the collapse of the tsarist regime, as they delayed supplies to Petrograd, which led first to the housewives demonstrating, then the workers. But it was a wonderful spring, followed by a very hot summer. Lots of big meetings were held and we had *papa*'s people from the cooperative movement, teachers and relations to stay. My impression is that 1917 was one long holiday; which ended with the October putsch.

We heard about it very quickly. The next day someone visited us from Petersburg and when we asked what was news he said: 'Oh, Trotsky's stirred things up, he's staged some coup. They've arrested a few ministers and declared a dictatorship of the proletariat. But it's all nonsense, of course. It'll be forgotten in a fortnight.'

Indeed, all through 1917, from the moment the Tsar abdicated, things happened that were superseded within a fortnight. The man's reaction was natural, therefore, but it turned out to be wrong.

What happened on 25 October [7 November] 1917 was no chance event. However, it intensified the interest in elections to the Constituent Assembly. My father explained to me that even Lenin dare not touch the authority of the Constituent Assembly and call the elections off. Once they had been held, the true master of Russia would be not the Tsarist, Provisional or Bolshevik government, but the Constituent Assembly. My father brought some placards from Volosovo saying 'Vote for the People's Freedom Party' (i.e. the Cadets) and hung them up where voting was to take place. One of the polling stations was in our recreation hall and the entrance was plastered with posters of the various parties. The public certainly went to look at them, as did I, because it was all so new and had not yet become boring.

At Izvary and its neighbouring villages everything went off well and the SRs won almost everywhere. This led to a lively exchange of views at the Volosovo-Kikerino Union, which I visited a couple of times with my father. Interestingly, the cooperative activists were politically divided, but most of them were SRs.

They liked to tease my father that basically he was a 'capitalist minister', i.e. one of the Cadets thrown out of the Provisional Government in the first months of the revolution. He in turn told them that the SRs were so busy theorizing that they would never have time to attend to agriculture.

At the beginning of 1918, when the Constituent Assembly was dispersed on its second day, everything became more serious, because a force had entered the Russian Revolution that believed in destroying its opponents physically. Shots were soon fired at Lenin and the Cheka was set up to fight counter-revolution and sabotage. In 1918 my father lost his political optimism as the picture darkened.

One day a representative from the commissariat of supplies of the Northern Commune turned up. He warmed to my father because they had both worked in technical engineering. He was extremely interested in the pupils who had been thieves, and grabbing one of them by the shoulders he asked my father: 'How long will it take you to correct this boy and turn him into a responsible citizen of our republic?'

'You are asking me like a mechanic,' replied my father, 'so I shall answer you like a mechanic. This boy isn't a lock or saucepan that was just soldered together. He is a young person. What you call 'correction' – forgetting his past transgressions and learning other ways of life – takes a long time and depends on the influence of the school, his comrades and teachers. So it would be wrong for me to translate that into figures such as three months or two years.'

The commissar liked this answer and said: 'You obviously know what you are talking about and we understand each other well.'

He certainly understood one of the school's problems: the growing shortage of food. Only a year before there had been no problem with meat, bread or vegetables. The commissar promised to help and actually sent more products from the ministry than were officially allocated, but as my father said, this was a drop in the ocean.

Then Lunacharsky, the People's Commissar for Enlightenment, visited the colony. He was going round the schools to acquaint himself with the world he was now in charge of. He visited us because he had heard a lot about the unusual nature of the school and apparently respected Bekleshov. My father had heard Lunacharsky speak in 1917 and was impressed by him as an orator and man of not extreme views. Lunacharsky understood the complexity of the situation, especially in education, better than the other politicians now on the scene.

An amusing thing happened to him whilst he was visiting us. The weather was pretty cold and he was wearing a capacious fur coat. First he had a word with the teachers. Very amiable and polite. He insisted on nothing and preached no new doctrine to them. Then he gave a speech to all the boys in the recreation hall. Afterwards, as a joke, he said to one of them: 'Well, do you like my coat?' – and enveloped him in half of it for about a second. Then they all adjourned for lunch, Lunacharsky talked to my father and the other teachers, and said that it was probably time for him to catch the train now, so he felt for his watch. It wasn't there. He was terribly surprised, but my father instantly knew what had happened: 'That's all right, don't worry, Comrade Lunacharsky, we'll find your watch in two shakes.'

He called the boy out and said to him: 'The Comrade Commissar is delighted with your skill. You unclipped his watch so quickly! Shall we give it back to him now?'

The boy grinned with pleasure and said: 'I was only joking. I wanted to show him how nifty I am.'

'Of course,' replied my father. 'We all realized that.'

Lunacharsky was incredibly taken by my father's handling of the boy and the fact that he managed to keep everything relaxed and humorous.

The school was in fact most at risk not from the top of the new Communist dictatorship, but from its lower echelons. A representative of the Committee of the Poor insisted on addressing the boys and getting them to change the system of sharing out their bread and sugar. They were unwilling. He then harangued the teachers with the most vulgar revolutionary mumbo-jumbo and said the Committee were carrying out a local purge and intended shooting Bekleshov, who had gone into hiding. On another occasion a group of workmen from the farm demanded that some of them share our flat, that the colony hand its vegetable plots over to them, give them more money and firewood, let them graze their cows in the colony herd, and goodness knows what else. The main problem, though, was food. One could do some barter with the peasants, who had produce but would not sell it for Kerensky banknotes, let alone Soviet roubles, but obviously that wasn't enough to feed a whole school. We ourselves survived thanks to the ducks and chickens that Nanny kept, and the school by culling its herd of cattle and breeding rabbits.

But they were dangerous times. The Cheka were making mysterious local arrests. At Volosovo station, on the board that used to display the train times, grubby lists of those executed were nailed up. Many extremely respected people from the area were branded 'speculators', 'counter-revolutionaries', and 'saboteurs', including the bosses of the big local trading firms that had supplied food and goods to the population in the war years. Suddenly they were seized and rumours flew that they were being killed. But *who* was sentencing them in this vile fashion, nobody could say.

We were particularly struck by the case of the shopkeeper at a small village nearby. We used to walk over there sometimes, call at the shop, and buy sweets. He was a typical small trader, with a somewhat rascally look: he had a red nose, a stiff ginger beard, and shifty eyes. I don't expect he earned very much, but he was a kind man. From time to time he would donate money to the little white church and primary school at Zapolye, a couple of miles away. He was arrested and suddenly to our horror his name appeared on one of the lists of people shot. Then the local Committee of the Poor confiscated his shop and all his stock, and his wife and five children were made paupers. Nobody we knew could understand why these actions were necessary.

The same thing happened to a man named Motylyov at a village five miles away. He was a peasant who had made a lot of money and built a People's Palace named after himself. Suddenly he was declared a capitalist who criticized Soviet power. He was taken away and shot. This had a devastating local effect. His village never forgave it, and in the Civil War they fought for the Whites.

My Nanny was particularly outraged by these goings-on. She regarded Soviet power as the personification of all the *bezobraziye* (disgrace) that had descended on the land of Russia since 1917.

The forms of this *bezobraziye* were indeed strange. At the beginning of 1919, in the recreation room next to my bedroom there was a meeting of the local cooperative and everyone attached to it, since it was the only organization that could distribute food rations when there were any. My father was away at the Volosovo-Kikerino Union and should have been back for it, but was late. The meeting started without him and became very stormy. I sat in my bedroom and listened with fear to the rising tide of voices and shouts of indignation.

My mother, who was also a member of the board of management, was reading out a financial report and the picture was depressing: there were no rations and it was getting more and more difficult to find them. I heard someone shout out that, because he wasn't doing anything and couldn't find any food, the chairman of the cooperative, my father, should have the accounts and a millstone tied round his neck and be thrown into a nearby lake. It was a ghastly thing to hear.

At that moment my father came in with two other members of the Volosovo-Kikerino Union. They went straight up to the podium and he announced that he had some good news: he had got hold of two truckloads of groats from the Ukraine and there would be about a pound and a quarter per person. The mood changed instantly, and the very same people who had been yelling that he should be drowned now thanked him with gusto for trying to feed the population.

The general mood had been unstable like this all through 1918. It upset me a great deal, and after this meeting my mother almost had a nervous breakdown. She was horrified at how people's emotions got out of hand, and although, fortunately, on this occasion everything had turned out all right, it might not have. The pendulum could swing from idolizing someone to threatening them with death. The powers that be were also beginning to unleash the incomprehensible actions termed 'proletarian terror'. What struck people most about the latter was that those who had any personal knowledge of these *cheka*'s ('extraordinary commissions') said: 'There are no peasants or workers on them. They are made up of strange, half-sick people.' In other words those whom Nanny called 'ne'er-do-wells and boozers'. Often they were not even Russian by origin, and spoke with an accent. But their actions led to the destruction of the fine, dynamic people who had created the wealth of this region.

In the winter of 1919 my father had to go to Petersburg on school business, and to my delight he took me with him.

On this journey I could not help comparing what I was seeing with what I remembered from 1917. *Then* the station at Volosovo had been ablaze with electric light, it was a building of exemplary cleanliness, well heated, with two buffets and hot and cold food. The buffet for third-class passengers was self-service and its tables had no cloths on them, but its prices were much lower than the first- and second-class buffets, whose tables had dazzling white tablecloths and napkins, and incongruous palms growing beside them in tubs, and the waiters were all elderly and wore white gloves and false shirt-fronts. *Now*, two years later, the station was badly lit and heated, and there were no buffets at all. The only thing you could get was free boiling water – a long-standing tradition of Russian railways.

The train was no better. There was no first or third class. The carriages were filthy and unheated. You could not see out of the windows for a thick layer of ice and grime. Instead of the noisy, cheerful throng of soldiers in 1917, the passengers were morose, withdrawn, badly dressed as if on purpose, with sacks, bags and parcels. I was amazed that the friendliness everyone had displayed then, and which had seemed the background to my whole childhood, had vanished completely.

We arrived at the Baltic Station and found Petrograd a half-dead city, buried in snow, with blocks of uncleared ice everywhere, and hardly any traffic. Snow-covered squares, snow-covered streets, frozen-up trams. Electricity here and there. Pavements like ice-rinks. A frightening sight. We had brought my uncle Kolya some potatoes and carrots – which would have been unheard-of before. We stayed two days.

When we got back to Volosovo, we were met by a coachman, who told my father who had been arrested, and tore into the government: 'What the hell's going on? We are simple people, we've worked all our lives, what have we done to deserve this? They're swindling us, there's nothing to eat, nothing to buy. And everything's falling to pieces. *Why*? Russia's such a rich country, it's got everything. But it's not two years since Nicholas abdicated, and there's nothing left!'

In 1919 the first of May was not celebrated, as the front was getting closer. At the end of April rumours began to fly that the 'Whites' would soon be here. But who were the 'Whites'? We did not really know, because the Soviet newspapers were strictly censored. The Whites were portrayed as bandits whom the Reds were always beating. Sometimes it was reported that the Whites had executed some prominent communist, or were hanging their own generals who had gone over to the worker-peasant army. The impression was that they were dastardly murderers.

Around the middle of May my Aunt Manya, Nanny, three or four other women, and I, set off for some neighbouring farmsteads to swap things for food. We had no workman with us and my aunt drove the cart. We had gone about six miles and were bartering away, when we suddenly heard rifle fire. We asked what was going on and the farmers said it was White partisans.

'What do you mean?'

'Don't you know? The Whites are coming. They have taken Yamburg and Vyra.' (The latter was a station about twelve miles west of Volosovo.)

Shortly afterwards, some men went past on horseback clutching rifles and with white armbands. These were the Whites' partisans.

'Right,' said Aunt Manya. 'We had better go home straightaway, or the White Army will be here and we'll get cut off.'

We reached home safely and that evening my father had a phone call from the Volosovo-Kikerino Union to say that the Whites had begun a major offensive. Early next morning, 16 May or a bit later, I was awoken by artillery fire. It turned out to be four-and-a-half-inch and three-inch field guns blasting in the direction of Volosovo and Gatchina. Around five in the afternoon there were tremendous whoops outside and people were shouting: 'They're coming, they're coming, our troops are coming!' Everyone ran to the main road and started waving handkerchieves and shouting greetings. Six carts came along with about eighteen soldiers in them, all young. Some were officers with epaulettes, which we had not seen for a long time, and they all had white crosses on their sleeves, or armbands with the colours of the Russian flag. They made straight for the manor house, and everyone followed them.

The captain made a short speech to the crowd from the steps. The White Army, to which they had the honour to belong, was fighting for the restoration of the rule of law in Russia and for the Russian people to be able to express its will through free elections rather than the dictatorship of one party or group of persons. He called on everyone to stay at their posts and carry on working as they were wont. There was to be no summary justice. If anyone had a grievance, they should put it in writing and address themselves to the military prosecutor, who would act according to the laws of Russia. Now, he proposed, we should all go to the church and like our forefathers before us thank God and ask Him for His continuing assistance. Whereupon bicycles were unloaded from the carts and some of the officers rode off we knew not where.

The church was actually in one of the recreation rooms. When the service was held, it transpired that a nineteenth member of the group had arrived, one Father Ioakim, whom we later got to know well. He was a colourful figure. He was tall, handsome, with a mane of black hair and a bushy beard, and he wore a thick Order of St George ribbon with his personal and priestly crosses hanging from it. He was an army archpriest and had been awarded the St George for leading a company into battle in 1916. He conducted the service very theatrically, declaiming the prayers loudly and clearly. It produced a great impression, even on those who rarely went to church; but the effect was spoilt by his sermon, which was not at all Christian. He exhorted everyone to fight the communists, and even used expressions like: 'I could throttle umpteen communists with my bare hands. Bring 'em in here and I'll show you.'

Many people did not like this. Later, when we got to know him and some of our teachers who went into the army sang with him, he turned out to be a very kind man indeed, and all his talk about himself as the spiritual and physical scourge of the enemies of Christ was pure theatre. But it looked as awful as the lists of people shot that were put up at Volosovo station. Why did the captain talk about the rule of law and say that there should be no summary justice, yet the army chaplain call for the immediate execution of all their adversaries?

During Bekleshov's absence (he was now permanently in St Petersburg), my mother had been acting principal of the colony school, because my father had had to concentrate on his work with the Volosovo-Kikerino Union. She thought it was now time to hand over to my father, especially as she had no experience of dealing with military men and got off on the wrong foot with them when she asked how many Whites there were and was told it was a military secret!

So my father was now acting principal and he broached with the captain the question of improving the school's food supplies. The captain said he would ask his superiors about it. The officers all said that at their base in Yamburg, whence the attack had been launched, the food situation was good, the bakeries were working freely, the market was open, and the army supplied itself separately without being a burden on the population.

A few days later my father received word that the Army thought it was possible for the school to receive rations from them. But this would best be organized in Yamburg, where the commandant, Colonel Bibikov, had the powers to authorize it. It was now the end of May. My father discussed it with my mother and decided to go. The situation seemed to have stabilized, although there was no news of further White successes and artillery battles were still raging beyond Volosovo.

He left for Volosovo with a lieutenant, who put him on a military train for Yamburg, as there were no passenger ones. Days passed, the weather was very good, nothing happened, but rumours were rife. It was said that the fantastic early successes were over, an artillery duel with the Reds was building up around Gatchina, and the Reds would soon counter-attack. This made everyone nervous and despite their obvious sympathy for the Whites most people did not know how to react. Should they leave? If so, where for?

Suddenly, on the evening of 6 June, a lieutenant turned up at our flat and asked to speak to *mama*. They went into the study and a few minutes later he left. *Mama* came out looking very worried and said that the lieutenant had told her that the Army was having to reduce its battle-lines and the post at Izvary was being abandoned. The soldiers would be leaving in a few hours. He had warned my mother because *papa* was well behind the White Army's lines and it might not be a good idea for his family to stay here. From the Reds' point of view my father would be compromised and my mother and the whole family could suffer as a result. He said, therefore, that if we decided to leave he would help us and provide transport away from the estate.

Mama conferred with Nanny, Aunt Manya and me and we were unanimous that we must not get separated from my father, that we had to try to catch him at Yamburg and all wait there, especially as, according to the lieutenant, the redeployment of the Army was temporary and all part of the plan to take Petrograd.

At about four in the morning my mother went to the lieutenant, who was awake sitting by the telephone, and told him that we were ready to leave. He brought round a cart and driver. It was full of hay and Nanny got into it holding my baby brother Arkadik asleep in her arms, followed by Tanechka with her things, then *mama* and me.

Of course, we did not know then that we were binding our lives to the fate of the White movement and thereby to emigration. Was that a good thing, or a bad thing? Perhaps only the subsequent history of the Andreyev family can tell.

5

1919: We Leave for the Unknown

We had not gone very far before we were stopped by a group of peasants.

'You're running away from something you've done there,' they said. 'You must go back and wait for the Reds to take over.'

My mother knew these peasants well and was appalled that they were already changing sides. But suddenly they all took to their heels: a detachment of White partisans with rifles was galloping towards us. These sent us safely on our way and we soon passed a couple of field-guns firing in the direction of Kikerino. When we reached Volosovo we heard shooting all the time.

I had never travelled by train in the direction of Yamburg before. About fifteen miles west of Volosovo we came into the station at Vyra. The train trundled past the platform and stopped a little way off. We could see that the whole platform was full of officers. In the middle stood a general of gigantic stature, who I learned was Rodzyanko, commander-in-chief of the army at that time. He was evidently travelling with Allied officers in foreign uniforms, probably English. There were at least fifty officers comprising his staff and the visitors' retinue. I was amazed at the magnificence of the Russian uniforms: Cossack uniforms, naval uniforms, Guards and Cavalry uniforms of different regiments, all of them full dress. In the centre was a guard of honour of twenty tall soldiers presenting arms. They wore superbly tailored field shirts and blue cap-bands with Romanov cockades in them.[11] This company looked fighting-fit, grim, and even a bit trigger-happy. To some extent they were the Guards unit of the White Army. All my life I have retained this last image of the imperial army, its uniforms, its magnificence, the troops throwing their chests out and their NCOs standing there very smartly saluting. It was a solemn moment. Within minutes our train was off again, leaving the brilliant vision behind.

---

11 'Romanov cockades' were cockades in the colours of the Romanov family, which were black and yellow. White was added to distinguish them from the Austrian colours.

We were crawling along a fairly monotonous line. It was all bogland, with the occasional small wood. There were a few stations, with not many soldiers and civilians on their platforms. Around eight in the evening we approached Yamburg. This was the first depot after Volosovo, so for about a mile before the station we were hemmed in by long passenger and goods trains which seemed to have absolutely no-one in them. Finally we began to pass the main platform, which had civilians and lots of soldiers on it. And suddenly little Tanya shouted: 'Mama, look! It's papa, papa!'

She was always very sharp-eyed, very quick off the mark. I must admit I didn't see my father at first, it was only when she shouted that I realized he was standing on the platform. We bumped over points and shot past him. 'Papa, papa!' Tanechka shouted. The train stopped, and then we could see that it was papa, and he was running towards us.

He was intending to leave on a train to Volosovo in a couple of hours' time and make his way to Izvary through the woods. He had known nothing about the front contracting, not a word had been spoken about it in Yamburg. If he had gone ahead, he would probably have walked into big trouble and been killed. But our family was not destined to be divided at that moment, and we were permitted to find our dear father again. The main credit for this belonged to Tanechka, whose beady eyes had spotted the father she adored. She adored everyone, but especially him, because she was a singer and so was he, and he had great hopes for her singing. She used to chirrup away from morning till night, and had perfect pitch like my father.

In Yamburg we discovered that my uncle Mikhail Nikolayevich, who had been headmaster of a big school there before being moved to Moscow, was a very popular man, and his successor gave us a free flat at the school. The town's commandant, Colonel Bibikov, dubbed us 'the first civilian refugees from around Gatchina' and gave us rations. We were all in good health. We kept practically open house for other refugees arriving and for the young White Army officers. Rodzyanko's northern corps had joined up with Yudenich, who had arrived from Finland, and the latter was to lead the army to Petrograd.

The town was charming. It had lots of small houses with wonderful gardens, in which we played croquet. It was June and the air was unforgettably laden with the scent of lilac and bird cherry. But even here the brutality of the twentieth century intruded. In the heart of the town was the cathedral, and when we arrived there was a gallows beside it on which we were told the former Tsarist general Nikolayev had been hanged for defecting to the Reds. Executions were still carried out, but in the churchyard. We sometimes walked here and I saw the remains of ropes on the trees.

On two occasions I also witnessed the funerals of officers killed at the front. The coffins arrived on horse-drawn hearses to the strains of a funeral march. They were then borne to the grave with the victims' caps tied to them, complete with Romanov cockades. After the graveside committal, a salute was fired and 'How Glorious is Our Lord in Zion' was sung – the unofficial hymn on such occasions of military grief. Then, like every army in the world, they marched off to stirring music designed to dampen the feelings left by the death of young people and look forward to victory. Of course, we did not know Bulgakov's *White Guard* then, but when I read it later I always recalled these Yamburg experiences.[12]

I liked the local custom of walking in the evenings when it was fine from the central streets along the side streets. Almost every house had seats outside, and the owner would sit out there with his friends. And they would invite you over: 'Come and sit with us, take a rest, have a chat...' Although I was young, I was very interested in politics. All of these people were disturbed by the armistice on the western front and the Paris Peace Conference, because it meant our allies were no longer interested in us and would support the powers that were breaking Russia up. The people who took part in these conversations were from all walks of life. There was a prison inspector, a very nice, elderly man who wore civvies in the evening, singers from the church choir, workers from the local factories, and a librarian. They all sympathized with the White Army and were terribly concerned about it.

Trotsky now brought up reserves and mounted a gradual counter-offensive supported by naval guns. One must give Rodzyanko's Northern Corps its due, not once did it suffer an outright defeat. It kept falling back, 'tightening its front', and during one such tightening Yamburg was surrendered. But by then we had gone. At the very end of June Bibikov handed my father a letter which said that we were being evacuated with other refugees by military transport to the Pskov area.

We travelled mainly at night, on pretty fast trains. First we were taken to Narva, then in goods wagons south towards Gdov. We were set down about three miles outside Gdov, near a village called Bragino.

We lived in a peasant hut in this very well-to-do village for four months. I was shocked that there was no privy, but there was a bath-house in the garden and good spring-water from a well. The food was quite reasonable and we made a long trip to the eastern shore of Lake Chudskoye (Peipus), where we bought fish for ourselves and our landlords. The only problem at Bragino was

12 Mikhail Bulgakov's *The White Guard* is a novel first published in Paris, 1927-29.

the sanitation. Epidemics broke out, of which the first was dysentery, and my brother Arkadik caught it and very soon died.

The whole family was devastated. He was a dear little boy, fifteen months old, blue-eyed, very good-natured, already scampering about, and he seemed to be musical. It was the first death that had happened before my eyes. Strangely, I cannot remember the details, but I very well remember feeling, for a long time, how unreal it was that he was no longer in the world. Tanechka and I were depressed and yet tried not to show our parents how upset we were, because they were suffering so much.

Fate is cruel, but perhaps God knew that we had many more tribulations ahead of us. My mother and I soon went down with dysentery, too. But the illness took our minds off Arkadik's death and I even wondered whether God had ordered things so that our worries about ourselves deflected our grief. We were treated by an amazing German *feldsher* (doctor's assistant) whom we had not met before my brother died and who practised herbal medicine.

Suddenly, in September, all the men were called up, including the category ('Reserve 2') that my father fell into. Probably because she was worrying about this – without my father our life would be much more difficult – my mother had a dream. She saw some gates, and beyond them a small, very old church. In the church was a remarkable Icon of the Holy Face. She knelt down before it, prayed (*mama* prayed every night, fervently, that God would arrange everything to the general good, as she put it), and she felt that her prayers had been heard. Next morning my father went to the army office in Gdov, where lots of people had gathered and the peasant women were wailing because they were losing their menfolk. My mother, meanwhile, went to look round the Kremlin at Gdov. To her amazement, inside it she saw the church she had dreamt about, and inside that was an enormous Icon of the Holy Face. She threw herself down before it and prayed, and suddenly understood that what she had seen in her dream was a prediction and would come true. So she kissed the icon passionately, left, and ran towards the army office. My father was coming out of it, ambling as always and smiling, and said everything was all right. He had been told that if he had been an officer, they would have taken him, but given the problems with his sight and his teeth he should stay in 'Reserve 2'. My parents went straight to the church and thanked God for not separating them at such a difficult time.

In October General Yudenich's offensive began brilliantly. His army was clothed by the British, it was well fed, and above all the Allies had sent him artillery and a few tanks. The Reds kept bolting and surrendering. Gatchina was taken, then Tsarskoye Selo, and Petersburg itself seemed within reach. My father even returned to Izvary for one day. He found that it had been ransacked and the school moved.

Then suddenly the White campaign ran out of steam. There was no permanent garrison at Bragino and usually only small cavalry or bicycle units passed through it. But one day we saw a vast column of troops on the move. They had arrived by the same branch line as us and disembarked at the same place. There were at least 2000 of them, wearing British greatcoats and accompanied by light artillery and machineguns. Obviously something was wrong at the front, and either the Reds had broken through it or outflanked it at Luga. The rumour was that Pskov too was about to surrender.

A few hours later, my father rushed in from the *zemstvo* where he worked, and said that we must leave immediately, Gdov was being evacuated and he had been given the necessary papers for us to entrain for Narva. We kissed the peasants farewell, and they were very sorry to see us go. They really loved my mother, they worshipped Nanny, they were kind to us children, and they respected my father. They gave us sacks of apples and immediately brought us a cart and driver to get to Gdov.

At the station it was chaos. Eventually my father discovered that the train was not leaving until noon the next day, so we were given a warrant to stay overnight in a flat that had been abandoned so quickly there was still food on the table. It even had a bath, and we slept beautifully. The problem was next morning: our driver had gone back to Bragino and we could not find another. So we got a handcart, my father loaded it with our things, and he and I pushed it. Tanechka had to walk, and we set off for the station, which was about two miles away. This was rather unpleasant. It was now November and a cold wind was blowing. We had to walk for quite a long time in the open and there was a huge crowd going in the same direction. Again we piled into red wooden goods vans, but the difference this time was that both platforms were full of soldiers and had guns with their covers off ready to fire. From this we concluded that nobody knew where the enemy had broken through, and our journey could be risky.

The train was very long, with engines at the front, middle and back, and it was packed with evacuees. It crept northwards all day and suddenly stopped during the night in what appeared to be open country. In fact it was a station appropriately called Nizy ('Dregs'), and we all had to get out. We were told that Narva was not accepting any incoming trains and this one had to go back to Gdov for more evacuees. We stayed in the station building for a while, because the crush of people made it warm, whilst my father went off to reconnoitre the village. He reported back that the school would take the whole family because he was a teacher, but they couldn't offer any food. Gradually it filled up as more and more refugees arrived on foot. Nanny had fallen ill and had to lie on the shelf by the Russian stove, where *mama* and a doctor tried to treat her. The rest of us were put up in a classroom.

We had been a few days at Nizy, when the situation suddenly deteriorated. The streets became a bivouac, with people sitting round fires everywhere as though it were the French retreat of 1812. All kinds of interesting people were there, including officers, and I remember one saying loudly and unceremoniously to another: 'What amazes me most is that not once in this campaign have I managed to take a shot at a Bolshevik. All the time it's been forwards and back, they never stood and fought us – and now we seem to be retreating.' My father also said that actually the North-West army had never been beaten in battle, each time it had to withdraw because of non-military complications at the front. Now the uncoordinated actions of the Estonian and Russian units had led to the Estonians abandoning the left flank at Pulkovo, which gave Trotsky the opportunity to start an outflanking movement. The rumour was that the retreat was the fault of General Vetrenko, commanding the Third Division. Apparently he was determined to be one of the first to enter Petersburg and therefore disobeyed Yudenich's order to advance from Gatchina to Tosno and cut off the Nikolayevsky Railway linking Petersburg to Moscow. This enabled the Red Army to bring up reinforcements from the Polish front. Whether that is true, I don't know, but people who worked with Vetrenko said it was.

Meanwhile, we heard that Gdov had fallen. All the roads were cut off, all the trains had left Nizy for Narva, and we had to leave too. But we had no horse and cart and Nanny was ill. There was no way we could walk the fifteen miles or so to Narva. It was cold and snowing. My father rushed hither and thither, but no-one would tell him anything – there was nobody in charge. The River Plyussa had not yet frozen, and there was a line of Whites on this side with machineguns and a line of Reds would come out of the woods on the other bank and fire back. I used to stand and watch them. Exciting, but dangerous!

My father was in complete despair and had already told us that we might have to stay here and hope that Nizy did not surrender, when he was walking down the street and saw coming towards him, shaven and immaculately turned out as usual, Colonel Bibikov and his adjutant Lira. Seeing my father, Bibikov saluted and said: 'Mr Andreyev, it's time for you to leave. This is now the front.'

'I'd love to, but there's nothing to go on!'

'I'll send a cart straight away,' Bibikov replied, and gave the order to Lira.

There were always some carts set aside for military needs in the North-West Army (they had been mobilized from the villages) and we got one from this reserve. We wrapped Nanny up as warmly as we could, laid her in the cart with all our things, and the four of us squeezed on as well.

Outside Narva we saw an incredible hotchpotch of carts and people camped around fires. Beyond them were barbed wire and Estonian guards. There were tens of thousands of civilian refugees and as many soldiers, but the Estonians were letting onto their territory only the medical or supply units that were based in Narva. Nothing my parents could do would help here, as Yudenich's government were already negotiating at a high level.

In the end an agreement was hammered out according to which some of the Russian troops would not go beyond Narva, so that they could assist the Estonians if Narva had to be defended against the Red Army, which it was assumed would try to mount a surprise attack, break the Estonian defences, and invade the country.

We remained in this camp outside Narva for the rest of that day, all night, and the following day until about 3 p.m., when it was still more or less light and they began to let us through the Estonian checkpoint. You can imagine the state of exhaustion, incomprehension and despair that we were all in. Why was our army, which was well equipped, well trained, motivated to fight communism, and had not once been defeated, now in retreat? Why did we have to go onto Estonian territory? Why were the Estonians demanding that our troops disarm, yet at the same time help them beat off a Red attack? All of these questions were loudly discussed and no-one found a proper answer.

The night was very cold. There was nowhere to sleep. Most people unharnessed their horses and slept on the carts among their belongings. They covered themselves with what they had. Fortunately, the troops cooked some hot food and took it round the groups of refugees, so that several times we had tea, soup, or kasha with bits of meat in. But in other respects it was dire, especially as Nanny's condition was worsening. My mother exerted all her energy, as always, and managed to get hold of an army doctor, who examined her. He decided she must go to hospital, and an ambulance came and moved her to a medical train. This took her to one of the Russian field hospitals on the line to Tallinn – at Yyevve, later called Yykhvi or Jõhvi in Estonian. So they started to treat her there at the beginning of November.

Now the order came for our group to move forward. We walked up to a wall of barbed wire accompanied by our carts, whose drivers were told to take us to the last border post and leave us there inside Estonia. We picked our way through a maze of barbed wire past Estonian sentries with rifles. There were even several machineguns trained on the Russian refugees and ranks of the North-West Army. An Estonian officer talked to us in Russian, but his soldiers probably did not know Russian well or did not want to speak it. They were very smartly dressed, mainly in sheepskin coats, and wore cockades and armbands in the national colours. They seemed to me very dour, these blonde-haired men with blue eyes, and they did not pay much attention to the Russians passing them. After this there were no baggage checks and they hardly looked at our documents. The officers merely noted down our surnames and how many people there were to a family.

Then the whole of our column, the Gdov town and district council to which we nominally belonged, set off with their belongings, women and children on a variety of carts. I walked beside my father. I regarded myself as fairly grown-up and thought that I should walk all the time I could. There was no knowing what was in store for us, but so far walking through the town was easy.

We went through the whole suburb, the Ivangorod *posad* (settlement), most of whose inhabitants were Russian, and then past the famous Ivangorod fortress. It was an elegant silhouette with splendid bastions. It was the very fortress built by Ivan the Great when he decided to fight for an outlet to the Baltic after throwing off the Mongol yoke in the 1480s. Here, opposite the massive Livonian castle of Narva, he built Ivangorod, 'Ivan's town'. Of course, I did not learn about this until much later, but even at the time it made a powerful impression on me. Dusk was falling on a winter's day and suddenly there was this 'vision' of the fortress.

Part II: Estonia

Map 3. Estonia.

1
Kurtna and Death

We walked across the bridge over the swiftly flowing River Narova. A few hundred yards from the bridge were the famous Narva waterfalls, supplying energy to the town and the Krähnholm Mills. We were now on the Estonian or, as it was once called, Livonian side of Narva. Later, when I lived there, I got very interested in the town's past, but even now I knew that Charles XII of Sweden had defeated Peter the Great's army here.

We went up Market Hill, crossed Market Square, and headed for the Tallinn road. There were lots of shops full of goods. A delicious smell of fresh bread wafted from the bakeries: you could see that they had rolls and even pastry, you really wanted to try them, but you were not allowed to stop. Our column of about 600 people was guarded by Estonian soldiers at the front and rear. The escort was a token one, but still there. The Estonians were afraid that once we got across the border we would melt into Narva, which was an army headquarters. Narva still had a military job ahead of it because it had to repel the attacks of the Red Army that were expected very soon.

We crossed the whole town and came out on the Tallinn road. This was not like the new military roads I had known around Volosovo, but old and with well-dug ditches for the run-off. Here and there bushes had been planted to protect it from the snow and wind. It was due to turn at some point and come out on the coast. We walked about ten miles and stopped where there was a farm and inn. The inn sold soup and some cooked food. My mother went in with my father and was lucky – she asked if they had any eggs and they sold us a dozen and even boiled them for us. So next day we had something to eat, which was very important because we never came to another place that sold food.

By now it was dark. The column was very tired and we were told that we would spend the night here in the village. There was a school near the inn and we could accommodate ourselves there. Fortunately, the school was well heated. There were no beds or blankets, but thanks to the warmth we slept well. In the morning the caretakers boiled water for us, the school management gave us free cups of tea, and we ate what we had originally brought with us. Then we set off and walked the whole day. It was pretty hard going. The dozen eggs came in very useful.

For some of the way the road was close to the shore and exposed to the wind off the sea. The Estonian coast in November was not a cheerful sight, the day was overcast, and the Gulf of Finland leaden and flecked with white horses. Eventually we reached the Yyevve area. My mother managed to communicate with the field hospital here and was told that Nanny had arrived, her temperature had gone down, and she was feeling better. She had had pneumonia, but it had been treated in time. We spent a terrible night in a cold uncomfortable inn at Yyevve. The landlord apologized that he had nothing to offer us, but literally all his provisions had been eaten, even the potatoes. He could only give us hot water. Next day we set out to walk the last eight miles to the estate of Kurtna, which was to serve as our base.

Kurtna was occupied by the headquarters of the First Division of the Russian North-West Army and a battalion of Estonian shock troops. When we arrived there both of the big houses – the manor house and the manager's home – were packed to bursting with troops. We were only let into the outbuildings, which were sombre, unheated rooms with nothing in them, not even tables and chairs. It was desperately cold, dirty and unpleasant in every sense. Representatives from our group went to the Russian and Estonian officers in charge to ask them where we could settle more permanently and what the food situation was, as none of us had any left.

The answer was not encouraging: the staff of the First Division had not yet received any orders about where we were to go, and the Estonian troops certainly did not want to vacate their billets for refugees. They had no stoves, firewood or food for us. We had arrived at two o'clock in the afternoon and by six in the evening we were frozen and dejected.

Between six and seven something happened that seared itself in my memory. My seven-year-old sister Tanechka was very hungry, but there was nothing to eat. She asked my mother for something, but my mother told her there was nothing. She then ran to my father, because he always did whatever he could for her, and said: 'Papa, papa, I want something to eat. Give me something to eat, papa, I'm very hungry. Mama says that I have to go to sleep, but I can't because I'm so hungry, I want something to eat. I haven't eaten anything since this morning.'

My father endeavoured to comfort her. He took her out of the room, tried singing with her, but that did not work and he rushed back into the room, where I witnessed him burst into terrible sobbing. I had never seen my father cry before and could not even imagine the sense of helplessness that would make a man sob in this way – helplessness at not being able to do something for the daughter he loved and give her at least a crust of bread so that she would feel her own father was helping her. It shook him very badly, and not just him. Several people heard and saw my father sobbing and it galvanized them. Everyone started saying it was time to do something.

A whole deputation went to talk to the Estonians. My father did not go. They told the Estonians that the children were crying from hunger and the parents crying because they had nothing to give them. It had an effect. Forty-five minutes later the deputation returned and said that the Estonians had understood the situation and were going to give us accommodation. They were cleaning out several rooms in the manor house and would feed us. An Estonian field kitchen drove up and actually began dishing out some very tasty pork and potatoes. We ate it, cheered up a bit, and two and a half hours later were transferred to the big house, where the Estonians had cleared two storeys for refugees and left only one for themselves.

This incident made a deep impression on me and may even be the reason that we never suffered from the 'generation problem' in our family – a problem that always disrupts and destroys family life and is very difficult to avoid. Perhaps this was because I could see so clearly the position my father was in; the fact that he was powerless to help me, that he had lost his social status, his material security, his national self-assurance, the strength of his convictions. All this happened before my very eyes. I never criticized my father in subsequent life, and the only time we had a disagreement about something it was entirely my fault. There was complete understanding between us, just as there was all my life between my mother and me. I have purposely dwelt on this incident, because I think it was a turning-point in my life.

So now it was the beginning of December. We had moved into the manor house and ended up in a large room. There were nine or ten of us refugees to five double beds. Our family had two enormous double beds, on which the four of us could sleep soundly. The food problem had been solved, because General Dirazhensky, the very amiable elderly commander of the First Division, ordered his staff to provide for the refugees and the staff took over the military kitchens. We were given two very good meals a day, tea was on tap, and some people, though not us, got hold of little kerosene and spirit cookers. We could live.

Then my sister fell seriously ill.

She was treated by an army doctor. She had influenza with complications to the heart. On 6 January 1920, Christmas Eve Old Style, Tanya, who had a raging temperature and was almost always semi-delirious, suddenly shouted 'Nanny! Nanny!' and stretched her arms out as though Nanny was standing before her. Later we discovered it was at that very hour that Nanny died in the military hospital at Yyevve, where my mother had visited her several times. We used to say afterwards that Nanny had come to say goodbye to her dear little ones, to her darling Tanechka. Nanny had loved her very much; they had lived 'soul in soul', as we say.

The next day Tanya died. She died unexpectedly. When her body was washed, she was found to have a mark in the area of her heart, and the doctor said it was because her aorta had burst. Two or three days later the news arrived from the hospital that Nanny had died. That was the third death in my life. I was suddenly visited by the sense of another world, an awareness that there was a world to which people like my brother Arkadik went. I couldn't believe that the little boy had committed any sin, so he must have gone to Paradise. Evidently there *was* another world, to which God called the righteous. Now Tanechka was going there, too…

Tanya died, but she could not be buried. It was quite impossible to make a coffin. She was taken outside and laid on the veranda, where it was extremely cold. The veranda was kept closed so that animals couldn't get in. She lay there and looked just like a little girl peacefully sleeping – she had a beautiful clear face, and my mother and father went to her every day, recited prayers over her, and wept. I went too. I had worshipped my sister. We were great friends and had never competed for our parents' love. I grieved for her. And I grieved for my parents, who were even more upset by her death than by Arkadik's.

My father approached the carpenters on the estate. They told him to wait, they would try to do something, but for the moment they had no coffin.

At this point disturbances broke out in the regiments of the First Division. The troops, as well as the carters and hands conscripted to help with the transport, wanted to return to the villages. They did not want to stay in a foreign country, Estonia. Some of the soldiers decided that come what may, in defiance of logic and their commanding officers' attempts to dissuade them, they would go home. It was January and the units of the North-West Army had fought well beside the Estonians to beat off all the Red Army's attacks. The heavy battles around Narva that the newspapers called 'Estonia's Verdun', were over, and it was clear that the Red Army would not be able to take Estonia. But logic does not count for much in such situations, and around 10 January 1920 two and a half thousand troops decided to set off for Russia.

When a colonel called Anosov and a group of other officers barred their way and tried to persuade them to reconsider, because the Reds would take their revenge on them – 'You are White soldiers,' he said, 'and we don't know yet what fate has in store for us, maybe the White Army will go back on the offensive' – a soldier shot him dead. The troops then made for Lake Peipus and the Estonian guards let them through. They crossed the lake on the ice, but when they got to the Soviet side they were fired on with machineguns, so they had to turn back. When they approached the Estonian side, they were fired on by the Estonians. Apparently, many of those who had decided to return to Russia perished.

These events were not reported in the Estonian press at the time, and even when people had occasion to remember them in the 1930s the Estonians tried to gloss over everything and consign it to oblivion. But Colonel Anosov had been killed and his body was laid out on the very same veranda as Tanya's. When the officers came to pay their respects and prepare a coffin, seeing the little girl there they said they would make one for her too. So twenty-four or forty-eight hours after Anosov's death, Tanya too was lying in a coffin. She had been almost a week out in the sub-zero air. She was put in the coffin and lay there exactly as though she were still sleeping; a very beautiful, crystal girl.[1] She was to be buried next to Nanny in the new cemetery at Yyevve. Whilst my mother and father were burying Nanny, Tanya's little body lay in its open coffin on the veranda. When they came back, they decided not to take me with them because there was a very hard frost and *mama* was afraid I would catch cold.

At the cemetery a terrible thing happened. My parents had taken a hold-all with them in which they kept not only what money they had left, but some of *mama*'s jewellery and all their documents. To get to where the new émigré cemetery was being set up, you had to cross rather a lot of open field. They carried the coffin with the help of the sledge-driver. But when they got back to the sledge, the hold-all had gone. It had been stolen. This was a double blow to the family. We had not only lost our dear little singer, Tanya, but our last links with our former life, and even the documents that are so vital in every person's life. The consequences of this bedevilled the whole Estonian period of my parents' life. They were not able to obtain copies of these Tsarist documents from the Soviet Union until 1940 or 1941, by which time Estonia had been incorporated into the USSR.

A typhus epidemic now broke out in the army and my father caught it. He was taken off to the hospital where Nanny had died. Shortly afterwards I went down with it too. When I arrived at the same hospital I was first put in a corridor. There were delirious patients with high temperatures everywhere. There were so many lice that they scrunched underfoot as people walked along the corridors where we, the new admissions, lay on straw. My mother already knew the nurses and military doctors, so she managed to get me moved to the same ward as my father. Not that I knew this, because I was unconscious. When I woke up, the crisis was past and I was lying in the next bed to my father, who was looking at me and smiling.

---

1   In accordance with Russian custom, the coffin was still open.

He had had an even worse time. His crisis had begun before I arrived, and his pulse had gone. He was lying there apparently not breathing and with his eyes turned up. A doctor said: 'He's dead, isn't he? Take him out then.' He was taken out immediately, because they were so short of beds. But a woman doctor who was also there remembered my mother and gave him two further injections to prevent a heart attack, and he suddenly sighed, closed his mouth, and turned his head. The crisis had passed. This was my mother's achievement: she prayed and prayed for him, but also kept visiting him. She walked eight miles there and eight miles back – at first every day, then every other day. This had an effect on the medical staff. They treated us differently, knowing that 'the schoolmistress' was behind us.

Just after my father was over his crisis, I was brought in. I was unconscious and talking gibberish, but the woman doctor came and gave me injections. When the crisis was over and I saw my father, I said to him: '*Papa*, I forgot to tell you: Tanechka didn't die, she just fell asleep, then got up, and whilst I was asleep we were together. I wanted to tell you this so much, but I was ill and couldn't.'

My father was stunned by this, and decided that I had lost my reason.

We came out of hospital on my twelfth birthday, 13 March 1920. My mother arrived to collect us with a sledge. By then she had moved to a small farm at Kurtna, rather than live on the estate, because the doctors did not want her to infect anyone and it was important for her to stay well if she could. There was deep snow along the route but the sun was bright, so we felt happy.

The farm was pretty primitive, not very well-off, it belonged to an Estonian family and adjoining it was a pigsty and cowshed. Inside was one large room occupied by the owners, and the bed at the other end of it was let to us for a sum. At night we put one mattress on the floor and two people slept on the bed. But now my mother fell ill, so my father and I slept on the floor. A few days later my father had to borrow a cart and take my mother to the doctor at Kurtna, and from there straight to the hospital, as she had typhus. Now my father went every other day to visit my mother. This helped a lot, because they already knew him, so my mother got more attention. The infection passed fairly quickly in her case and she had no acute crisis. To that extent she was lucky.

It was a wonderful spring. Every day we went to the estate and were given terrific army food. The cook fed us and gave us a second helping to take away for supper. The snows were thawing fast, and the woods, which came right up to the farmhouse, were full of life – animals, birds and plants were waking up.

Once when we were out we heard church bells ringing. There was a convent five miles away and when the wind was in the right direction the sound carried.

3.   Tatyana Andreyeva's grave (taken in 1932).

For us it was like a message from God. My father and I were overcome with emotion and crossed ourselves and broke out into prayer. All his life my father had a strong sense of prayer; I think I was born with the same, but I was also brought up to have it. At this moment our perception was heightened. We gave thanks to God for His help in these terrible events. So many thousands of people had died, but we had survived, despite our great losses.

2

School at Last

Everyone was leaving the estate at Kurtna. The staff of the First Division was disbanded and General Dirazhensky departed with all his men. The army kitchens closed down.

My father found lodgings in one half of a small house on a road through the forest about two miles from Yyevve. The forester who owned it would take no rent, because he said he would welcome the opportunity to keep up his Russian by visiting us every so often. My mother came out of hospital to this new home. Another Russian family soon moved into the other half, and there were other Russian ex-teacher refugees living nearby, so it became a small Russian colony, which sometimes went on forest walks together, or sang Russian songs conducted by my father. The summer we spent there was very important for us, because we were recuperating from the typhus and my father was very badly affected by all the upheaval in his life and the complete lack of money.

We survived entirely on American philanthropy. Members of the Young Men's Christian Association – sensibly-dressed, six-foot-tall Americans with large spectacles – brought us food.[2] The American missions also supplied us refugees with underclothes of the right size, shoes, and if need be a coat, often of military cut. Twice a week we went to Yyevve and the Americans gave us food parcels, which greatly supplemented our diet. The contents varied. There was always sweet evaporated milk in tins, which my father and I particularly liked, and thick slabs of American army chocolate. Then you got rice, peas, or beans, ready to cook or already cooked in tins, delicious smoked rind of fat, packets of flour, and sometimes freshly baked bread and biscuits. It was extremely generous and intelligently thought out. Of course, they also distributed various vegetable oils and sometimes fats. I mention this in some detail, because most people have completely forgotten it by now but it saved thousands of us from starvation. You must not forget that Estonia was a young country and there wasn't the abundance of food on the farms that there was a few years later. Lots of cattle and fowl were slaughtered during the war years. Gradually it

---

2   See H.H. Fisher, *The Famine in Soviet Russia 1919-23* (London, 1927).

recovered. Meanwhile, thanks to the well thought out American effort we got more or less everything we needed. As a result, people began to come round again from their terrible war experiences and diseases.

But no-one gave us any money, not a kopeck, and we needed money if only to write letters. After everything was stolen from us at the cemetery, we were left literally with the change in our pockets. So my father started making toys and selling them through stationery and book shops in Yyevve. He cut out figures from plywood, smoothed their edges, and painted them. One set of animals was called THE FARM, another WILD BEASTS. They were done with humour and, I would say, art, and they really sold quite well. They did not cost much to make, and the retailers did not pay him much, but my father was glad of the ready cash.

At the beginning of September 1920 a Russian school opened at Yyevve intended for the children of refugees like us; but I attended it for only three weeks because we moved to the estate of Paggar, about eight miles away. We joined the labour colony there. This was a group of former officers of the North-West Army, led by Colonel Vilyashev, who were taken on by Count Shtakelberg to renovate a factory on his estate which he wanted to make into a vodka distillery. We as a family were put up in a well-heated wing of the manor house, and my father's job was to install most of the machinery and get it running. After this he went lumberjacking with a Russian team in Shtakelberg's forests – but he did not earn much money there, either.

Come the beginning of 1921, then, he was looking for better work further afield. He went to Tartu to see ex-senator Nikolay Shmeman, who had once been in charge of the St Petersburg Agricultural Colony and Training School. He was very pleased to see my father but no longer had any influence. In Tallinn my father saw Andrushkevich, headmaster of the private Russian High School, and Yanson, head of the Russian teachers' union. They both knew perfectly well what my parents' position in Russia had been, but more teachers had come out of Russia with the army than they could cope with, and these teachers' papers were all in order, whereas my parents' had been stolen. My father was shocked by what he called the 'pedagogic perfidy' of Andrushkevich and Yanson, who would not even certify to the Ministry that they knew him as a teacher. After that, he turned his back on teaching for good.

At about this time, it was decided that I would start as a boarder at the Russian émigré school in Narva, so I had to prepare for the entrance exam.

You must remember that almost all my education so far had been at home. My mother taught me to write Russian properly, and she taught me mathematics, which I was good at. I had been a voracious reader since the age of six, had deeply experienced all the Russian and Napoleonic history I had read, and had learnt an impressive amount of geography from the novels of Jules Verne! My parents had adult conversations about history, culture, politics, from which I was not excluded. Now, whilst he was visiting Tartu, my father bought some excellent textbooks, including Platonov's classic pre-revolutionary one on Russian history. I really enjoyed studying for this entrance exam at home, and I passed with flying colours.

The boarding-house was run by Father Pavel, the future Bishop of Narva and Izhora, who was also acting headmaster. He was a wonderful priest and an excellent teacher. He had no system of punishments. If someone did something wrong, he would ask to see them and talk it through. I always remember the service and sermon he gave us on the first day. He spoke very well about knowledge, science, and the idea of God: he told us that whenever God was mentioned in Newton's presence he took his hat off, and that Kant had devoted half his life to a proof of the existence of God, despite being an out and out rationalist. And knowledge, Father Pavel said, fleshes out our idea of God. He developed this theme without any false pathos, logically, step by step, as though analysing these phenomena. It had a strong effect on our young minds. We respected him no end.

There were five dormitories in the boarding-house, which was on the top floor of the vicarage next to the cathedral. I was in the youngest group, with six others in my dormitory. Every morning before breakfast we sang grace. You could drink as much tea and eat as many white rolls as you liked. We then walked to the school, which was five minutes away down the main street towards the Castle of the Teutonic Order. Morning break was twenty minutes, during which we dashed into the confectionery shop next door and bought our own pasties, pies or rolls, which were good. For lunch we were taken across the road to the girls' boarding-house, where we had ordinary soup, or *shchi* (cabbage soup) with a piece of meat in, and bread of course; very tasty chops with macaroni (fish on Wednesdays and Fridays); and kissel, compote or fruit to finish with. Pure Russian cuisine. You could never say we went hungry! The teachers ate with us and had the same-sized portions. It was totally democratic.

I was friends with a boy called Gleb Rodionov. We had a lot in common, in particular he was passionately interested in Narva's past. To my astonishment, he told me that the town was riddled with tunnels. At first I did not believe him, but then he showed me various old guide-books that described them. One fine day we went for a walk beneath Narva. It was a Sunday, when we were more or less free. We explored the tunnels for two or three hours. They were

4.   Nikolay Andreyev aged 13.

probably excavated in the sixteenth century, when they were important to the defenders of the Castle if it was besieged. The emergency exits then were well beyond the town limits, but now they were within them. We made several exciting expeditions through the tunnels, carrying lights of course and a coil of rope. Once we came upon a door. We heaved it open and found ourselves in someone's cellar, surrounded by barrels. We quickly withdrew, in case we were mistaken for young thieves. I think what we were doing was quite risky, because if anything had happened no-one would have guessed that we were underneath Narva all the time. Gleb had a terrific imagination, which fed on the books of Fennimore Cooper and Mayne Reid that he had and which I borrowed from him. Two years later, he died from meningitis at the age of sixteen, before he could graduate from the high school.

After I had been settled in Narva, my father took decisive steps to find a job. He went to Tallinn, where he applied unsuccessfully for various advertised posts. Then he called at a factory about a job which turned out to be already taken. The secretary, a German lady called Aleksandra Ivanovna, who spoke excellent Russian, fell into conversation with him. She was full of sympathy that he had to fell trees miles from anywhere. He told her about the losses in his family. Suddenly her heart went out to him. She asked him where he was staying and said: 'I'll ask some people I know about a job. I've heard that a new factory is opening here.' She was referring to a tobacco factory owned by a Russified Englishman called Lange. That evening she visited the factory and next morning was able to tell my father that Lange would like to see him. Lange engaged him on the spot. Although my father could not stand tobacco, and never smoked a cigarette in his life, he worked as the engineer at this Tallinn factory for almost ten years. His salary was pretty good and in those days there was a custom in the Baltic States (an English custom, it was considered) of paying employees double at Christmas, as a present. My father began at Lange's in October 1921, received double pay in December, then my parents moved to Tallinn for good.

Tallinn was overcrowded and it was terribly difficult to find a flat. They rented a room in the basement of 24 Zheleznaya Street, which was quite a modern block for the times, complete with lift. All accommodation in Tallinn was expensive, and after being without money for so long they had to buy new clothes, so they were still hard up. The only job *mama* could find was sticking together boxes of *papirosy* (Russian cigarettes with a hollow cardboard mouthpiece) at a factory called 'La Ferme', where she eventually became a quality-controller. She worked there for over a year, but then started giving private lessons to children taking entrance exams – she partly reverted to her profession.

When I left Narva in June 1922 I took with me a school report that gave me five out of five for every subject. I was going to join my parents in Tallinn and attend the private Russian High School there.

My parents were still living in their basement room sub-let from the Kupriyanov family. Mr Kupriyanov was a cobbler, Russian but married to an Estonian, they spoke Estonian a lot at home, but he had kept his Russian. They were pleasant people, but not educated. They thought that the film *Robinson Crusoe* was a series of real events that had been photographed on some far-flung islands! Kupriyanov was terribly shocked when, with all the effrontery of a fourteen-year-old, I explained to him that they were actors and the whole thing was directed. But he was a nice man, who rejected Bolshevism because he saw that when the Bolsheviks passed through Estonia they looted and murdered wherever they went.

The Kupriyanovs could not understand our situation, however, and how difficult it was for my father and mother, having worked with their brains all their lives, to be suddenly reduced to being a simple engineer or worker in a tobacco factory. The fact that they had come down in the world did not affect anyone else, so most people were indifferent. The general attitude was that what had happened could only happen in Russia. Bolshevism was peculiar to Russia. 'When the Bolsheviks tried to take over Estonia, we threw them out. We now have a free democratic republic. But the Russians are so barbaric they can't understand that and have accepted Bolshevism. On their own heads be it!' But people did not discuss the subject very often.

Because of my report from Narva, I was taken into the Russian High School in Tallinn without sitting an entrance examination. It was run by the Russian Schooling in Estonia Society as though it were a pre-revolutionary Russian *gimnaziya* (grammar school/high school). Thus the school year started on the last Monday in August.

When I arrived that day at Narva Street, where the school was situated, I gasped: it was blocked by a crowd of people, including about 400 pupils waiting to be let in. They were all chattering and shouting in Russian. I felt very small and frightened. These supremely confident young people looked physically dangerous and mentally superior to me in every way. Finally a door opened and the janitor appeared – Uncle Fedya, as we called him. He raised one hand, said 'In orderly fashion now!', and to my amazement the whole crowd started walking demurely into the building and upstairs, as the assembly hall was on the top floor.

Amongst the teachers were a first priest, a second priest, and a deacon. They sang a short service, then the headmaster L.A. Andrushkevich thundered out a very effective speech. He said that a new school year was beginning and we should be happy and grateful to the Russian Schooling in Estonia Society for caring about us; that we should always guard against wasting our energy on messing about; that we should study for the benefit of our Country, which sooner or later would call its sons back. This was the universal theme of the first emigration. We were always being told that we were working not for ourselves and our own selfish interests, not in order to earn a lot of money, own a lovely flat and marry a beautiful woman, but in order to accumulate knowledge that would be useful to our Country.

I then marched off to my classroom with my form-teacher and forty-one other pupils. I did not know a single one of them.

The first friends I made lived in the same neighbourhood as me, then I began to make friends with boys I felt an affinity with, for example Kostya Gavrilov.[3] He and I were friends for the rest of our lives, but the way our friendship began is interesting.

One day a leg on the teacher's chair, which stood on a podium, was broken. The inspector, Ivan Stoleykov, a Latin-teacher and typical administrator, came along to the classroom and demanded that the culprit own up. It was a malicious act, he said, the teacher could have sat down and fallen off. Fortunately, teachers generally moved this chair back, which one of them had done, the leg had fallen away, and everything had been prevented. But Stoleykov spat fire and brimstone and demanded a confession.

'Who is on form duty?' he asked.

As luck would have it, I was.

'You will inform me by the end of the last lesson who broke this chair-leg, and if you do not, you will be held responsible for it yourself.'

When he had gone, I said to the class: 'You heard what the inspector said, so if anyone wants to give me his name, I'll pass it on to the inspector.'

---

3   Konstantin Gavrilov and Nikolay Andreyev remained close friends all their lives. They went to Prague together and Kostya by a lucky chance left Prague for Argentina the day before the German invasion. There he continued to work as a biologist and was elected a member of the Argentinian Academy of Sciences. He and Nikolay Andreyev continued to correspond. When Kostya Gavrilov heard of Nikolay Andreyev's death, he was very depressed and died not long after.

I went back to what I was doing, which was cleaning the blackboard for the next lesson. At this point Kostya Gavrilov, whom I hardly knew, got up from the back row and came over to me.

'I broke it,' he said. 'Go and tell the inspector.'

All Gavrilov's body language told me that he was just provoking me. Moreover, I had a theory that no-one had broken the chair, the leg had simply snapped off because the teachers were always jerking it back and the chair was not in its first youth, in fact it was a veteran chair. Some teachers even rocked about in this chair on that leg... So I stared at Kostya and said that if he really had broken it, he could go and tell the inspector himself.

'No,' he said. '*You* must tell him. You said we had to give you our name, so you can go and tell him it was me.'

I said I had examined the chair and reckoned it had happened simply because teachers were always balancing the chair on this leg and some of them even rocked about on it. So that's why it broke. And I was not going to collaborate with our inspector's police investigation, but if someone considered themselves guilty they could go to him themselves.

Gavrilov was taken aback by this and said: 'You're wrong. I broke it.'

'Maybe you were sleepwalking when you broke it,' I said. 'I don't know, so you go and tell him. Explain when you broke it, how you broke it. Nobody saw you break it. When did you break it? You even leave before the rest of us every day, because you live so far away.'

When the inspector came back and asked me if I had found the culprit, I replied: 'There cannot be a culprit, sir, because – ', and explained my theory.

Now it was his turn to be taken aback. He was an *ancien régime* inspector and therefore bellowed at me for form's sake, but eventually said: 'I see you are all as clever as monkeys, but I'm no fool either. I shall get to the bottom of this! Now you can go home.'

Of course, we understood this was an empty threat. After he had gone, Gavrilov came up to me and, beaming all over, said: 'You handled that well. You're a real friend. I was testing you. I thought you would grass, but you didn't. You behaved like a true comrade. Let's be friends.'

And he gave me his hand and we were friends.

3

Life in Tallinn

In the summer of 1923 we moved from our basement to 51-A Poska Street. Poska was the Estonian diplomat who negotiated peace with the Soviet Union in 1920 and got a number of Russian areas, including Pechory and Narva, included in Estonia, which was a great blessing for them. According to official statistics, Estonia now had 1.1 million inhabitants, of whom 10 per cent were Russians.

Number 51-A consisted of two blocks. The first, which fronted the street, had four apartments, with a family in each. In the second block there was a yard with a strange building in it where the caretaker had lived before he moved to the basement of block 1. The little building had an empty room with an oven, a stove and a flue, and if you lit the stove the flue warmed up and heated the whole room. This was the 'apartment' which we now moved into. We had to renovate it, buy furniture for it, use a screen and a dresser to create privacy, but above all be obsessively tidy. When naval officers visited us, they used to ask which of us had served on a battleship, it was so 'shipshape'.

This home was incredibly popular. There was a constant stream of people to it after eight o'clock in the evening. All sorts of people. For instance, the very tall poet Igor Severyanin was friends with my parents and my father used to say that when he visited them he took up all the airspace in the apartment.[4] Another writer who came to see them was Vasily Nikiforov-Volgin,[5] and they were great friends with Sergey Shilling,[6] who tried to help them in every way when they were short of work in the thirties. Then, of course, there were all our old friends. *Mama* made two very good pies on Sundays, one with cabbage, eggs and meat and the other a sweet one with jam, because she always knew there would be guests. Often we could not start until one of our bachelor or divorced friends had arrived.

Altogether, despite its primitiveness, we considered that we had gained by moving into this building. First, it was next to a tram stop, which saved *mama*

---

4   Igor Severyanin (1887-1941), whose real name was Igor Vasilyevich Lotaryov, was a very popular poet during the 1910s and 1920s. He moved to Estonia in 1918 and died in Tallinn in 1941.

5   Vasily Akimovich Nikiforov-Volgin (1900/01-1941), who was of peasant origin, wrote short stories, many of which had a spiritual content and were influenced by his interest in Russian religious culture.

6   Sergey Mikhaylovich Shilling was secretary to the Russian National Society and the Russian Teachers' Union.

The room on Poska Street, Tallinn.

5.   Nikolay Andreyev at the window – late 1920s.

6.   Yefrem and Yekaterina Andreyev – 1930s.

time going to lessons or the market. But Narva Street was close by anyway, and it took me only twenty minutes to walk to school. Secondly, not far away was the beach and a beautiful promenade with seats, lilacs, bird cherries and other fragrant plants. If you walked to the eastern end of it, you came to the *Rusalka* ('Mermaid') Monument to the Russian man-of-war of that name which sank in the Baltic with all hands in 1893. The monument was designed by the sculptor Adamson and was extremely impressive. The names of all the victims were inscribed on it in Russian and it had an angel on top holding a cross and appearing to bless the dead at sea. All the Russians who went for walks in this area visited the monument. We loved to walk along the shore here in the evening, because there was hardly a sound and we could breathe the sea air and calmly discuss whatever was on the Andreyev family's mind.

A no less pleasant place was the enormous Katharinental park, a beautifully laid out palace garden that was the equal of anything I have seen in Europe. Its main avenues were lit by electric lamps and as you walked along, some of these avenues looked as though the sea was just at the end of them. The park had two centres of attraction, the large palace that Peter the Great had built for his wife, Catherine I, and Peter's Little House, a building in the Dutch style which documents show was built by Peter himself before his official residence was finished. The first was superbly furnished in the eighteenth century and for roughly the last seven years of the Estonian Republic the president lived there. What surprised me about the second was its low ceilings, given that Peter was over six feet tall.

In 1924, I think, Peter's Square still existed; it was later renamed Liberty Square. In the middle of it was a life-size statue of Peter the Great in a cocked hat with a sword at his side and holding a spy-glass. He was looking westwards. It was a fine example of eighteenth century monumental art, and one of the most human statues of this statesman. Unfortunately, when nationalistic passions were running high it was decided, in spite of protests from the Russian press and Russian members of parliament, not only to remove the statue but to cut it in half and melt the lower half down for coinage. The top half was taken to the Katharinental and lay around on a trestle outside Peter's Little House for years. People visiting the house usually touched the nose, which having copper in it began to glow red. Then the King of Sweden visited Tallinn, asked to see Peter's Little House, and beheld the Tsar's figure in this lamentable state. It was re-established vertically on a plinth. You could still touch its nose, which people did, but at least it was upright.

For me personally, the Katharinental park was associated with the 'lyrical' side of my life. More than one heroine met me there beneath its spreading branches,

7.   Catherine Andreyev on Poska Street in 1994

and 'lyrical' delight filled the souls of those participating in such trysts… In a special sense it was our park, my park. I also walked there many times on my own, I read a lot there, and dreamed of the future – in uncertain terms. The Katharinental park always reminded me of Russia and things Russian, because it was associated with Peter, who in my consciousness stood for the Russian factor in Europe.

Going back to 51-A Poska Street, the tenants of block two were always changing. At one point the family of Captain Malevich lived there, who commanded the Estonian Navy. Although this was his real name, he used a different, Estonian one, because he was of Estonian extraction. He had been a Captain First Class in the former Baltic Imperial Fleet, his son was taught by my mother, and we made his acquaintance as a result of the events of 1 December 1924.

It was a rather frosty morning. My father got up first, as usual, put some logs in the stove, and had his breakfast. Then he made the sign of the cross over *mama* and me, and left. Twenty minutes later I left for school. I always walked very fast, especially in winter, because in the manner of the times I wore short trousers and knee-length stockings (it took the personal intervention of the headmaster to persuade me to go into long trousers!).[7] I shot down Solomennaya Street, came out on Narva Street, and was surprised that I hadn't bumped into any of my fellow-pupils. In fact there were very few pedestrians about at all, and no policemen. Even at the crossroads, where there was supposed to be a policeman, there was none. Well, I did not give this any more thought and went on to school.

There, as always, it was very warm, cosy and well-lit, but there was not the usual throng streaming into the building. Two or three schoolboys were standing about, talking to Uncle Fedya, but no teachers, just the headmaster. Then I went over to the coat-hooks for our class, and someone said: 'Why have you come in? Don't you know there's no school today?'

'No, how should I?'

'There's fighting going on in the town.'

'What do you mean, fighting?'

'They've seized the Post Office. There's shooting there, and around the station, so the trains haven't come in from the suburbs, and there's nobody here.'

---

7   Nikolay Andreyev wore shorts for so long for financial reasons – they were cheaper.

About thirty of us had turned up on foot. The headmaster telephoned somewhere and told us there would be no lessons: 'If you want to, you can stay here, or if you don't live far away you can go home.'

I preferred to stay at school and wait for more news. Gradually people came in and it emerged that some groups of Communists, so-called 'detachments of armed workers', had staged a coup. The Estonian Communist Party was not very numerous, but it was legal, although there was constant trouble with it because some of its members kept committing illegal acts in support of the Soviet Union. At night they had attacked the home of the head of state, Dr Akel, the war ministry, the station, the main post office, the telephone exchange, and the barracks of the police reservists. A man came in from the latter district and told us it was chaos there, they were virtually tossing bombs about, but it was being brought under control. The territorial army, police and self-defence units had already occupied the town centre, they all had rifles, and they were winning. No newspapers were published, so we did not know what was going on. By eleven o'clock we started to disperse. There were no trams running and the streets were empty. I went home.

The result of this insurrection was that for a short time Estonia was ruled by a military dictatorship under General Laidoner. The following day, when all the newspapers reappeared, Laidoner published an address to the nation, in which he categorically stated that the fate of the country had hung by a thread, because these people had wanted to overthrow the state by force. They had not succeeded and they had evidently been dealt with pretty harshly. Most of them were killed on the spot. Some of the bigger names were put on trial. Of course, most of the population, who knew what Communism was like, if only from a distance, if only very slightly, felt no sympathy for the ringleaders or those who had carried out the putsch. It became clear that the Estonian nation was of one mind on the matter, and they dealt with these people severely. The situation during the night had been extremely serious, because everyone was afraid that Soviet troops would attempt to support the conspirators, so Estonian military units were not brought up to Tallinn but stayed in strategic positions where they could engage with the Soviet forces if these appeared on Estonia's borders.

That evening Captain Malevich came to our flat.

'Yefrem Nikolayevich, come and have a drink with me,' he said.

'What is the occasion?' *papa* asked.

'We've won the lottery! We can carry on living! You see, I took the whole Navy out today – two and a half tubs, a couple of torpedo boats, and an antiquated submarine – and if the Red Fleet had turned up there would have been nothing left of us in ninety minutes. And you know yourself what things would have been like after that!'

As a final tribute to our 'villa' on Poska Street, I should mention that it was in this room that I wrote all my first articles for Russian newspapers and edited the school magazine. When I was already in Prague, Sergey Shilling, the secretary of the Russian national minority in Estonia, invited me to become editor of *Nov* ('Things New'), an anthology of young writing and the first of its kind in the Russian emigration. We edited and published from our 'villa' the issues for 1928, 1929 and 1930. So our 'villa' deserves a place in the history of diaspora literatures. It is where I wrote my essay 'Sirin' (1930) about Nabokov's prose, which caused a stir at the time because it was the first extended piece about his art.

The unpleasant sides of our life here – the crampedness, the absence of any opportunity to have a proper summer holiday, my father's social dissatisfaction, my mother's disappointment at not being able to return to teaching on a large scale until the Soviet period – none of this hindered the creative growth and activity of the youngest member of the Andreyev family. 'The spirit bloweth where it listeth' – this ancient truth was often recalled by us in our 'villa' and sums up our whole Tallinn existence.[8]

4

'The Call of Russia'

In June 1924 the literary circle at the High School organized its first tour of Estonia. The itinerary was Tartu - Valga - Pechory - Old Izborsk, the last two of which had previously been part of Russia.

It was a great success. There were about forty people in the group, including friends of mine from the literary circle and the theatrical productions I had acted in, and some teachers. We were always in high spirits, always singing. The travelling was done largely by train and we had a whole carriage to ourselves. We were welcomed wherever we went. We stayed in primary schools and high schools, because our leader, Vladimir Sokolov, had teacher-friends everywhere.

We liked Tartu very much. Sokolov had been a teacher there before coming to us, and he was popular in Tartu. A banquet was given in our honour. We were taken round the famous university and Sokolov, who had studied there, explained to us that many Russian poets had been associated with Dorpat, as it was then called, and Zhukovsky had written about it.[9] We also discussed why

---

8   Russian version of the Gospel according to St John 3:8.

9   Vasily Zhukovsky (1783-1852), a romantic poet and translator, was a friend of Pushkin.

the town came to be called in Russian Yuryev, and why Ivan the Terrible looked upon Yuryev as his, despite the fact that the Livonian Knights owned it.

From here we went to Valga, a small town divided between Estonia and Latvia. We joked that one of us jumped over a ditch in the town and it was only later, as he was walking along, that he noticed all the signs were in a foreign language. He took a closer look around him and realized he was in Latvia – the ditch was the border. He very soon jumped back into his native Estonia!

Pechory, which we visited next, astonished and enchanted us. It was a completely different world: not Estonian, not Latvian, not Swedish-German-Russian like Tartu, but a typical Russian provincial town. The Pskov-Pechery monastery was breathtaking: we had not expected such beauty, such a unified whole. The ancient walls, towers, loopholes, secret passageways (not really secret at all, but we imagined they were), original gates, even the lay-brothers in black cassocks and skull-caps who opened and closed the gates, all seemed part of an historical landscape. The monastery was called the 'Assumption' monastery after its amazing Cathedral of the Assumption built into the side of a hill. I had occasion to visit it several times later in life, when I was studying its history. In 1924, of course, I had no idea I would one day be researching its history, I looked upon it as a picturesque piece of Old Russia that had survived by a miracle for our consolation outside Russia's borders in tiny Estonia.

From here we went to Izborsk, which also made a tremendous impression on us. The weather was fine and we could see Pskov in the distance, or to be more precise we could see that Pskov was there, because a hazy image of roofs and the belfry of the Cathedral of the Pskov Holy Trinity hung in the air. We were shown over the monastery at Izborsk by Aleksey Bulatov, who was chairman of the local circle for the preservation of ancient monuments. He was dressed à la russe, in an embroidered shirt and high boots. He had a beard and what struck us at the time as crafty eyes. A colourful man, he seemed to embody Pskov's independence in the past, and ancient Novgorod, which were associated in our imagination with Rus. It was all a very profound experience for us.

The following summer Sokolov organized another brilliant expedition, this time to Finland. We visited Helsinki, Vyborg, Imatra, Sveaborg, and ended up on the shores of Lake Ladoga, whence we were to sail to the Valaam Monastery which I had last seen with my parents in 1915.

A quite large motorboat came to pick us up, and we were surprised and delighted to see that its name was written in Cyrillic: *The Saint Nicholas*. Its crew consisted of three monks, who spoke both Finnish and Russian. The trip had a stronger effect on me than before. The lake slightly depresses you. You sense this huge volume of water beneath you, and it is not well-disposed towards you (I've noticed this about lakes generally). The surface is vast. At some point the Finnish shore disappears behind you, but the Valaam Islands have not yet come into view. You feel you are on a boundless sea. How long the voyage will last, you don't know. You can't help thinking of the transitoriness of your existence, that this could be your last journey anywhere, and your soul is filled with pity for the world, penitence, and thoughts of mortality. I was not the only one who felt this way.

We headed straight for the archipelago, which contains about forty islands, some small, some large. On one of the main ones are the monastery buildings, around a big bay into which we sailed. The rocky shore, the shimmering perspectives and the ethereal outline of the main monastery's bell-tower, were stunning.

I could not help comparing things with how they had been in 1915. Then, evidently, the monastery had been very well off. There were thousands of pilgrims, or tourists as they would now be called. The hotel in 1915 was full. Steamers and people arrived and departed like clockwork. Several hundred people sat down to eat in the refectory at a time and there were four sittings per meal. The monastery's big two-storeyed steamers plied to and fro from Petrograd with 300-400 passengers. The churches were full of people praying, of course. The pilgrims went to the remote parts of the monastery in large groups mainly by motor-boat. So it was much more open to the public then. Now there were hardly any visitors. The monks regarded our group as very large; it got special attention; they were particularly pleased that we were all Russian, and from another country, Estonia. In the refectory, which we visited several times a day, we were seated separately from the monks, as there were women amongst us, but we were given the same to eat as the monks. As before, we were allowed to talk during the meal, and each day a different monk read monotonously and not very clearly from descriptions of holy places or the lives of the saints. If anything, the impact now was stronger, as there was not the smart set with their *haute couture* as there was in 1915.

The monastery choir was much smaller now, but sang just as finely. The services were just as long and there is no doubt that the monastery's setting surrounded by water and severe conditions, cut off from people, disposed the monks to concentrate on the main tasks of their calling – serving God and mankind.

We stayed there two and a half days. First we toured the main island with the monastery, then we were taken to the various cells of the monastery on other islands. Usually we were rowed there in the boats which the monks themselves used to get about, and sometimes we went in motorboats, as when we visited hermit Yefrem.

He lived entirely alone on an islet, in a small cell next to a beautifully built and decorated little church. He was wearing his *skhima*-monk black and white vestments.[10] He was tall, well-built, bearded and with kind, clear eyes. We spent a few hours with him and gathered from his stories that he had once been confessor to Grand Duke Nikolay Nikolayevich. He led a very ascetic life; although we looked around everywhere, we could find no signs of food. He lived on what the monks brought him. He held services several times a day in the little church, and slept in a coffin. He had already dug a grave for himself next to his cell. He explained to us that he was not expecting to die soon, but believed that when you die you should cause others the minimum of trouble, so he had prepared everything in advance.

We realized he was a man with great experience and understanding of life. The services he held were powerful. He gave a short one on our arrival and for the first and last time in my life I heard in the Orthodox liturgy the words: 'For our enemies, who hate us, let us pray unto the Lord.' That day the lake was calm and the sky seemed a pure, endless blue above us. The deep blue sky, the fathomless waters of the lake, the clumps of trees growing on this islet, all combined to make a strong impression on us, like the wise monk himself, who took a very level view of life and was completely free of the falsity that could sometimes be felt in the preachers in Tallinn's churches, who struck you as saying things because they had to and living quite differently from how they told you to. There was nothing of that here.

When we finally left, he blessed us. And that is how he remained in our memory – standing on the shore blessing us as we went away again in a motorboat to the main island.

Meeting him, and experiencing what I think we all experienced on Valaam, left us more serious and subdued. Up to then we had spent most of our time larking about, telling jokes, and thinking up facetious couplets. But after Valaam our attitude was different. We were undoubtedly spiritually enriched and partook of the monks' search for God and truth. I can't say to what extent it took root in our souls, but it certainly remained there a long time.

10 A monk who has taken the strictest monastic vows, the 'great *skhima*'.

It was best expressed in a poem written afterwards by one of our literary circle, Irina Kaigorodova, and published in the first issue of *Nov* in 1928. The last verse read:

> *How clearly then we saw, how faith awoke!*
> *We heard the mighty call of Russia here.*
> *So this is where our Russia now is hid,*
> *Her soul unscathed beneath the weight of chains.*

5

1927: I Leave for Prague

The sixth form focussed my mind on two vital questions: what was I really interested in, and what was I going to do after leaving the high school? By now I was definitely inclining to the arts. Literature, the theatre and history inspired me much more than the prospect of becoming an average engineer and building concrete bridges for the rest of my life.[11] No decisions were yet taken, but in the lower sixth I started learning Latin, in case I needed it later.

The exams went well and I even got a five for Estonian, although to be honest I don't believe my Estonian was ever of that standard.

Between the exams and the leaving assembly, the school had to send a boy and a girl with the headmaster to the head of state. This was a tradition established by Estonian presidents, who received representatives of all the secondary schools at the end of the academic year, gave them a meal, made a short speech wishing them well in life, and thus as it were bonded with the future intelligentsia who were going to work for the good of their country. The day before this was due to happen, the inspector dropped in out of the blue and told me that next day I must come to school wearing my best suit and my school-leaver's badge, as I was going to see the president. I was surprised – usually it was the year-leader's privilege – and I even had the temerity to ask the inspector whether he had got the right person. He raised his eyebrows: 'Do you think I would joke about such a serious matter?!'

Next day, I turned up at the appointed time and was pleased to see Tamara Golitsynskaya representing the girls. She looked Circassian and was therefore almost unique in the school-leaving year: most of the girls had blonde, auburn or chestnut hair. She had two beautiful, raven-black tresses, a wonderful figure, dainty feet, and misty, languid eyes that promised goodness knows what

---

11 The majority of young émigrés tried to get qualified as engineers as it appeared that this was more likely to guarantee employment while abroad. Those who were later arrested by the Soviet authorities at the end of the Second World War were more likely to be taken off to the Soviet Union to build factories. Nikolay Andreyev was lucky in this respect.

– heavenly bliss! Fifty years later I saw a photograph of her sent from the USSR and she still had the same elegance and stylish beauty. Gossips said the headmaster had chosen her because she would throw all the other girls into the shade; but she was a very good student and had been awarded *cum laude* like me.

We arrived at the presidential palace, which was smaller inside than it looked outside, and saw several hundred young people from schools all over Estonia. We all felt shy in each other's presence and were on our best behaviour. The president spoke with feeling and expression, which was not common in Estonian everyday life. Then we gave a rousing rendition of the national anthem: 'My fatherland, my happiness and joy, how wonderful thou art...' After that we were given a goblet of wine each, fruit and pieces of torte. We tried something of everything, then were whisked away to have our photograph taken. It was a relief to leave the palace, because all the time we were there we had to stick by the side of our headmaster. All the headmasters exchanged remarks, but we schoolchildren wouldn't risk opening our mouths in this holy of holies of the Estonian state.

It became clear now that I would be leaving Estonia. I could train as an engineer in Estonia, but it was a small country with few opportunities and I knew from my father's experience that engineers there were always pushed around by the people who owned the firms. The only alternative seemed to be to scrape a miserable living on one of the newspapers. But I really wanted to study the history of literature and possibly history itself. The question was, where? And how was I to pay for it?

At Tartu, Slavonic languages and Russian literature were taught on a limited scale. History there either meant Estonian history, or European history from a German angle. Personally I was only interested in the Russian approach to history. Tartu, therefore, was not an option. I could have studied law there, but it would have been foolhardy for a Russian to count on getting enough work as a lawyer in Estonia.

Another idea, suggested by my grandfather in Torzhok, who maintained a lively correspondence with us, was that I should read history at Leningrad or Moscow University, as they were 'probably best', it was not difficult to get into them, and I had uncles in both cities. These uncles, however, did not share my grandfather's optimism. From the beginning of NEP until 1925 people travelled fairly regularly from Estonia to Russia and back again, but it was obvious by 1927 that NEP was winding down. Everyone my parents spoke to said that if I went now I could find myself in trouble fast, because I had different habits, I was used to the free exchange of opinions, I would be regarded as a product of bourgeois culture, and this would be very dangerous. So the Soviet option was not on.

France and Belgium were out, too, because I did not know French well enough – I had not studied it since the year I spent at Narva High School. My German would be adequate, but Germany was extremely expensive and there were no scholarships. People tended to go to Germany to get the best technical education, knowing that the job prospects were also better in German industry.

There was one option left: Czechoslovakia. This was the most promising. For a variety of reasons, Czechoslovakia in the early 1920s was pro the Russian émigrés. The first president, Professor Masaryk, took under his wing scholars expelled from the Soviet Union, and the Czechoslovak government decided to help students finish their education who had been exiled mid-course by the Civil War. The so-called 'Russian Action' was initiated and the Czechs awarded thousands of scholarships to Russian students. A large centre was set up for them in Prague, and a number of strong educational and research organizations sprang up beside it.

However, by 1927 the situation had changed. Most faculties were not taking young Russian émigrés any more and the few who got in had to sign a promise that they would not ask for a scholarship. There was only one route available to me: through the agricultural cooperative institute which taught in Russian. These people were still advertising for students to graduate as civil and agricultural engineers, and their advertisements were tempting because the degrees were worth something, tuition was in Russian, and the institute would arrange the entry visa. The year before I left the High School Kostya Tennukest, Volodya Rimsky-Korsakov and others had gone to Prague on this ticket, and they sent back very favourable reports. If things turned out well, you could get financial support once you were there. You soon began to understand Czech, although speaking it was more difficult. There were masses of Russians, Russian centres, and Russian organizations.

My instinct told me I should go; I would probably have to go; but where was I to find the money?

The main event on my 'lyrical' front at that time was Rita Ulk, who had come out of the USSR with her father and brother. Her mother, who was dead, had been German, her father was Estonian, and the children were completely Russified. Rita was a pretty blonde with a beautiful plait down to her waist. She was lively, liked a good laugh, but could also discuss serious things. She was in the year below me at school, although it turned out later that she was a year older.

Possibly because I was not one of the horde of boys running after her, Rita noticed me and appreciated me as a person more and more. Through the summer of 1927 she saw off all her rivals and we were soon going everywhere together. It culminated in a trip to Pechory with other high school graduates, when we declared our love to each other. The relationship was so wonderful that it pushed all my problems out of the way, even what I was going to do next and whether I would get the money to go abroad. But Rita was a more experienced person than me (she had lived in the USSR), and she took the initiative. She had words with Zinaida Dormidontova and Margarita Kaigorodova, two ladies who knew me well, and persuaded them to set up a fund for me and collect money. I did not know anything about this, but in September they suddenly announced that they had enough to cover the first year and a half of my study in Prague and my travel.[12] So this was the result of Rita Ulk coming into my life.

Kostya Gavrilov and I were to travel to Prague together. As soon as the decision to go was made, the world of Estonia began to fade. The school year started up and Rita disappeared into the sixth form. Kostya and I attended the service for the first day of term, as did many other recent graduates. But when first the pupils and then the teachers went off to their classes, we felt completely estranged from it all.

As the day of departure approached, my parents grew very sad. I was the only child they had left, now I was grown up enough to be going away for a long time, but how would it all turn out? They did, however, completely approve. They thought it was necessary for me to leave 'provincial' Estonia, and Prague seemed the right place to get a good higher education because, fortunately for me, the Soviet regime had exiled a lot of Russian professors there. My mother packed two suitcases for me and in true Russian fashion put in enough food to get to Mongolia. A service was held for Kostya and me in the Church of St Nicholas, and we were blessed on our way.

We left Tallinn on 15 October on a Finnish vessel bound for Stettin. There was a circus travelling with us and the animals were in cages on deck covered with tarpaulins. During the night we came out into the Baltic and hit a storm. Goodness knows what the animals went through. It was the first time I had been to sea and lying in my bunk I could not work out what was happening. I got dressed quickly and came up on deck. Massive bottle-green waves were breaking over it, and there was absolutely no-one there. I went to the dining-room for breakfast and apart from me there were only two passengers, a couple

12 The history of the creation and evolution of the Russian academic community in Prague can be found in: C. Andreyev and I. Savicky, *Russia Abroad. Prague and the Russian Diaspora 1918-1938* (Yale, 2004).

of sailors, and the captain. The captain waved and greeted me as a future sailor. Poor Kostya, despite the fact that his uncle was a famous White admiral, made the mistake of not coming on deck as soon as he woke up, and was terribly sick. The whole ship was ill. I walked around all day and watched the prow plunging so deeply into the waves the captain's bridge was nearly swamped. In the evening I wondered how things were below decks, so I went down to see. I took one look at the victims, and threw up!

The storm delayed us by twenty hours, but now we were coming into the Stettiner Haff. It was interesting that as soon as we neared Germany we saw an increase in the number of structures associated with technology: wherever you looked there were factory chimneys, shipyards, and signs of industrialization. Unfortunately, wherever we looked in Stettin there were also incredibly long German words which we could not understand. We began to feel that our acquaintance with Schiller at the High School had ill-prepared us for everyday German... This had interesting consequences when our train reached Berlin.

On board the ship there was a group of monks from the Valaam Monastery who were on their way to Yugoslavia. We had not seen them, even on board – presumably they considered the food sinful. We had helped them through Customs at Stettin, because they did not know German, and when they got off in Berlin their exotic appearance attracted quite a crowd. The Berliners were given to mockery in those days and shouted provocative things at the monks and had a good laugh at their expense. The monks were frightened, they did not understand what was going on, and they looked very forlorn. But we did not have much idea, either. We knew that we had to go to another station, the Dresden, for Prague, and that we would have to take the monks with us, but how were we going to negotiate it all in German?

At this point a tall, smiling, ruddy-cheeked young policeman arrived, went up to the monks, and said something to them in Russian. They were overjoyed and almost covered him in kisses.

Hans explained that he had learnt a few words of Russian when he had been a prisoner-of-war on the eastern front. He looked up the train times for us, organized two taxis, and helped us load our own and the monks' luggage.

Kostya and I were intrigued to know what it was Hans said to the monks that sent them into such transports of delight, and we discovered when we went with him to the third class buffet, because he repeated it to us:

'How are you brothers, f...k your m.....s!'

Hans was sincerely convinced this was a friendly Russian greeting that can be used in various situations; it even contained the word *Mutter*. As soon as he said it, of course, the monks felt at home.

8.   Yekaterina and Yefrem Andreyev in their room in Tallinn.

Part III: Czechoslovakia

Map 4. Czechoslovakia as well as places visited in Estonia and Russia.

9.   Kostya Gavrilov and Nikolay Andreyev taken on the day they left Tallinn for Prague – 1927.

1
Prague Beginnings

The train came into Prague's Wilson Station at six o'clock in the morning. We got out and were overwhelmed by the smell of carbolic acid. All Prague's stations were washed down with this in the morning and for years afterwards I associated the smell with arriving in Czechoslovakia.

Waiting for us on the platform was the tall, imposing, dark-eyed and black-haired Volodya Rimsky-Korsakov, who always stood proudly and statuesquely and was equally capable of representing his high school class, the school generally, or Russia itself. At his side was the shorter figure of Kostya Tennukest, who had already found us a room, but not in Prague, where it was much dearer and foreign students were not allowed to settle straight away, especially if like me they had only a Nansen passport.[1] So we would be living in a village twenty-five miles outside Prague. He had also found out how I could enrol at the Philosophy Faculty, and that the university did not mind in the least if I was simultaneously a student of the Russian Agricultural Cooperative Institute (RACI). While Volodya took Kostya Gavrilov off to enrol, Tennukest helped me register at the Philosophy Faculty. I had to get a large official stamp from the Estonian Consul to prove I was Andreyev, but since I had graduated from the High School *cum laude* Charles University waived my first three months fees.

Before deciding which lectures I was going to attend, I thought I had better visit the institution that I was legally attached to, RACI. I was not intending to tell them I'd joined the university – it did not concern them – but I had obtained my visa through them. The director of RACI was Professor Marakuyev, a Don Cossack. I had previously thought Cossacks spend all their time charging around with lances. Marakuyev was an amiable, very educated, elderly man who was a specialist in agriculture and the cooperative movement, had published a lot, and was highly respected in the south of Russia.

All the teachers at RACI were Russian. The syllabus was large and contained a lot of more general topics. There was a very interesting course of lectures on political economy delivered by a former professor of, I think, Kharkov University, called Dmitry Ivantsov. Mathematics was taught by Marakuyev himself. The courses in general descriptive and systematic botany were taken by a great expert, Professor Vladimir Ilin. Economic geography and certain branches of economics associated with Russia were taught by Pyotr Savitsky,

---

1 Dr Fridtjof Nansen became the first High Commissioner for Refugees on behalf of the League of Nations in 1921. The 'Nansen Passport' was a document designed to provide some kind of legal status for refugees and eventually was accepted by fifty-four governments. For many Russian refugees, whose Imperial Russian papers were no longer valid and who did not wish to have Soviet papers, the 'Nansen Passport' served almost as a symbol of loyalty to Russia and opposition to the Bolsheviks.

one of the leaders of the 'Eurasians', an interesting and constructive mind to whom I owe a great deal. The lectures on the history of the cooperative movement were given by Professor Totomiants, who also lectured in Berlin and Paris. Book-keeping, accounting and the principles of cooperative management were taught by Aleksandr Zenkovsky, brother of the famous philosopher Father Sergy Zenkovsky. And so on. I can honestly say that the lectures at RACI were not a waste of time. They broadened my horizons.

My main focus, however, was the Philosophy Faculty of Charles University. In Russia we would probably have called it the Faculty of Languages and History with philosophical subjects attached. Here everything was combined under 'philosophy'. The courses were four years. You could choose what subjects you liked, and therefore pitch your course in a particular direction. If you wanted to become a Slavist, the assistant lecturers would suggest which subjects you should sign up for as starters. In my case these were the introduction to philosophy, with seminar, led by Professor Kozak, and Professor Weingart's introductory lectures on Slavonic philology. In addition, of course, I attended lectures and seminars on Russian literature and history.

The lectures were of a high quality. Professor Vladimir Frantsev, who was a specialist on the Slavophiles and led a seminar on eighteenth and nineteenth century Russian drama, was a member of the Russian, Polish and Czech Academies and lectured in Russian and Czech. By this I mean he might start in Czech, change to Russian, and finish in Czech. Perhaps he did this because his audience was the most mixed – it contained a lot of Czechs. Frantsev's lectures were very useful to me because they were specific and easy to follow, even when he was talking in Czech. If he had expressed his main point in Czech, he would repeat it in Russian, and vice versa, which was a great help in mastering Czech.

Yevgeny Lyatsky lectured on modern Russian Literature, by which was meant nineteenth-century. He lectured in Russian and was often very amusing about critics and authors. Not many Czechs attended his lectures. To appreciate them you had to have complete command of Russian, which not many Czechs at that time did. He had an abstract style of lecturing which was sometimes difficult to follow, but always interesting.

The seminar he led was so impressive that I can still remember when it was held: at two o'clock on Tuesday afternoons. I arrived and was amazed to see that it was taking place in his large study, where all twenty-four chairs were occupied and some people were sitting on the floor. Lyatsky was in a good mood and announced that the theme of the seminar, which was the first of the season, was the new 'formal method' of literary criticism fashionable in the Soviet Union. A paper on it would be read by Rostislav Pletnyov, who would then lead the discussion. Pletnyov was a postgraduate writing a Ph.D. thesis on nature in Dostoyevsky. The range of his knowledge and interests was great and he was four or five years older than me. He was a descendant of the Pletnyovs in Pushkin's circle.

He read an interesting paper that not only described what the Formalists believed, but looked at how they had evolved their theories. I had never encountered such erudition before. Pletnyov referred to the views of dozens of famous people, cited bibliographical references from memory, included an enormous number of quotations, and made it all not only clear but extremely interesting. We realized that he was showing us a genuinely new approach to literature. The older students then asked him questions, including a girl who knew all of Potebnya's theories and insisted that he had played a decisive part in formalism.[2] Pletnyov answered questions and criticism convincingly and with profuse quotations and references. He more or less agreed that the Formalists were going too far and, although their theory was interesting and in some cases true, to explain literature only in terms of authors vying to outdo their predecessors in the use of 'devices' was somewhat risky.

I came out of the seminar reeling and with a strong sense of inferiority. My God, what knowledge, what language! Lyatsky, Pletnyov and the girl had been juggling with concepts and nuances of concepts that I knew nothing about and had simply to take on trust. This baptism of fire forced me to treat literary scholarship seriously. To be a literary scholar, I decided, you had to know a lot and take a systematic approach to your work.

As leader of the seminar, Lyatsky set the subjects that students could study. I was attracted by the theme 'Gogol as an historian', which Lyatsky mentioned in passing was contentious and under-researched. I thought it might be interesting because I loved Gogol and here was an opportunity to find out more. So that I could research it in full, Lyatsky gave me a letter of introduction to the director of the Slavonic Library.

This library had a fantastic selection of Russian books. It was based on the personal library of Vladimir Tukalevsky, a bibliophile close to the SRs who before the Revolution had been very well off. His library had been outside Russia and he sold it to the Czech Foreign Ministry for a good price on condition that he remained director until his retirement. Tukalevsky set about expanding the library by buying up books in the Soviet Union and bringing them out. For instance, after Academician Platonov's arrest in Russia his library was sold and found its way into Prague's Slavonic Library.

2   A.A. Potebnya (1835-91) was a Russian critic concerned with the literary image.

Eventually the library moved to the Klementinum,[3] which was very convenient because it was next to the University, but when I went to it in 1927 it was still in Stromovka and treated as the personal property of Tukalevsky.

He was passionate about his library. His main concern was to keep the uninitiated, those unworthy of 'her', away. He immediately tried to persuade me to leave, saying that it was too far for me to come, other Russian libraries had all these books, and Lyatsky must have sent me 'because he is a professor and absent-minded'. I was a bit perturbed, but remembered that he had been described to me as an eccentric, so I did not give up. I explained to him calmly and earnestly that I had already been through everything the other libraries had on Gogol, and if I was going to write this seminar paper I needed to explore the depths. And the 'depths' could only be plumbed using the books assembled by him in his library. This mollified him, but he said some other strange things: 'If we give you permission, you must not smoke in the building, there is no smoking here… and you mustn't get grease-marks on the books.' I replied calmly, even smilingly, that I did not smoke, I did not eat fat, and I never carried food with me. This reassured him and at last he said to his lady secretary: 'satisfy his library requirements!'

I spent many hours there and out of my reading grew a paper in which I sought not to ridicule Gogol the historian as Vengerov and everyone else before me had, but to rehabilitate him and show wherein lay his charm – why he tried to synthesize and generalize in what he wrote, rather than just list the facts, which was all Vengerov seemed to think history was.[4]

The seminar was set for the second half of February. Before it I experienced a profound crisis and was even going to commit suicide because I felt I had no talent.[5] But I didn't *want* to kill myself! I was in a state of despair because I was so tired: every hour of the day was taken up with something, I was always rushing from one end of Prague to another, and although I was young and quick on my feet it had worn me out.

The seminar went extremely well. Lyatsky was delighted. Pletnyov opened the discussion by praising my paper, and the others found virtues in it that I had

3   The Klementinum was a former Jesuit monastery which, in 1781, became the National Library and Czech copyright library.

4   S A. Vengerov (1855-1920) was a literary critic and biographer.

5   Nikolay Andreyev was trying to think of a way to commit suicide which would look like an accident as he thought it would be less upsetting for his parents.

not noticed myself.[6] I had a great success; it was the birth of my reputation in the University. An unknown lad from the Baltic region suddenly became a promising student; I acquired friends, starting with Pletnyov; all the older students noticed me; and Lyatsky gave me the highest award that could be made for a paper: a hundred Czech crowns, first prize for a seminar contribution. This was trumpeted from the noticeboard of the 'Slavonic Seminar'. The suicide option, which I had hidden from everyone, now fell away.

In the second semester that year I had a similar success in Frantsev's seminar with a paper about foreign influence on Griboyedov's comedy *The Misfortune of Being Clever*, and the following year I won a hundred crowns for a paper in Professor Horák's seminar, on Tolstoy's *Khadzhi Murat*. So I had established my reputation with three leading Slavists: Lyatsky, Frantsev and Jiři Horák, who would play an important role if I wanted to stay on at the University as a postgraduate. Subsequently it turned out that I had a good reputation among very different university teachers who rarely agreed with each other, for instance Frantsev and Lyatsky, who were always at odds.

I had no great triumphs in history during my first year, although I attended Kizevetter's lectures and passed the exam satisfactorily. Paul I and Alexander I were both taught in the first trimester, but at the oral Kizevetter kept asking me about Alexander I. Here I discovered an interesting thing about Kizevetter: he wanted students to repeat *his*, Kizevetter's, conclusions and ways of formulating them, which surprised me because later I did not always agree with him. Of course, this was sheer impudence on my part and now I understand that pedagogically he was right, because he wanted to leave in his audiences' mind a certain interpretation of Russian history. This interpretation was a liberal one; the one Kizevetter served all his life.

Since I was very interested in Russian literature, when I arrived in Prague I tried to find out what was happening where in this field and I soon discovered that there was a literary society called '*Skeet*' (literally, 'the retreat', or 'the secluded monastery').[7] Some people called it 'The Poets' *Skeet*' because most

---

6   This paper, on Gogol as a historian, was published posthumously. 'Gogol kak istorik' in
     Transactions of the Association of Russian-American Scholars in the USA, vol XIX (1986),
     pp.189-202.

7   '*Skeet*' was a group of young writers which generated a great deal of interest, but most of
     the material is in Russian. See O.M. Malevich, *Vokrug Skita, Ezhegodnik Rukopisnogo
     Otdela Pushkinskogo Doma 1994 goda,* (St Petersburg, 1998) and L. Beloshevskaia,
     'Molodaia emigrantskaia literatura v Prage (Ob"edinenie "Skit": tvorcheskoe litso)'
     in L.N. Beloshevskaia and V.P. Nechaev (eds.), *"Skit": Praga, 1922-1940: antologiia,
     biografii, dokumenty* (Moscow: Russkii Put', 2006).

of its members wrote poetry. I did not write poetry, but I was interested in the society so I went to one of its meetings.

The members met in the Russian Pedagogical Centre, and it was in this three-room institution crammed with books, newspapers and current magazines that an idea was born which later spread through the whole emigration: celebrating Russian Culture Day on Pushkin's birthday. This was a genuinely national celebration in the Russian emigration, because it united *everyone*, although even here, of course, people later managed to disagree, and put forward St Vladimir's Day instead; but this idea did not win, and by and large Russian Culture Day was associated with Pushkin.[8]

We met in the evenings and the background of books and periodicals formed an appropriate setting. In the middle of the room, at a table lit by an electric lamp, sat a short man with a beard and enormous cranium, looking very much like Dostoyevsky. This was Alfred Bem. He was later called 'Professor', but strictly speaking he was not one. Back in Russia he had worked at the Academy of Sciences as a bibliographer, and in emigration this was a stumbling-block to him because it meant he had no official teaching experience in Russia and his dear colleagues did their utmost to prevent him getting a job. However, at the end of the day he became a great expert on Dostoyevsky and was awarded a doctorate for his books on him published in Czech. Formally, though, he remained a lecturer and taught Russian to beginners.

Bem was extremely interested in modern poetry and had come to Czechoslovakia from Warsaw, where he had been involved with Russian writers in another society, called 'Taverna'. He was a good literary critic and it was interesting to hear his opinion; he always endeavoured to speak to the point, objectively, without reference to the author's personality or 'tendency'. He simply analysed a work read at '*Skeet*' in terms of how it was written – well or badly in technical terms, if badly what were its negative sides, and if well, what was done well? Bem encouraged everyone to join in the discussions at '*Skeet*', which he ran. '*Skeet*' itself had been founded earlier, before Bem, but it was he who gave it stability and kept a record of its meetings: who spoke, what was discussed, how. Apparently this record still exists in one of Prague's archives. One day someone will write an interesting study from it.

---

8   Pushkin was chosen as someone who could unite the emigration. Everyone of all shades
    of opinion could admire Pushkin's achievement and contribution to culture. Interestingly,
    Stalin also used Pushkin as a symbol of Russian culture and the centenary of Pushkin's death
    in 1937 was marked as a great event. I know of no evidence to show that Stalin borrowed
    this idea from the emigration. (Ed.)

I was invited by Bem to read a story that I had written literally in one day, called 'The Youngest Sister', based on one of the many letters I had received from Estonia that year. It was well received and published in *Nov* (Tallinn) in 1928. However, I was not fully accepted into '*Skeet*' until 1930.

The summer of 1928 found Kostya Gavrilov and me wending our way back via Berlin and Stettin to Estonia for a long holiday. We had the cheapest steamer tickets available, which meant sleeping on deck. This was not so bad, however, as we were given reclining chairs, which were very comfortable, and travel rugs.

Sitting on deck in this chair, I mulled over what I had achieved in the past year.

Despite the initial difficulties and living twenty-five miles outside Prague, I had become a student and proved myself not only in the study of literature but also at RACI. I had passed all my examinations with the grade of 'excellent'. I had acquired confidence that I could study well, and had ended up near the top among the many Russian and Czech students at the Philosophy Faculty. But in addition, thanks to the presence of the Russian Free University, all of us had been able to take such subjects as beginner philosophy, the history of the First World War, which interested me greatly, and developments in Soviet literature, which we did not know much about before leaving for Czechoslovakia. All of these were pluses.

Another plus was the fact that Lyatsky, for example, did me a number of important favours. He said that in the autumn he would take me on as a member of staff of the Russian courses which he ran at the Russian Free University. When he paid me on behalf of the Slavonic Seminar for my paper on Gogol, he suddenly stared at me and said: 'I very much hope that this remuneration will enable you to buy a civilized European hat and part with that cap, which to many Russians suggests things that have nothing to do with what you actually are.'

The cap in question was just a typical Finnish/Swedish sailor's cap, but in their ignorance some Russian émigrés regarded leather caps like this as Cheka issue. For a time it was rumoured that I was a Chekist, a very young one, but still a Chekist who had been sent to Prague! These rumours had evidently reached Lyatsky. To my surprise he added: 'Would you be offended if I offered you my old suit?'

The suit was actually brand new and I looked good in it. He gave it to me and I was now taking it home to have it altered to my measurements...

Obviously, neither Estonia, nor Tartu, nor all the Russian and Estonian celebrities in Tallinn, could compete with the academic line-up in Prague. At that time Charles University was attracting the best Slavists in Europe.

An even stronger and more important aspect of my Prague experiences to
date was the constant presence of the 'Russian theme'. The problem of Russia
haunted the place day and night. It was looked at from various political points
of view, but also from the heights of academic knowledge. I was keen to expand
the negative impressions I had acquired from my mother and father, and from
my own experience of the Civil War, by listening to the general discussion about
Russia as it was now. What would happen to NEP? Would it bring Russia
freedom, or was it an illusory stage in an illusory evolution? Most people
thought that the Soviet regime would stay the same, or even get worse. This was
the feeling, but of course we did not know it would take the form of the Stalinist
terror. The Eurasians and the 'westernizers' disagreed in their interpretations
of what was happening. Nothing said in Estonia on the subject, either from the
right or the left, could compare with this discussion, because there everything
came down to emotion, whereas in Prague the clash of opinions was based on
analysis; and that attracted me.

Finally, there was the question of the Orthodox Church. Prague was the
only place in the Russian emigration that was not under bishops of different
jurisdictions, i.e. Synodal or that of the Patriarch of Constantinople. The head of
the Russian Orthodox Church in Prague was Bishop Sergy (Korolyov), who had
come to Czechoslovakia against his will. He had been consecrated a bishop in
Poland by Patriarch Tikhon and before the First World War had been active with
Archbishop Yevlogy in trying to persuade the Uniates to rejoin the Orthodox
Church. After 1917 the Poles would not let him stay in Poland as they regarded
him as engaged in Orthodox propaganda inconsistent with the interests of the
Polish Republic. So he came to Prague, without knowing anyone there, and it
was wholly thanks to him that the church in Prague was spared a schism.

I met the *vladyka* ('lord bishop') in the autumn of 1927. On my mother's
birthday I went to his church (it was a Sunday) and said that I would like
someone to celebrate a *moleben* (short service for a special occasion). This
reached the bishop and he came out to see me. 'Why do you want a *moleben*
said?' he asked. I explained that it was because it was my *mama*'s birthday, and
he was very interested to know who *mama* and I were. Years later, in Berlin, I
learned that I had made quite an impression on him and he had even told people
in different places that there were still young Russians who thought about their
mothers and had *molebens* said for them on their birthdays.

After that *Vladyka* and I became friends, he remembered me, and used to
invite me to his open house on Thursdays, when he offered tea and anything that
people had brought him as a gift – tortes, jams, and delicious pies. His complete
lack of formality won me over straight away. He understood you immediately

10.   From left to right – Melnikov, Andreyev, Khokhlov, Gavrilov in Prague – late 1920s.

and tried to cheer you up spiritually. He officiated very seriously and devoutly, with great inner concentration. He was able to create a powerful atmosphere and he had splendid young deacons assisting him: Badya Novgorodtsev, Ivan Georgiyevsky and others. There was an excellent choir, and every time I came to Bishop Sergy's church I felt my soul leap up, and I knew that my parents were praying for me at that time and we were communicating through prayer, despite the hundreds of miles that separated us.

2

A Defining Event

The ship came into Tallinn Bay, the churches appeared on the horizon, we entered the harbour, and I could see my parents standing on the quay. Kostya too started waving his arms: his sisters had turned out to meet him! The longed-for moment came, we were on dry land, and *mama* and my father were hugging me. We set off on foot for our dear Katharinental, but then my father decided to take a taxi, saying as he always did: 'You only live once, money exists to be spent, as Karl Marx said!'

My first impression of Tallinn was that everything had shrunk: the distances were shorter, the parks were not as grand as they seemed before, and the houses were tiny. I was very pleased to be home and I felt completely secure in my parents' house – I mean psychologically secure, because at the end of the day my life in Prague was like a military campaign on every front, whereas now I was deep in the rear and could be myself. On the other hand, my personal life now took a different turn from how I had dreamt of it on the ship.

When I left Tallinn for Czechoslovakia, it was perfectly clear to me that I should not make any solemn vows and promises to Rita. To bind someone at such a moment, even the girl you loved most, seemed to me precipitate and simply unrealistic. If our feelings for each other survived the test of separation, then let's see how things would develop in that new situation, I told myself. We exchanged a lot of letters, but hers had dried up in the spring. I assumed this was because she was taking her school-leaving exams. But now I learned the real reason: in the spring she had got married! I was felled by this, and even lay motionless for several hours on our sofa...

Shortly after my arrival, however, I was visited by my parents' good friend Sergey Shilling, the secretary of the Russian minority in Estonia, who proposed to me a project that I enthusiastically accepted and that kept me fully occupied for the rest of my stay. This was to edit the first issue of *Nov* ('Things New'), a collection of new Russian writing for Russian Culture Day, which in Tallinn was timed for the beginning of the next academic year.

It was Shilling's idea that the contributions should be from the younger generation. He felt that the usual émigré contributors to such anthologies were beginning to repeat themselves. He insisted on the title *Nov*, but I did not like it because of its other meaning 'Virgin Land' associated with Turgenev's novel and *narodnik* (Populist) feelings. Worse, he proposed an epigraph from Korolenko: 'There *are* lights ahead.' I thought this would make our publication look rather jejune. But perhaps he secretly thought such an epigraph would sell more copies because it was accessible to young people in the villages, the village intelligentsia. His view was that our magazine should not be urban, purely aesthetic, cut off from the land. I acceded, partly because I knew he did not really like some of the material I wanted to publish, and altogether we produced something that people said was alive and comparatively interesting.

One of my own contributions was an article on Tolstoy for the centenary of his birth, and the high point of my 1928 visit to Tallinn was taking part in the official celebration of Russian Culture Day in the Estonia Theatre in October, at which Tolstoy was also a major theme.

Kostya Gavrilov and I returned to Prague overland, via Warsaw. Thanks to some complicated jiggery-pokery, which cost me a lot of money, I managed to exchange my Estonian Nansen passport for a Czech Nansen one, which gave me the right to live in the centre of Prague, and this in turn made it economic to take up Lyatsky's offer of giving Russian classes two evenings a week at the Russian Free University.

As I began my second year in Prague, however, it was clear that I had to find some way of becoming financially more independent. Although my Estonian patrons were well-disposed to me, I could not carry on relying on them: the first time round a lot had contributed, now there were far fewer. Mrs Kaigorodova gave me to understand that everything hung on the generosity of one person, a Mrs Vakhman, who was her friend and the wife of a director of a large factory. She had heard my talks, and seen me perform in theatre productions, and therefore donated a sum that would certainly help me, but my future was still far from secure.

Then, in November 1928, something happened that changed my whole life. I was coming out of a lecture when somebody told me that there was a Dr Rasovsky wanting to see me. I did not know a Dr Rasovsky, so the news did not excite me. I was very tired that day and had had nothing to eat since early morning, when the landlady of my incredibly cold bedsit had, as stipulated in the lease, given me a cup of coffee and a roll. Rasovsky was short, skinny, not very prepossessing, but intellectual-looking.

'I am Dr Rasovsky,' he said, 'secretary to Professor Kalitinsky, who is director of the Academician Kondakov Seminar.'

I must admit that this also left me cold. I had never heard of Kalitinsky and although I had vaguely heard of the Kondakov Seminar, I was struggling to remember what. Nevertheless, I politely said I was at his service. Rasovsky told me that Professor Kalitinsky would like to meet me next day for a chat, and if it suited me Rasovsky and I could meet after lectures next day and he would take me there. I consented, and asked him why Kalitinsky wanted to see me.

'He'll tell you himself,' replied Rasovsky. 'I think he wants to ask you about your academic interests.'

That evening and the following morning I asked people about Kalitinsky and the Kondakov Seminar, but they were unable to tell me anything concrete. I learned that Academician Kondakov, who had died in Prague four years ago, was a great scholar, the Seminar was therefore continued in his honour, and his magnum opus *The Russian Icon* had now been published. Kalitinsky was a Moscow professor, a very dynamic man, who had succeeded in getting *The Russian Icon* published and whose research interests were similar to Kondakov's.

The next day I had again eaten hardly anything by the end of lectures, partly because I was extremely hard-up, and partly because my lecture timetable was so tight that I could only grab a glass of milk and a roll at midday. Dr Rasovsky appeared and we set off across Charles Bridge, the oldest and most beautiful bridge in Prague, decorated with all manner of historical figures and symbolic beasts – an amazing medieval confection. I preferred to listen to my companion than talk myself, but he had no particular questions to ask me. We entered Mala Straná and ascended its narrow medieval alleys, then climbed the enormous set of steps to Hradčany, where we walked into an area of old private palaces – not the official ones which the nobility built after the Middle Ages and where during the Republic the Foreign Ministry was situated, for instance. There was a set of wonderful arches here, through which we passed, and suddenly Rasovsky said: 'We've arrived.'

We went into a strange enclosed courtyard. Each storey had its own staircase and a gallery, there were many flats or rooms, with their front door onto the gallery, and a staircase down again – a design that was common in Prague and probably all medieval towns. We went up to the first floor and into a flat that consisted of two small rooms. The first was full of books and before I could take a closer look at them we were in the second room, which also had a lot of books, several desks, and cupboards.

This was the home of the Kondakov Seminar and also where Aleksandr Kalitinsky and Dmitry Rasovsky, his secretary, lived. Like everyone else's in Prague at that time, their accommodation was cramped. It was pleasantly warm, though, and they immediately gave me tea, rolls and butter, which was also very pleasant, as I was starving. Kalitinsky had previously been head of the Moscow Archaeological Institute and was married to the famous Moscow Arts actress Mariya Germanova. Possibly he was on tour with her when they got stuck behind White Army lines and ended up abroad. Whilst Kondakov was alive, Kalitinsky was part of his seminar, which comprised not only students but an array of professors including the historian Georgy Vernadsky. After Kondakov's death they decided to continue his research and seminar, which from having been 'Kondakov's seminar' became 'the Kondakov Seminar'. They published a superb collection of articles in memory of him. In his *History of Russian Archaeology* Academician Zhebelev called Kondakov the 'Archistrategos' (Captain of Hosts) of Russian archaeology and art history. Kondakov also played an extremely important part in the global study of Byzantium, since he was the first to propose a chronology for the development of Byzantine art. No-one before him had thought of studying the miniatures painted in manuscripts. All the manuscripts had been dated, so they showed development through time as the miniatures reflected the salient features of the artistic period in which they were created.

Kalitinsky filled me in on all this and explained what the Kondakov Institute did. He had his two young assistants sitting next to him – one with a thin moustache, a nervous look and an intellectual mien, Nikolay Belyayev, an art historian, the other Nikolay Toll. The latter struck me as very gloomy. He looked at the floor, said little, was carefully shaven, and his slightly curly hair stood up on his head. Belyayev smiled and Kalitinsky was polite, affable and shrewd. From time to time, with penetrating curiosity, he asked me about my studies and interests. I told him that I wanted to become a Slavist, with special reference to Russia and Russian literature, that so far I had studied the modern period, and that in the faculty not much was done about the pre-modern. He listened graciously. We finished our tea and he said that now he would show me what, basically, was determining the future of the Seminarium Kondakovianum, namely *The Russian Icon*. He briefly related how Kondakov had collected material for the book and ordered a series of coloured plates in Prague to illustrate it, since he was planning to bring it out under the aegis of the Imperial Academy of Sciences.

Kondakov had studied the icon for thirty years and brought his manuscript out with him in emigration. The Czechs had made the colour plates during the War, and afterwards approached Soviet Russia, the Soviet Academy of Sciences, for payment. However, Party representatives at the Academy replied that they did not want colour plates of icons and could not pay for them anyway. The Czechs were thrown by this, and even offered the plates to the Pope, who declined them. Then a miracle occurred.

Kondakov emigrated. First he was in Bulgaria, where in one of his seminal studies (they all were that) about an archaeological expedition through Macedonia he demonstrated the Bulgarian, rather than Serbian, nature of Macedonian culture, and appeared thereby to substantiate Bulgaria's claims to Macedonian territory. The Bulgarians were so pleased they even named a street after him. But it became impossible for him to stay in Sofia: Bulgaria had been an ally of Germany's in the War, it was now a very poor country, there was nothing he could do there, he was hard up, and he began to think of leaving for France.

All of this came to the notice of Czechoslovakia's president. In the 1890s Tómaš Masaryk applied for a chair in Slavonic Studies at St Petersburg University. He was elected thanks in particular to Academician Kondakov. Then the diplomats stepped in. The Russian Imperial Ministry of Foreign Affairs learned of the election and was horrified: to appoint Masaryk would be a slap in the face to Austria, as Masaryk had already been active in the cause of Czech independence and opposed the Austrian government on a number of issues. The Ministry of Foreign Affairs therefore recommended the Ministry of National Enlightenment not to confirm Masaryk's appointment. Academicians such as Pypin and Kondakov expressed their respect for the candidate and their regret that they could not appoint him.

Masaryk remembered this. He understood the tragedy of Russian academics who after the Bolshevik putsch were left without a job, or were wiped out, or had to flee the country. Masaryk helped them by setting up a number of personal scholarships. Hearing that Kondakov was languishing in Bulgaria, he invited him to be a guest of the Czech Republic, gave him a personal pension, and set up a lecture course for him at Charles University. Kondakov lectured in Russian and basically it was a unique 'synthetic' course on the history of medieval painting and culture. Masaryk even arranged for him to teach his own daughter, Dr Alice Masaryk, who was interested in the history of art. So Masaryk did everything possible in the circumstances, and when Kondakov died Masaryk was very sympathetic to the idea of continuing the study of Byzantium and the Middle Ages in the direction set by Kondakov. He again endeavoured to provide personal pensions, for example for Professor Kalitinsky as director of the Kondakov Seminar. Then he arranged for the grants of certain young academics who had just graduated, such as Belyayev and Rasovsky, to be extended. Nikolay Toll was paid from an American source.

Masaryk regarded it as wholly unlikely that the Soviet regime would survive, since it was devoid of all logic, reliant on brute force, and opposed the morality, traditions and Christian culture that Russia's development had been based on. Politically, this meant that whilst he was president Czechoslovakia did not recognize the Soviet government *de jure*, only *de facto*. As Masaryk saw it, helping young scholars was providing for the future. The day would come when Russia would return to normality and the Russian émigrés in Czechoslovakia would go home. If they had received an education in Prague, had had contact with Czech culture, and with Czechoslovak political and cultural circles, this would be to the benefit of both countries. On top of everything else, then, he decided to set up two scholarships at the Kondakov Institute for young scholars who would facilitate future Russo-Czech relations in that way. As Kalitinsky himself later told me, on hearing of Masaryk's decision he made inquiries about Russian students at the Philosophy Faculty who might be suitable and were still in their second year. He asked Academician Frantsev, Professor Lyatsky, and Sergey Gessen, who was a friend of his and had been involved in training scholars, and he also approached the Office of Russian Student Faculty-Groups. They all put forward only one name – mine! Kalitinsky and his staff were so struck by this that they decided to meet me straight away, hence Rasovsky's mission.

So now I was sitting before them. When we had looked through *The Russian Icon* and I had said nothing, Kalitinsky announced: 'And now, gentlemen, we are all going to have supper at Princess Natalya Grigoryevna's.' He explained that Princess Yashvil was in the first place a great friend of the late Academician Kondakov and a pupil of his in icon-painting, and secondly was active in the running of the Kondakov Seminar and had set up a string of foreign contacts that could be useful for the future and already had been in organizing the collection of articles in his memory. So we all – Professor Kalitinsky, Dr Belyayev, Dr Toll, Dr Rasovsky, and I – stood up, washed our hands (I approved of this), and picked our way through the dark alleys of Hradčany to a villa in a street nearby. To my surprise, Princess Yashvil's flat was in the basement.

She was really quite an old lady; but she had a lively, educated face, and kind, penetrating eyes. Her daughter, Tatyana Rodzyanko, lived with her. She was about forty and had been married to, I think, the eldest son of the president of the State Duma. Later people told me that Tatyana's extreme nervousness and the Princess's grey hair both dated from the same moment: when some drunk soldiers in Kiev in 1918 had killed two officers who had just returned from Austrian captivity – Princess Yashvil's son and son-in-law. But I did not know that then and was simply charmed by her very kind treatment of me. Actually I had never before experienced such treatment in Prague, because most of my dealings with people were 'business' ones. Here I was asked to sit down, I was immediately offered unpretentious but delicious Russian food, given a glass of wine, and the princess inquired how our meeting had gone. Kalitinsky said he was satisfied, he had found out all he needed, but added: 'Nikolay Yefremovich looked at *The Russian Icon*, but didn't say anything. I could see that it made an impression on him, but he didn't comment...' This alarmed me and I was about to explain why I hadn't commented, but I let it pass. Which was all to the good.

From Kalitinsky's, Toll's and Belyayev's conversation with the princess (Rasovsky hardly contributed) it transpired that I was a serious candidate for one of the scholarships.

'I think we shall get on together,' Kalitinsky said to me, 'and in a couple of days' time we will work out with you what we would like you to do for us. If possible, call at the Seminar during the day.'

I thanked them, although I was not terribly sure whether it was a good or a bad thing that I was getting involved in this work: I hadn't a clue what the work was or whether I would be any good at it. I understood that it was not literature, which I was some good at, that it was concerned with serious problems, with an empirical approach to studying antiquity – icon-painting and archaeology – and history in a different sense from that in which Kizevetter lectured on it. However, I did not mention any of this yet. I was just pleased, and could see that they were upstanding, amazingly nice people (as was amply confirmed later), and that they were treating me extremely amicably. They seemed to like my youthfulness, my serious-mindedness, my desire not to put my foot in it, and even the carefulness with which I ate. The latter cost me an effort, as I was as hungry as a wolf but knew that the princess and Kalitinsky belonged to the upper stratum of Russian life and I must therefore exhibit some table manners. They also seemed to approve of the way I kissed the princess's and her daughter's hand, perfectly naturally and not like a trained bear.

The next day I consulted my fellow Russian students about what I should do. Kostya Gavrilov was totally in favour, but from the rest I received mixed messages. Unfortunately, I felt I could not ask people like Lyatsky, so I fell to thinking about what my parents' attitude would be. I regarded what had happened as possibly the hand of fate, because just at this time my funds were running out, and although Lyatsky had kindly offered me some secretarial work and I was teaching Russian twice a week, these were drops in the ocean. If I was offered a scholarship and, as Kalitinsky put it, a flat in the same block, that would solve my problem. I mention all this because I was still very young and solving these practical problems, whether something was good or bad, whether it would lead somewhere or not, was difficult. I really could not tell. I am not a churchy person, to my shame I never have been, but I am a believer. I prayed fervently that evening and I asked God to give me understanding and guide me when, the day after next, I would be talking to Kalitinsky.

Kalitinsky was captivating. He was very tall, the breeding shone out of his face and manners, he had tremendous presence, and people looked at him wherever he went. It is not surprising that Germanova, one of the most beautiful women in Moscow, and a first-rate actress, married him. He told me now that the Seminar had thought everything over, and wanted to offer me a scholarship. They could give me a room. I might have to share it with another Russian student, who might be coming over from Poland. Whilst I was living elsewhere, I would receive 650 crowns a month. This was an incredible sum – two and a half times what I was receiving from Estonia. And I would have no special obligations at the moment, other than to arrange with Rasovsky to turn up twice a week from ten till one, say, to help him pack the books in special cardboard boxes for despatch to customers and be initiated into the postal and correspondence side of things. All of the Seminar's members also had practical duties; it was a condition of everyone's employment. As for prospects, Kalitinsky could offer two alternatives: either I could change courses to archaeology and history, or I could remain a Slavist but add various subjects on.

'What do you think about this yourself?' he asked.

I said I was a very cautious person and thought it would not be sensible to throw away the ground I had already conquered; Slavists now knew me, whereas there was no telling how I might fare if I went over to archaeology. Secondly, I was intending to expand my learning programme anyway. I had already started taking notes at lectures on Byzantine and Russian art, I had brought my registration book with me, I showed him that I was attending them but had not yet taken the orals on them, and if necessary I could take the written examinations as well. Kalitinsky said that was excellent, and if I needed to add on subjects to feel more comfortable within the framework of the Kondakov Seminar, it would be quicker to do that in-house. For example, Toll could give me an introduction to archaeology and recommend books. Where the history of Russian archaeology was concerned one of them could give me a reading-list, tutor me, point me in the right direction. The same for Byzantine Studies. So that is what we basically agreed.

When I wrote to my parents for advice, they said they were afraid to take upon themselves responsibility for the decision, but they thought it would be good for me to get involved in Russian archaeology because it would give my historical knowledge of later periods a firmer foundation. I liked this view: it gave me another strong argument in favour.

The reason I have allowed myself to go into some detail about all this is that it was the most important event in this period of my life – and ultimately in my life as a whole. In retrospect, it is interesting that this generous proposal caught me so unprepared. Strictly speaking, I should have been proud that I had been chosen, but I wasn't: I was worried and even frightened. Would I manage to pack everything in? I saw before me people who were experts in their field putting their trust in me, and their trust gave me a sense of obligation. On the other hand, there were going to be massive changes. Obviously, RACI was going to take a back seat, it was going to be even more difficult to get to lectures there, but I would try to get all my credits within two years. It would even be difficult to attend my University lectures, because I had to go two or three mornings a week to the Seminar. My attempts to change these hours to afternoons failed, because technically everyone worked for the Seminar only till lunchtime, then got on with their research.

All of this put me in a difficult position. I was, after all, still a student. Of course, I could have missed some lectures, but that was risky in the long run. So my path was not strewn with roses. I had no sense of triumph and elation at getting this scholarship, because it created so many problems. How was I to combine the freedom and exuberance of being a student with my duties vis-à-vis the Kondakov Seminar? I must admit I even pined for the gay abandon of my student days, which now seemed gone forever. Eventually everything sorted itself out and I was able to satisfy my diverse interests. But the first months were a bit difficult – character-building perhaps we should say.

Many people envied me. It looked to them as though I had won the lottery. I doubt, though, whether most of them would have coped with the problems that I had to overcome.

3

Academic Life

Of all the scholars at the Kondakov Institute, as it later became, Nikolay Toll gave me the most practical help. For my doctorate from Charles University I had to choose a subject associated with Old Russian written literature, but it also had to fit in with the Kondakov Institute. I was at a loss. Then Toll suggested: 'The Clerk Viskovaty Affair as a Literary and Ideological Phenomenon'. This proved a very rich theme and the work I did on it is still used today. It was a new synthesis of the ideological problems of the sixteenth century (my speciality)

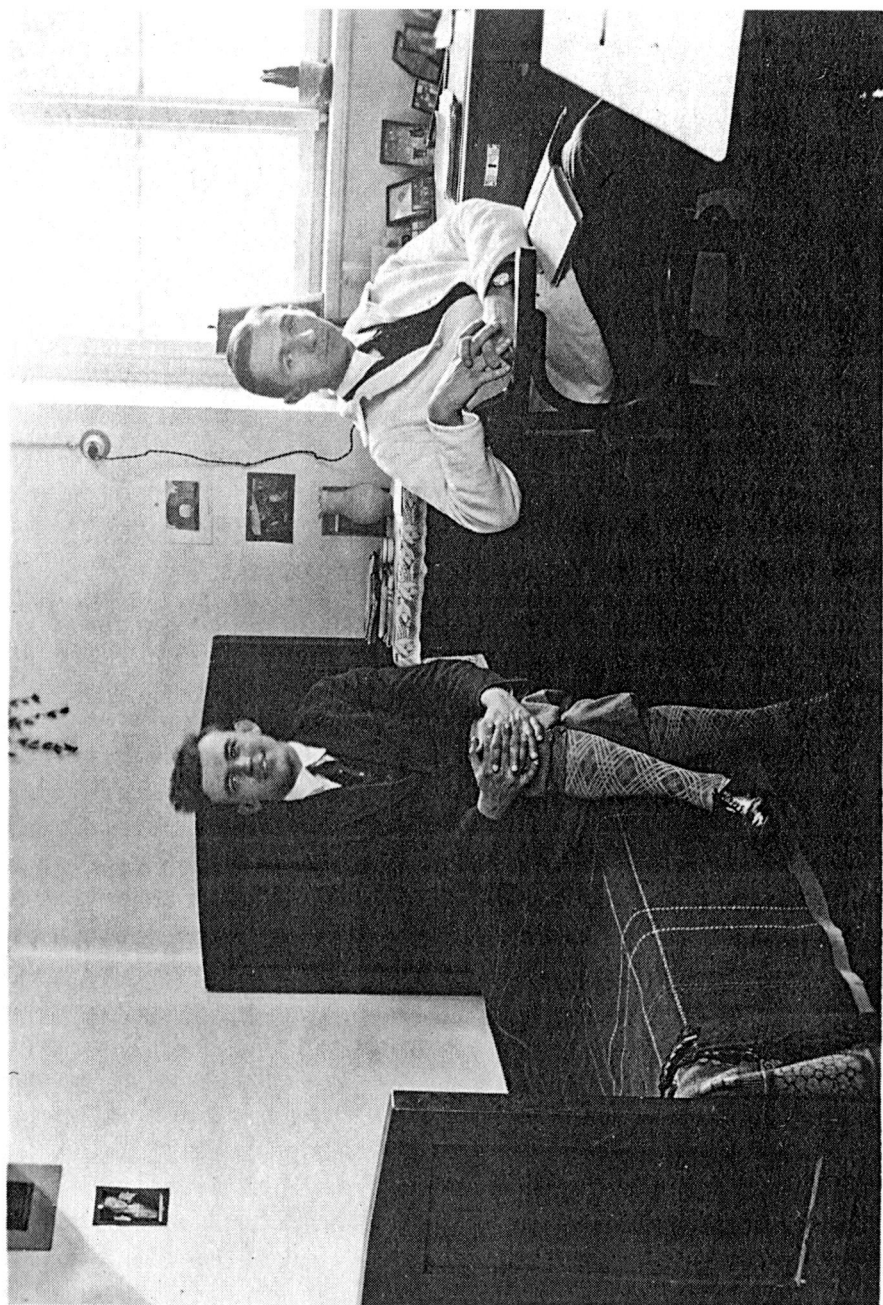

11. Andreyev and Melnikov in the Kondakov Institute.

with aspects of Russian icon-painting. I owed my approach here entirely to Toll, who also became a personal friend and introduced me to a research environment.

The Seminar met every Friday to discuss its members' research, papers by invited specialists, or new books. Everything was subjected to rigorous analysis, but to my surprise no-one took offence when criticized. For a start, the object of criticism could calmly answer it. If the criticism stuck, he could say: 'I will think it over, and next time tell you whether I agree with your critique.' This approach seemed to me constructive. I was extremely lucky to have joined a fully-fledged research team.

Within this Kalitinsky had a special role. His research was not wide in scope, but its methodology was always absolutely watertight, which meant that his theories usually could not be refuted. He thus made a vital contribution to the Seminar's meetings. By asking two or three questions, in the most friendly manner, he would suddenly reveal, without saying so outright, that the speaker's approach was not fully thought out, was vulnerable in places, and needed revising or supplementing. At the Philosophy Society he was feared for his ability to pull a brick out of the foundation of a paper, bringing the whole edifice down. He was also a regular attender of the History Society, to which I was later elected.

I recall an incredible public discussion at this Society on the popular theme 'Was the hermit Fyodor Kuzmich really Alexander I?'. A couple of books had just come out in Europe on this subject. The introductory paper was given by a lecturer called Sakhanev and then various eminences including Kizevetter and Zavadsky contributed. The general feeling was that there was no physical evidence that Fyodor Kuzmich was Alexander I, and Kizevetter even declared emotionally that the Emperor of All the Russias was not a needle that could be easily hidden in a haystack – it was all a legend. Kalitinsky basically asked two questions. If, as circumstantial evidence suggested, Fyodor Kuzmich was not Alexander I, then who was he? As long as no answer was found to this question, the legend would live on. And why, immediately after he ascended the throne, did Nicholas I spend so much time investigating the circumstances of his brother's death? Nicholas I's behaviour seemed to suggest that the government was unsure about something; but what? The Decembrist revolt had already been crushed, so why was there so much tension until Alexander I's remains had arrived in Petersburg from Taganrog and been buried? This needed looking into, Kalitinsky suggested, because one had the impression contemporaries thought differently from today's experts. Kizevetter had said that a secret like this could not have been kept by so many people, but he, Kalitinsky, thought that at such a high level, and with the kind of loyalty to the tsar that then existed, such secrets could be kept. He gave a string of examples from the eighteenth century of events whose details we do not know, precisely because the people who did – a small inner circle – considered themselves sworn to silence.

Kalitinsky's contribution encouraged Nikolay Belyayev to say that he did not agree with Sakhanev's assessment of the portraits and death masks. As an art historian, Belyayev considered that the portraits of Alexander I and the mask of Fyodor Kuzmich could be of the same person. This stirred things up and the organizers were unhappy because, as always after Kalitinsky's interventions, they felt the ground slipping from under them. He had a unique methodological power! I shall remain grateful to him for the rest of my life for directing my attention at such an early age to the importance of *how* you tackle your material, irrespective of *what* it is. Here Kalitinsky made a great contribution to my understanding of scholarship.

Unfortunately, in 1930 his wife left him for someone else, he had a nervous breakdown, and had to give up the directorship and recuperate in Paris. This was a blow for the whole Seminar, which had not yet been reorganized, and worst of all it precipitated a power struggle. Before Kalitinsky, there had been a duumvirate of Kalitinsky and Vernadsky, but the latter now lived in the United States and was merely a figurehead. Toll probably had the best prospects, because he worked on a lot of publications and was an archaeologist. But Belyayev was certainly not going to work under Toll, and vice versa. There was enormous conflict, which did not affect me because it was going on above me and mainly had to be dealt with by the Princess.

It ended very sadly. Belyayev was doing desperate and not very ethical things: he had declared war on Toll, he would not listen to Vernadsky's remonstrations, he rejected the Princess's attempts to solve the conflict peacefully, and he joined forces with some Czech professors who were willing to support him if he got them jobs in the Kondakov Institute. Then he suddenly disappeared. It turned out he had been killed. On 23 December 1931 he had been run over in the street by a lorry. Apparently he had had no documents on him, so he was eventually identified in a morgue. This had a shattering effect on us: the conflict had been resolved, but in the manner of a Greek tragedy...

Toll now had no rival, but he was not intending to seize power, he wanted to find a director. In the end one was found: Aleksandr Vasilyev, an Academician and an expert on Byzantine and Arab history. He was in the USA at the time and even accepted the post 'unseen'. This solved the problem: Toll remained assistant director, the Princess became treasurer, and Rasovsky secretary. By then I had almost graduated and was doing various library and other jobs in the Institute, although my main task was to get on with my doctorate. Running ahead, I have to say I was extremely grateful to Kalitinsky that despite his

enforced absence he remained on good terms with us, and when I published
part of my dissertation in 1932 he wrote me an interesting and very useful letter
analysing my work.

However, if I had to put anyone at the head of the Kondakov team, it would
be Princess Yashvil. She was an exceptional woman, of a kind that Russia today
can hardly produce. She belonged to the aristocracy and was a lady in the highest
sense of the word. On her father's side she was descended from the Scottish
Philipsons, who had entered the Tsar's service in the seventeenth century. The
violent deaths of her son and son-in-law had had such a terrible effect on her
that she still wore mourning. Her life was an amazing blend of nobility, high
ideals, and ceaseless toil. Nothing was too much for her, and everything she
touched acquired nobility, because she was driven by purity of soul and motive.
I am not idealising her moral nature – I was fortunate enough to know her for
eleven years, and all that time she was the embodiment of kindness, wisdom and
spiritual clarity.

Her life story was phenomenally interesting. She married Prince Yashvil out
of love, and since he was descended from one of the conspirators who murdered
Paul I she had a mass said secretly for the latter every year on 11 March, the
anniversary of the assassination. I attended two of these masses myself. They
were not an act of hypocrisy or a mere gesture, no, they were acts of very deep
spiritual conviction, both she and her daughter believed that Prince Yashvil's
ancestor's involvement in the murder of Paul I was not only un-Christian but
disloyal to the emperor, incompatible with the concept of monarchy; and the
Princess was a monarchist in the noblest sense of the word. So she prayed with
all her soul for the sins of the original Prince Yashvil to be forgiven and even, I
think, believed that the tragic events that had befallen her were a kind of rebound
from the enormity committed on 11 March 1801. She was absolutely selfless.
Before the revolution, as a very rich landowner, she had built schools for the
peasants, provided them with training in various crafts, and supported whole
communities of artists. During the War she had been active in the Russian Red
Cross at an international level. Her calming influence in the Seminar was crucial.
She completely trusted everyone who worked there and did her utmost to keep
them, creating the kind of spiritual and psychological ambience necessary for
this kind of work. And since she was not seeking anything for herself, she was
able to ask all kinds of people to take an interest in our publications, buy them,
and later become members of the society called the Kondakov Institute.

I not only finished my dissertation, I also continued to research a number of
phenomena associated with the icons and frescoes of the sixteenth century, and
although I could not complete my research into the whole Muscovite period

12.   Members of the Kondakov Institute.
From left to right – Melnikov, Rasovsky, Andreyev, and Toll.

before I was forced to leave Prague, I essentially succeeded in mapping out an important hitherto unstudied subject: how the ideas behind Muscovite Rus were reflected and developed in icon-painting.

My dissertation was accepted in December 1932 and I was allowed to proceed to the oral examination for the degree of Doctor of Philosophy. In Prague the oral examination was still run on medieval lines. There were *rigorosa* on general subjects, for example the history of philosophy and the fundamentals of psychology, that went on for hours. If you were not a philosopher, you still had to have a *rigorosum* on the subject lasting an hour; and on your main subjects, which in my case were formally still Slavonic Studies, the *rigorosum* had to last two. Both were before a board of examiners.

I took the 'little *rigorosum*', as it was called, first, on the history of philosophy. I had to answer everything in Czech. Philosophy is the kind of subject you can't actually 'know': it is not a collection of facts, you may be able to remember a philosopher's general message, but you can hardly memorize the nuances of his thought in a short time, for that you need to be steeped in him over a long period. I boned up the history from a text-book, but I was also greatly helped by Sergey Levitsky, a follower of Lossky. I had chosen Hume as my special subject. Levitsky took me through Hume in detail and helped me master Kant, Hegel and Schelling.

On the day, I had a stroke of good luck. The chief examiner was supposed to be Professor Kozak, an extremely unpleasant man. He was an elementary positivist and for some reason did not like Russian émigrés. He regarded them as a reactionary presence and was in the habit of asking us with a smirk why we were in Prague. But he was on study leave in America, so I was examined by people who were more interested in how much I knew. The exam went well and I particularly shone with Hume.

So now, in the summer of 1933, I was to take the 'big *rigorosum*'. This was a serious and gruesome business. First you had to know the fundamentals of Slavonic philology. I was not a philologist, but I could still be asked questions on the subject. Then there were *all* the Slavonic literatures: you had to know the movements, authors, works, and critical literature, for which you needed an encyclopaedic memory. And finally there was history.

Formally, history was reduced to Czechoslovak history, but of course the examiners always asked you about things connected with the subject or period of your dissertation. Since I was Russian, I could be asked about contacts between Russia and any Slav nation during the latter's history – an immense subject requiring a good memory and a very clear head. I devised a system of sheets of paper with all the information about a particular subject on, and set about learning them. I slaved day and night, but the longer I was at it the less I seemed to know. The evening before the 'big *rigorosum*' I pulled out the sheet on Tolstoy. I had a splendid knowledge of his works, I had delivered papers on him, and published on him. But I couldn't remember a single fact about him! At that point I realized I must stop. My father had been right when he wrote to me: 'To hell with the exam, look after your health.'

The examiners were Horák, who was dean of faculty and chairman of the board; Lyatsky; a professor of Czech history; and one other. Two other candidates were being grilled at the same time. First I was examined in Russian by Lyatsky, which was good, and at the end he said; 'Calm down, you know everything perfectly well, I'm going to give you *cum laude*.' Then I was passed to Horák, who also made the concession of talking to me in Russian, probably because he could see I was tired. I answered all his questions well, but there is one I still do not know the answer to. He asked me about an article on the early Polish Romantics. I had not read it, but was able to summarize its contents. 'Y-es...' he said, 'but there's another important point in it, isn't there?' I hadn't a clue what he was referring to, so I repeated what I had said using different words. 'Yes,' he said, 'but what else does he say?' I went through the process again and he gave up, disappointed. Later I realized what the problem was: obviously he had talked about this point at one of his lectures, but I wasn't there. Unfortunately he was one of those literary historians and examiners who like to hear their own opinions spouted back at them. With the Czech historian I had an interesting discussion about the possible influence of the Cossacks on the Hussites.

Two hours and twenty minutes after the examination started, Horák informed us that we had all passed. I was so exhausted that when I staggered into the restaurant on Wenceslas Square where Kostya Gavrilov and others were waiting for me, I was deathly white and they thought I had failed. After celebrating here I went home and crashed out on my bed for two hours, fully clothed. When I woke up, I suddenly remembered I was meant to be at a dinner for me given by Toll and his wife. I rushed off without changing, and when I got there I found everyone in dinner jackets and evening dresses.

General Chernavin, who was closely involved with the Kondakov Institute, summed up a lot of people's feelings when he said to me afterwards: 'Nikolay Yefremovich, I congratulate you on having completed a certain stage in your life.'

I think I had vindicated the trust that so many had put in me, and the good references they had given me. A new chapter in my life now began, because Czechs addressed me as 'pan Doktor', and to them that really was something.

But what had the different university courses and professors given me?

If we take philosophy, philosophically they gave me little. Although he was so unpleasant, Professor Kozak's lectures and seminar were quite useful from the point of view of terminology, chronology and methodology. The lectures by Professor Kral, the chief examiner of the philosophy rigorosum, were the most impressive. But the core of my philosophical education was acquired from Professor Lapshin's lectures in the Russian People's University, whose Philosophy Society I was a member of.

I never became a philologist, but I did attend Professor Weingart's lectures and seminars, which gave me an introduction to Slavonic philology. Professor Murko's lectures on folklore were pedagogically poor, and I never became an expert on folklore, but he did leave me with respect for this discipline. Instead of folklore, I studied icons.

Where Russian history was concerned, I attended all of Kizevetter's lectures and absorbed his interpretations and methods. He was mainly an expert on the eighteenth century. He embodied the liberal view of Russian history, and I subsequently discovered as a researcher that this did not always tally with the facts. For example, his attitude to Ivan the Terrible and his times was negative, because, understandably, he could not overlook all the cruelty and spilt blood that comprised the 'stench' of that period, the essence of the Oprichnina (Ivan's state). Even as a student, though, I was interested in R.Yu. Vipper's opinion in his book *Ivan Grozny*. Vipper was the first to look at the period against the background of European events in the sixteenth century, rather than purely in terms of developments inside Russia. The Russian events then suddenly looked like an echo of what was going on in Western Europe, not that there was any collusion between Moscow and the West, it was all simply the trend of the times. I found this fascinating. At the same time, I read an extremely harsh review of Vipper's book by Kizevetter in the journal *Sovremennye zapiski* ('Contemporary Notes'). Subsequently I studied this period myself. I could see that Kizevetter was absolutely wrong, and this reduced his authority in my eyes. What I thought wrong about the liberal view of Russian history, particularly the Muscovite period, was that it always seemed to assume that the Russian government did not care about the country's development.

Of the other historians, Professor Bidlo was particularly interesting, as he was extremely anti-Russian. He was a Byzantium scholar, but he lectured on

13.   Nikolay Andreyev after award of doctorate, 1933.

Czech history. His underlying assumption was that Europe ends where the Catholic faith ends. This was somewhat true of Muscovite Rus, but certainly not of the Kiev period or the eighteenth century. The most exhaustive lectures were by Professor Novotny, who gave an interminable course on Czech history. They were rather boring, but he had huge audiences because he was such a conscientious historian.

As for the literature courses in the faculty, Horák had a big Czech following for his lectures on the history of Russian literature from Radishchev onwards, but he hardly seemed to understand such Russian phenomena as Slavophilism or Dostoyevsky's religious beliefs. He was imaginative: he once said to me that I ought to write something about the influence of folklore on icons, but this merely revealed an amateurish understanding of Russian icon-painting. Then there was 'the Academician' – Frantsev. He had a floating kidney and this sometimes made him grotesquely irritable. Personally in time I found his bilingual lecturing style tedious, but his seminar on Russian literature was *de rigueur*, sometimes he was in very good form, and there was no doubt that he was an international authority on Czech literary scholarship and Slavonic Studies.

I owe a very great deal to Yevgeny Lyatsky. Before the revolution he had not been a university teacher – he had been in charge of the ethnography section of the Alexander III Russian Museum in Petersburg. In Prague Russian academics were always running him down behind his back because he had been made a permanent professor of Charles University and director of a large state publishing house, was married to a research student half his age, and had generally done well for himself. The gossips said he owed all this to the fact that his first wife was Academician Pypin's daughter and Pypin had, with Kondakov, supported Masaryk's application to St Petersburg University. I found all this slander unsavoury, because to me he was a perfect gentleman. When I first encountered him at his seminar on the Formalists, he immediately struck me as an important figure. He was the first professor to give me work, which he always paid for. He was very well disposed towards me and took an interest in my literary activity. After I got my doctorate, he even said to me: 'Nikolay Yefremovich, what I wish you is that you find your true métier. One of your vocations is to be the editor of a "fat journal", because you've had an all-round education, you've got taste, and you would make a good job of it.'

Of course, there was a downside. Once, when I was collaborating with him on the first publication of some of Tolstoy's letters in a volume edited by Horák, he actually got me to prepare them for publication, complete with notes and variants, and I spent many days deciphering them because, as is well known,

Tolstoy's handwriting is virtually illegible. When the book came out, I was astonished to see there was no mention of me in it! He had paid me very well, but he put the work out as his own. But as someone told me, this kind of thing was common in academic circles and I had to get used to it. All in all, Lyatsky was for me a positive phenomenon. I could always go to him for help and advice.

4

1934: Political Changes

After I received my doctorate, Toll informed me that I had been elected a full member of the Kondakov Institute. I would have the post of librarian and researcher, would be able to undertake my own research, and the scholarship that had been paid to me as a student by the President's Office would now become my salary. This was very welcome news, but on top of that the Institute decided to give me a long holiday because I obviously needed it. I asked for the whole autumn, i.e. from October to December 1933, including Christmas. This fitted in very well, as Rasovsky and Toll were away all summer doing fieldwork. The Princess was also away, so I had to manage the Institute almost singlehanded until about 20 September. It gave me a chance to regain consciousness and do some writing even before I left for Estonia.

Meanwhile, I had a letter from Sergey Shilling in Tallinn inviting me to give a course of lectures on contemporary literature at the Russian People's University there, of which he was head. I accepted and we agreed that they would be called 'Russian Literature after the Revolution'. There were to be three lectures of two hours each, with a break in the middle, and the first two were to be devoted to Soviet literature and the last one to émigré literature. When I arrived in Tallinn there were posters up advertising the lectures and featuring me for the first time as 'Doctor of Philosophy of Charles University Prague'. Not everyone understood what this meant, but I was the apple of everyone's eye because obviously it was an achievement and proved that local people hadn't thrown their money away.

By coincidence, Ivan Bunin had just been awarded the Nobel Prize for Literature, so before the first lecture I said a few words about him and the significance of the event. Since Bunin was in emigration, the prize gave spiritual sustenance to those Russians who were outside their native country but were continuing to create values that the rest of the world was interested in. I began the lecture proper by quoting Trotsky, who had said in 1922 that if a qualitatively new literature had not sprung up within ten years, one different from the bourgeois kind, then the methods the proletarian writers were using must be wrong. My view was that anything of any quality produced in Soviet literature in the past ten years had grown out of the classical tradition of Russian literature, and all the rest was either threadbare experiment or artistically so inadequate that it died soon after it was published. I then described the feuding between the main literary movements. There was some interesting discussion afterwards, in which a few speakers expressed pro-Soviet views, but I was able to use concrete examples to show that these were Utopian. My lectures were published in abridged form for Estonia's 1934 Day of Russian Culture.

I managed to stay on in Estonia until 15 January. When I got back to Prague, Lyatsky rang me. 'I have something extremely important to tell you,' he said. 'We – Frantsev, Horák and I – have been discussing who to put forward for the lectureship in Russian and Slavonic literature when Frantsev retires in two years time, and would you believe it we all agreed it should be you.'

'*Me?*'

'You. We all agree you are the most deserving candidate. Keep quiet about it for the time being, but you must choose a subject to specialize in. What about Avvakum? There's a new wave of interest in him and you know icons well, so you could link the subject to icons and then discuss his literary techniques. Think about it and let me know. If we three put your name forward, the dean's office will accept it.'

I thanked Yevgeny Aleksandrovich for such a demonstration of friendship towards me, and hurried off to tell Toll. He was highly excited by the news: 'Fantastic! It will give you a foothold in the Czech world, of course you will remain at the Institute, we will make you a member of the board of management, and financially your future will be assured.'

I did not tell any of my colleagues about it, but I did tell Kostya Gavrilov and my parents in confidence that there was a proposal to put me forward for a lectureship because I had the right specialisms. Professor Horák also talked to me about it and even persuaded me to give him a typewritten document in Czech offering my services, so that it could be instantly produced when required. Frantsev told me he was very pleased and hoped that I would soon be declared the candidate, write the piece I had to submit, and the matter would be settled within a twelvemonth.

So these were the prospects now before me. I started thinking about the subject and came up with some interesting approaches to Avvakum that did involve icons. I spent about six weeks familiarizing myself with the literature and deciding how to present the theme in a way that would be new to Slavists and interesting to historians. With great enthusiasm I wrote most of a first draft. Then suddenly there was another phone call from Lyatsky. I could tell

14. Nikolay Andreyev on the Estonian border in 1934 – Russia in the background.

straightaway that he was depressed. He said: 'Nikolay Yefremovich, I am ringing you on an important matter. I am ringing to suggest that you withdraw your candidacy for the lectureship that we offered you.'

I decided he had gone mad. In complete stupefaction I said: 'I'm sorry, I don't understand. Six weeks ago you yourself told me I must apply, I've even drafted what I would submit, I wanted to talk to you about this, and now you are telling me I must withdraw. Why?'

'You are a young man, at the beginning of your academic career, and you want as few failures and rejections on your c.v. as possible.'

'Failures and rejections? Has something happened?'

'No,' continued Lyatsky, 'but it is about to. The fact is, the Czechoslovak Foreign Ministry is contesting your candidacy.'

'What has it got to do with the Foreign Ministry?'

'Would you believe it, when the Foreign Ministry heard what we were planning, they said we couldn't appoint a Russian émigré as Frantsev's successor, it would have to be a Soviet or Czech scholar, so that there were no complaints from the Soviets that the Philosophy Faculty is run by émigrés.'

'But that's political interference!'

'Yes, as you know the Czechs have done a volte-face and even recognized the Soviet Union *de jure*.[9] Masaryk's line has been abandoned, they regard Beneš as a realist, so everything's being changed. If you don't withdraw your candidacy, they will turn you down. It would be quite easy: they replace us with another board of electors, this board says that you don't know Czech well enough, you don't know this, that and the other, and your views are retrograde. They'll say anything. Then all that will go in your official c.v. We can't let that happen, so it would be better for you to withdraw.'

'Who will be the candidate, then?'

'No-one. The job will have to be split up. You could have filled Frantsev's post completely, you wouldn't have been a full professor to begin with, just a lecturer, but all you would have needed was a few years experience. The Czech candidates don't know Russian or the Russian subjects well enough.'

It was a disaster. Not for the first time, I reflected that one should never count one's chickens. I wished I had not told Kostya or my parents. It was an exact counterpart to Masaryk's treatment in Petersburg. I recalled this and was

9   Czechoslovakia extended *de jure* recognition to the Soviet Union on 9 June 1934. See I.
     Lukes, *Czechoslovakia between Stalin and Hitler* (Oxford, 1996), pp. 37 *et seq*.

amazed that almost forty years had passed and nothing had changed: a Foreign Ministry could alter the course of a scholar's life.

The year 1934 made me look differently at Prague and everything that was going on in Czechoslovakia. The whole of the so-called Russian Action in Czechoslovakia, i.e. direct financial aid to young Russians in the first instance and academics in the second, the whole of this page of Czech-Russian cultural friendship was prompted by rejection of the Soviet Union. President Masaryk had not recognized Soviet power *de jure*, and since tens of thousands of Czech Legionaries had fought the Bolsheviks in Siberia these Czechs were anti-Soviet. This is why the 'Action' was possible – the Legionaries understood perfectly well that the Soviets were no friends of the Slavs, that Communist power was different from national governments, and therefore that if the smaller Slav states needed to lean on Russia for support it should be anti-Bolshevik Russia, or at least not Communist Russia. Thus in Czechoslovakia the Communists were a persecuted minority. When I was at high school, it was the same in Estonia, Poland, Latvia. The whole of eastern Europe was anti-Bolshevik.

In 1933, when I was giving my lectures in Tallinn, I found that the Soviet Union was exercising strong pressure on the cultural life of the Baltic States. The lectures on post-revolutionary Russian literature were well received and I was rung up by prominent cultural figures in Narva, Tartu and Pechory enthusiastically inviting me to repeat them there. But not one of these trips came off, because the Estonian political police would not permit them. Sergey Shilling knew the head of the police, Ivan Kaban, well, as they had been at school together. When he asked him why I wasn't being allowed to go on my lecture tour, he said: 'It's not my call, it's the Soviet Union's. If Andreyev takes a positive line towards the Soviet Union, the Estonians don't like it. If he takes a negative line, it's even worse, as the Soviet diplomats will say the Estonians are engaging in anti-Soviet propaganda.'

So although they authorized these lectures in the capital, they could not possibly permit them in the border areas and elsewhere. What Kaban said was convincing, but I was dismayed at the implication that the Baltic States had fallen under Soviet influence. Encouraged by the French, Czechoslovakia also took a pro-Soviet line. Beneš visited the Soviet Union and was greeted with open arms. He came back with some remarkable icons he'd been given, and the Czechs recognized the Soviet regime *de jure*. Soviets started turning up in incredible numbers. A Soviet air squadron flew in on the very day that Nikolay Astrov, the last freely elected mayor of Moscow, was buried. Even Czech newspapers pointed out that as the cortège was shuffling to the cemetery General Unshrift was arriving from Moscow with a whole Soviet military mission.

My experience in the matter of appointing Frantsev's successor displayed the same features of fear of the USSR, although there was not yet any direct intimidation. The climate was changing. The emergence of Hitler had provoked more and more pro-Soviet feeling. 'Well,' people said, 'the USSR is at least a Slav state.' Absurdly, in 1938 some Czechs started ranting that Stalin was the greatest Slav who ever lived! When Kostya Gavrilov said to them, 'What do you mean "Slav", he hasn't a drop of Slav blood in him, he's Georgian', they nearly beat us up.

The first stage in the Russian Action in Czechoslovakia, which lasted from 1921 to 1925, was before my time. By 1926/27 fewer Russians were arriving. The seven years of Prague life that I have described saw the Russian Action shrink on every front. The only exception was the Kondakov Seminar, which enjoyed President Masaryk's special attention.

Experts have told me that the Russian population of Prague was about 6000. The Russians continued to live there and integrate into Prague life. In about 1925 a new wave of students appeared, the one to which I belonged. They were young people who felt constricted in the new small states with their inverted chauvinism. They felt there were few prospects for them there, so they set out to obtain an education abroad and reach the cultural centres. It was an instinctive rather than conscious process. I too felt instinctively that I could not get anywhere in Estonia.

5

Russian Prague

In 1927 the Russian world in Prague had several nuclei.

One of these was the Russian church headed by Bishop Sergy, whom I described in chapter one. Every Saturday, because public transport was better than on Sunday, this nucleus filled to bursting with Russians coming from all over the place for vespers. They re-established contacts lost in the week and basically comprised a Russian community. This community was largest during Lent. For the Easter Vigil several thousand Russians came together and it was virtually impossible to get into the church. There were also throngs of people at Christmas and Trinity. *Vladyka* did not have many priests, but he had a faithful helper in Archimandrite Isaaky, a much-decorated former officer of the Drozdov division. Later he was always assisted by Father Mikhail Vasnetsov, son of the famous painter. There was a good choir and the church was a centre of life right up to the end of Russian Prague.

Some authors have said that it was only in Prague that the Social Revolutionaries congregated and received state support. This is not so: in fact Czechoslovak aid was for individuals, although the SRs were certainly the biggest of the Russian groups in Prague. In particular, they had Zemgor, the remains of the All-Russian Town and Country Union, whose chairman in Prague was the SR Fyodorov-Mansvetov, and all the leadership and employees of Zemgor were associated with the SRs. This does not mean, however, that only the SRs were accepted by the Czechs. Prague had émigré political movements of every hue, the whole spectrum of Russian political and social organizations.

SR journals like *Volya Rossii* ('Russia's Will') were not the only ones published in Prague; there were also independent journals such as *Studencheskiye gody* ('Student Years'), almanacs, and a whole publishing house called '*Plamya*' ('The Flame'), which was subsidized by the Czechs and had nothing to do with the SRs. Later, there was for many years a newspaper called *Novosti* ('The News'), published by Kirill Tsegoyev. Countess Panina's organization '*Russky Ochag*' ('The Russian Hearth') also deserves mention. In the first place, it had a fine library, smaller than Zemgor's but excellently selected; the fiction and art history sections were particularly good. 'The Russian Hearth' also had a cafeteria, where you could get breakfast, lunch and supper at a very reasonable price, and tea to drink at any time. It also had assembly rooms, where the History Society, the Committee for Russian Culture Day, the Union of University Women, the Union of Doctors, and others, met.

Countess Sofya Vladimirovna Panina was a Constitutional Democrat ('Cadet'). Before the revolution she had been a well-known philanthropist. For instance, she set up the Nicholas II People's House in St Petersburg – a major cultural centre with a good theatre where prices were much lower and it was easier to obtain tickets than at the Aleksandrinsky and Mariinsky theatres. People said that Countess Panina had got married when she was young, but had left her husband on her wedding night and requested the Emperor to give her back her maiden name; apparently Alexander III had signed her petition with the comment: 'Regard as virgin.' At least, this is what people said.

For a long time a significant organization was the Union of Russian Writers and Journalists, which occasionally met at 'The Russian Hearth' and sometimes at Zemgor or the Russian Free University. At one time this Union was presided over by Nikolay Astrov, Countess Panina's partner and a former mayor of Moscow. An honorary president was Vasily Nemirovich-Danchenko, the oldest of the Russian writers in emigration.[10] Yevgeny Chirikov was also a

10 Vasily Nemirovich-Danchenko (1844-1936) was a novelist and brother of the co-founder of the Moscow Arts Theatre.

prominent member.[11] The important thing about the Union of Russian Writers and Journalists was that it gave grants to young poets and writers – not large grants, but a help if you earned more on the side. This organization had nothing to do with the SRs either. It contained all kinds of people, and those in its key positions were more right-wing than socialist.

The Russian People's University, which was also independent of the SRs, was a large organization. It consisted of two groups. First there were almost all the academics who received individual grants from Czech sources, then there was its executive, which was small and led by Mikhail Novikov, the last freely elected rector of Moscow University. The number of people attending the Russian People's University varied: many came to high-profile discussions like the one about Alexander I and Fyodor Kuzmich, but at the specialist seminars there were sometimes only five or six. When the Germans arrived and war was in the air, attendance shot up, especially when the sessions were about Russian history. Then there were hundreds in the audience. There were some societies in this university that were extremely important, such as the History Society, which was really a separate organization, and the Philosophy Society, which contained famous names such as Lossky, Gessen, Lapshin and Chizhevsky.

There was an amazing seminar on the history of the First World War. I enjoyed it enormously, made reams of notes, and greatly regret that I had to leave them all behind. Most of those present had been in the war, some of them were very prominent, generals, and what they said and discussed was exceptionally interesting. They did not know the Russian Imperial Army from books – they had been part of it. Unfortunately, I could not always get to this seminar, as it was held on Fridays, when there were compulsory meetings at the Kondakov Institute.

These cultural centres in Prague formed an essential part of our Russian life there. For anyone with intellectual interests it was a rich field. Moreover all kinds of authorities and experts kept arriving from other countries to address us. From time to time Milyukov would come and give public lectures before hordes of people. He also read papers on specific subjects at the History Society. Occasionally Berdyayev came, and I heard several of his lectures. He was difficult to follow, because he had a tic: his tongue kept shooting out. If you didn't know this, you could get a bit of a shock. But each time it happened he would regain control of it, the tongue would disappear, and he would carry on talking normally for a few minutes, then suddenly it would pop out again. S.L. Frank came from Berlin and I remember quite a few visits by F.A. Stepun from Dresden. Big figures like General Denikin also came; he was a very good

---

11 Yevgeny Chirikov (1864-1932) was a playwright and prosewriter.

lecturer, but of course most of what he had to say was about politics. For the centenary of Tolstoy's birth, Maklakov was invited. He spoke in the hall of the Czech National Museum in Masaryk's presence, as did Horák. Cultural life was extremely active.

The military organizations were another important component. The main one in Prague, as everywhere else in the emigration, was the Warriors League based in Paris. This had been conceived by Wrangel and developed by Kutepov. It was very necessary in order to prevent the Russian forces from falling apart. It was doubtful that they would ever be called upon for positive action in the Soviet Union, but I think some sort of professional, national association was useful, although later the Warriors League's ideology became rather crude. At the beginning of the emigration, in the twenties, the League was good, but by the thirties it had become odd. Nevertheless, the organization was active and included most of the former members of the White Armies. Even people who were sceptical about a 'spring offensive' in the USSR continued to pay their subscriptions and turn out on various public occasions. Celebrating the anniversaries of the Battle on the Ice, or the Kornilov, Markov and Drozdov regiments, or the founding of the Volunteer Army, was all pseudo-military activity, but I repeat, it made a psychological contribution to keeping the emigration together.

It was interesting to observe that people who had only been in the White Army a couple of years and then become engineers, doctors or academics, still considered themselves soldiers. This phenomenon seems to have scared the Bolsheviks. They exaggerated its significance. They kidnapped General Kutepov because they were sure that if a country like Germany decided to attack the Soviet Union the Warriors League could play a part. In Prague the League was headed by General Kharzhevsky and had a restaurant called 'Ogonyok' ('The Glimmer') which was open to the public. The general might be dining there, with some of his friends from the League, or just a colonel dining there, and a young man who was now a scientist and once a captain would come in, go first to their table, click his heels, and say: 'Your Excellency!', or 'Colonel, Sir!', 'Permit me to sit down!'. At first I thought this was hilarious. Of course, he would be given permission, and he would sit down somewhere. They often had large banquets in this restaurant, with rivers of vodka and wine, and would then give rousing renditions of Volunteer marching songs.

There were lots of other military groups in Prague, for instance the Don Cossacks, of whom there were several thousand living mostly in the provinces. They married Czech girls and became agricultural workers or even farmers, until the Germans rooted them out and told them that in spite of their Czech passports they were still émigrés. There were some high ranks in Prague from the staff of the Don Army, including their commander, General Sidorin. I did not know him personally, but I did know someone from that circle called Pyotr Skachkov, with whom I had some interesting conversations about Sholokhov's *And Quiet Flows the Don*, which was just then coming out in instalments. These Prague Don Cossacks were highly qualified to read the novel, as they were nearly all described in it.

Another interesting group were the Denikin generals, starting with General Shilling, who had once been military commander of Odessa. His reputation had been savaged by the press, but he himself was a very respectable person, a general of the old school. One of his assistants, General Viktor Chernavin, was a member of the Kondakov Institute and a good friend of mine. He was an interesting and well-informed military writer who had a feel for military problems and was a born military historian. He worked in the Russian Historical Archive Abroad, which was an amazing institution.

It was maintained by the Czechoslovak government, but 95 per cent of its personnel were Russian émigrés. It attempted to bring together all the Russian publications that had ever appeared abroad, whether pre-revolutionary, left-wing, or émigré post-revolutionary. It was enormous, excellently organized, and always receiving memoirs and other private material which it undertook to preserve. General Denikin donated to it at least fifty boxes full – the whole of his gigantic archive as commander-in-chief of the Volunteer Army.[12] He had brought it out of Russia in one piece and donated it on condition that it would be made available some time after his death. Evidently he did not want his contemporaries to be too disturbed by what they found in it.

General Chernavin had access to a lot of the military material that was coming in. By 1936 he was retired and asked me if I would collaborate with him. He needed a secretary he could dictate to and who would stop him if he said something that wasn't clear. He invited me to write several articles with him for *Segodnya* ('Today') and the Warsaw newspaper *Za svobodu* ('For Freedom'), offering me a third of the payment. The pieces were to be signed by him and of course my collaboration was not to be mentioned. This suited me fine and I willingly helped him. I checked the final draft for him of a report commissioned by the Hoover Institute that was a completely documented study of an episode hitherto unknown to me in the last cavalry battle fought by General Pavlov, who had Don and Kuban Cossacks under him and might still have turned

12 Denikin's archive was given to the RZIA (Russian Historical Archive Abroad) on the understanding that Denikin's papers would be returned to Russia once Communism had been overthrown and freedom re-established. Czech Foreign Military Archive, 181, 24.6.1935.

Fortune's wheel in Denikin's favour if he had smashed or halted the onsurge of Budyonny's cavalry. However, as Chernavin demonstrated in his study, a series of completely unforeseen circumstances prevented Pavlov from doing this: his cavalry did not have time to feed their horses, and they had been riding so long they could not give them the rest that they needed to win the battle. It proved fatal. I was stunned when I read this: it transpired that Denikin had every chance of winning, even Pavlov's cavalry force was not smaller, maybe larger, than Budyonny's 'bands' advancing to meet him.

There was also a large group of Kolchak's generals, chief amongst whom was General Voytsekhovsky, who at one point had commanded Kolchak's army and was now active in the Czechoslovak army: he had been in charge of Brno military district and then transferred to Prague. It is interesting that when Soviet military representatives attended Czechoslovak manoeuvres for the first time, Voytsekhovsky asked the Czechoslovak Army to supply him with Russian interpreters. Everyone was amazed: what did Voytsekhovsky, himself Russian, want them for?

I asked him about this later, in the German period when he had retired, was living in our block, and we became friends. He replied: 'There was a very simple diplomatic reason. I did *not* want to conduct confidential conversations eyeball to eyeball with Soviet generals, because then the Czechs could have accused me of anything. When I rang them about it, they said: "Are you sure you want an interpreter? You speak Russian, don't you?" I replied: "There is nothing in my contract with you to say that I have to know Russian, I might have forgotten it over the years, and I might have certain reasons for not speaking Russian, so please be so kind as to send me an interpreter." But in fact I did it to protect my position in the Czechoslovak Army.'

Actually, until the Germans arrived, many Czech officers, the general staff, and even the CIC General Syrovy, could speak Russian because they had been in the Legion. Syrovy, as the Russian emigration liked to recall, had sold Kolchak for thirty pieces of silver, having turned him over to be shot in Irkutsk. Moreover, many officers married Russian women in Siberia and brought them out, as people put it, along with their mahogany furniture on the American freight ships sent to rescue them from Vladivostok. I myself knew several Czech households where Russian flourished. Consequently the Czechoslovak top brass at that time, if not actually well-disposed, did at least understand the predicament of the émigré military organizations.

Another of Kolchak's generals who was now in the Czechoslovak Army was Inostrantsev. He had been a general in the Guards and was rather full of himself. I knew him quite well, because he often came to see the Princess and noticed me there. Some of his comments were interesting; he had even published something defending the Czech legions in Siberia, which was why, gossips said, he had been given a job in the Czechoslovak Army. He argued against the widely held view that the Czechoslovak legions had got their hands on some of Russia's gold and wanted therefore to get out of Siberia and Russia with it as fast as possible. It was said that this gold was used to start up the Legio-Bank in Prague, that the Russian Action was funded out of the interest from it, and the Russians who knew about this were given more than the rest. Goodness knows what truth there was in it, but one cannot ignore the books by General Sakharov and others, who were explicit about it. These books were banned in Czechoslovakia.

In Prague you could find every colour of the Russian émigré political spectrum, and whatever happened anywhere in Russian political life abroad was echoed here. But which groups were specifically associated with Prague? The SRs, and left-wing SRs particularly – I don't mean the Left SRs proper, but the left-wing part of the group that was abroad: Sukhomlin, Lebedev, they were all further to the left than Avksentyev, Rudnyov and Kerensky. Mark Slonim also sided with them; he was fairly left-wing until 1927. These SRs played an important part, because until 1927 the foreign delegation of the Socialist Revolutionary Party was still alive and kicking. By that year, however, Stalin had dealt with the SRs inside Russia, and for that reason, evidently, and others this foreign delegation gradually disappeared, although the Menshevik delegation carried on for a very long time, even after the Second World War. At any rate, the SRs were in Prague and at one point Chernov, the 'peasant minister' and hapless theoretician of the SR party, lived there. But he was no longer the idol of the young. The SRs were fading out, but all the while their journals existed, especially *Volya Rossii*, the SR spirit made itself felt.

I think there were very few Mensheviks in Prague. Why that was I don't know, possibly because they were based first in Berlin, then in Paris, and then in New York, giving the Slav countries a wide berth. So the socialist sector here ended with the former SRs.

The mistake that all the émigré politicos made was to target the intelligentsia, as they had before the revolution, each wooing it in its own way within its own ideology. The group *Krestyanskaya Rossiya* ('Peasant Russia'), which was very large and active in Prague at one time, had grown from SR ideology, but its leaders (Maslov, Argunov and others) decided they must be realistic. In the Russia of the twenties and thirties the bulk of the population were still peasants, who protested, rebelled, and did not want to become socialists. The Tambov and other uprisings of the 1920s were peasant protests, and the fact that

Stalin had forced collectivization on them, that millions had been deported and died in unspeakable conditions, showed that the peasants were a social force to be reckoned with. 'Peasant Russia' attracted the most unexpected people, for instance Bem, the Dostoyevsky expert and leader of '*Skeet*'.

The Eurasians were also closely associated with Prague. They belonged to the very highest echelons of the Russian intelligentsia abroad and were active as early as 1920, when there was a group of them in Bulgaria, although they were not called Eurasians at the time. The first person to write a book on Eurasianism was Prince Nikolay Sergeyevich Trubetskoy, the famous philologist and later a professor in Vienna. They included some brilliant minds: the historian Georgy Vernadsky, the geographer and economist Pyotr Savitsky, the jurist and political scientist Nikolay Alekseyev, and the theologian Father Georgy Florovsky. There were also historians amongst them, for example Sergey Pushkarev, who was very young then, and Prince Chkheidze, as well as Tartars and Kalmyks.

The Eurasians believed that the reason the Russian Empire declined and collapsed was that in the reign of Peter the Great the national consciousness began to split, because the leadership had been westernized and the masses remained as they were. The course of civilization in Russia needed to be slightly adjusted by taking into account not only the European models, but the Asian influences and roots which as the Empire grew naturally became an organic part of the state. This was their basic idea; philosophical layers were then added. The Eurasians were an interesting phenomenon, but they very quickly split. Florovsky wrote a famous article about them, entitled 'The Eurasian Temptation'. Some left, including Pushkarev. I was in the lobby of the Russian History Society when on one of Milyukov's visits to Prague Pushkarev suddenly said to him: 'Pavel Nikolayevich, I have left the Eurasians', to which Milyukov answered like a grandfather: 'Good boy, good boy'!

Many people in Prague sympathized with the Eurasians, even Toll was one at some point, and Tatyana Rodzyanko and Marina Tsvetayeva flirted with it. It was a fresh and somehow organic movement that opened certain perspectives and forced one to rethink Russian history; which was interesting. Savitsky's publications and Vernadsky's *Sketches of Russian History* were particularly stimulating. They published a lot. Savitsky's writing was provocative. For instance, he published in Czech a work called *A Sixth of the Earth*, in which he described the past and future achievements of Russian industry and was one of the first to say that Russia could be economically self-sufficient. He was right: in a way he anticipated the economic development of the Soviet Union.

I was present at the Eurasians' stormy public discussions in 1927/29 and even wrote about them in a Tallinn newspaper. I had never seen such passions at a political meeting before. For example at one point Savitsky shouted: 'Pyotr Struve is making a whore of Russia's sacred name in his rag of a newspaper!' Kizevetter and Gessen spoke against Eurasianism and tried to say that there was nothing new about it, it was just a form of Slavophilism. I think they were wrong there: it was new and lively. In the thirties the Eurasians published a broadsheet called *Yevraziya* ('Eurasia'), then they split along political lines. Some of them became pro-Stalin, others were even recruited by the OGPU.

There was another group that was pretty active, though not very numerous, and that was the RDU, the Republican-Democratic Union. It was based in Paris and led by Milyukov. The Prague chairman, I think, was a history lecturer called Boris Yevreinov, and the secretary Dmitry Meisner, who had edited *Studencheskiye gody* and been on the left of the student body; for instance he opposed the Warriors League, Wrangel and Kutepov. From time to time the RDU had public gatherings, usually involving Milyukov, who gave long and interesting talks which were often politically contentious and unleashed terrible passions. Lots of people went to these gatherings. Whether they all supported the RDU's ideas, I don't know. The main idea was that it was inevitable Russia would evolve, and in fact it already was evolving; even some aspects of Stalinism they interpreted as evolution. This turned out to be profoundly wrong. But they were sceptical about revolutionary action in Russia, which the Warriors Union and right-wing sections of the emigration favoured. All this was hotly discussed and the RDU made an impact.

The NTS (Popular Labour Union) believed that young people had to be given the idea of an armed struggle, a terrorist campaign if necessary, against the Soviet Union. Apparently members of the Warriors League were in at the birth of NTS, but the latter very soon dissociated itself from the Warriors League because it found the marriage oppressive and its young people preferred to organize themselves. I knew a lot of NTS people in Prague quite well, and for an amusing reason: I was 'lyrical' about Irina Vergun, the sister of the chief NTS man, Kirill Vergun. After 1933 the NTS worked hard on its ideology. You have to remember that the spectre of fascism was now haunting Europe. NTS was affected: it produced a mixture of Russian-style Civil War 'leaderism' and the modern versions. What caught their imaginations was that there really had been great changes in Germany, which previously had been in danger of going Communist. Suddenly we had seen a lurch to the right with the appearance of the Nazis, but not just them, other national groups too, away from the ideas of social democracy, which had predominated in the so-called Weimar Republic, and the working classes who had been so communistically inclined had gone to the other extreme: they had become nationalists.

I used to argue about all this with Vergun, who was one of the leaders of NTS's youth organization. We often paced about for hours on the waste ground behind the Baikal Cinema. Within his family he had immediately become a leader and ideologist with definite ideas, but here we could discuss ideas seriously. I told him that there was a lot in their beliefs that was too abstract: they seemed to think Russia was a *tabula rasa*. I thought they should combine Russia's historical roots with the results of the revolution, they needed to pursue a synthesis, and I did not see this in their 'green novels', in NTS's ideology.[13]

The NTS usually held their meetings in a building by the '*Ogonyok*' restaurant. The leading figures and a few interested persons would be there and the talks and discussions were stimulating, if a bit basic sometimes, as they were training their future agitators and ideologues. Suddenly one fine evening the Czechoslovak police burst in, arrested everyone there, and drove them off in black Marias to the Central Police Station. It was unheard of: Czechoslovakia permitted freedom of thought, this was a closed meeting, so obviously the authorities were making some point. Experts immediately decided it was done to please the Soviet embassy, which frowned on all White Guard organizations, especially this one. Didn't one of NTS's songs promise that the 'whole country' would 'rise up' when the NTS terrorists sparked the 'final struggle'? Coming from such young lips, this must have put the wind up the Soviet representatives.

Most of the NTS were let go next morning, but Vergun and some other leaders were held until late evening the following day. When they were released, it was suggested that they leave Czechoslovakia. This was nasty and showed that we had entered a new phase, in which the Czechoslovak police were going to harass the emigration. It was a lesson to the whole emigration – as all the Russian newspapers abroad realized – and even Meisner, an opponent of NTS, wrote in the Paris émigré paper *Posledniye novosti* ('Latest News') that the rumours about NTS's ideology and significance were grossly exaggerated and Soviet diplomats had put incredible pressure on the Czechoslovak government. Similar things were happening in the Baltic States, where arrests and expulsions had already occurred and in Estonia NTS members had been exiled to some islands – a vicious action brought about by Soviet diplomatic pressure.

NTS nominally disappeared. It sort of went underground, it stopped holding meetings in public places, and its activity became more clandestine. Its members split up into small groups, they became tougher, of course, and various daft things were said about them, for example in private conversations they were compared to the Decembrists. This simply made me laugh. Even their wives

13 'Green novels' were little booklets which explained aspects of the NTS programme. The colour green alluded to the Green Lamp society and the Decembrists.

were called 'Decembrist-wives'! After a while, Vergun left for Yugoslavia, where I think he got a job as an engineer and was fully occupied in the central organs of NTS. Eventually he wrote me a very interesting letter, in which he thanked me for arguing so much with him about the organization's ideology. Not that my criticisms had influenced him at all, he hadn't changed his essential beliefs, but my attacks had made him think about his beliefs more carefully and find different arguments. Involuntarily, then, I had been a polisher of Vergun's ideas and those of his organization.

Later, under the Germans, NTS was still illegal and was smashed in two stages with enormous loss of personnel. Vergun was transferred to Germany and continued to work on the one hand as an engineer and on the other as one of NTS's ideologues. It was an organization that even influenced Vlasov's ROA (Russian Liberation Army). Vergun was arrested, like most of the NTS leadership of that period, and would probably have died in a German concentration camp like some of his comrades, but for the fact that Himmler decided to recognize Vlasov and Vlasov immediately requested the release of a number of these people so that they could work with him. They were freed, but fate always played an important part in the emigration: Vergun and others were on their way back to Prague to recover from their imprisonment, when their train was hit by American bombers during a daytime raid on Pilsen and several were killed, including Vergun. So I never saw him again, which was a pity. He had a lot of experience of handling Soviet Russians – Vlasov and his fellow-soldiers – and I was hoping that he would be able to give me better information about such things than I got in Prague.

Everyone predicted that NTS would not last long. They said it had arisen not of its own free will, but under pressure from the Warriors League, and had no original ideas, having borrowed them either from Europe's military organizations or from the new nationalist or even fascist movements. But things turned out differently. The social democrats have gone, the SRs have gone, there are no active monarchist groups left, or any other post-revolutionary movements amongst the emigration. Of all the émigré organizations, NTS is the only one that survived the Second World War and exists to this day. And it is not even because NTS was younger – youth passes, NTS split just like the other organizations, but obviously it had something that was more alive than the rest. I would not say it was its ideas, because in many respects I find these doubtful. But there it is: one of history's paradoxes. I don't mean to imply it is some kind of bluff, because I greatly respect the people in this organization; they were not interested in money, they were idealists, they believed in their ideas with all their might, possibly because they had experienced enormous changes in the political temperature all over the world during their lifetime. Most of them were my age, of my generation, and their mistakes were the mistakes of my generation.

Although politically the Prague Russians may not have produced anything new, developments in the émigré movements that started elsewhere always had their repercussions in Prague. Moreover, as I have tried to show, although all the groups in Prague appeared to be separate, in reality they had many points of contact.

6
My Pskov-Pechery Hypothesis

After my chances of acquiring a lectureship had been blown away by Soviet pressure on the imagination of the Czechoslovak Foreign Ministry, I had to concentrate with all seriousness on making a name for myself as a scholar.

I began by developing my doctoral research and publishing two large articles on Russian icon-making and veneration in the sixteenth century. This led me to reconsider those icons that Kondakov in his classic *The Russian Icon* had termed 'mystical-didactic'. What were the mystical-didactic subjects and where did they come from? Mystical-didactic compositions did not spring from the Byzantine tradition, because that tradition did not know this kind of pictorial ideology. As I showed in a paper at the Institute, even the arch-enemies Avvakum and Nikon were agreed about icon-painting: they both adhered to the Byzantine traditions of icon-painting, they both rejected naturalism and the trend towards so-called realism, which came from the West and was infiltrating Russian icons. It all made me wonder where these western influences originated in the Russian icon-painting world. Where were the actual sources of the western innovations?

All the material I looked at suggested that there was a big difference between the theory of the educated people and the practice of the icon-painters. The icon-painters may even, therefore, have undergone western influence without noticing it; but where? I thought this influence had occurred 'without prior permission' and probably in the Pskov area. But how could I test this hypothesis? Pskov was in the Soviet Union and inaccessible to me. Naturally, I therefore turned my attention to the only site this side of the border – the Pskov-Pechery monastery inside Estonia. I began to read up about it and got the distinct impression that the monastery must have compositions displaying signs of western influence. In a publication of 1899 Professor Petukhov of Tartu University even said there had been talks between Protestants and Orthodox on territory close to the monastery. So there had been contact with westerners and the monastery was perhaps a more open point for communication with the West than other areas. From this it seemed quite logical that the Pskov masters brought these innovations to the

Moscow Kremlin at the end of the 1540s, as the 'Clerk Viskovaty Affair' (the subject of my thesis) demonstrated. This was what a reading of the literature suggested.

At this point a new factor appeared, which made it possible to move these theoretical speculations into the real world.

The famous American aviator Charles Lindbergh, the first man to fly the Atlantic, flew into Prague. He was on his way back from a visit to the USSR and Princess Yashvil was invited to a dinner in his honour at the American Embassy. She spoke fluent English and the whole diplomatic corps in Prague was on friendly terms with her. Lindbergh said he had been terribly depressed by everything he had seen in the Soviet Union, disappointed and disillusioned. The Princess therefore asked him if he would like to visit our institute, for a glimpse of a different Russia, and he came. He was delighted with our publications and bought some. Most important of all, though, he said to the Princess: 'You know, I think I would be doing the right thing if I asked you to accept some money for your young scholars, who I should think have to travel to various countries to see things' – and he gave her $200. Of these, I was awarded fifty, which enabled me to make two trips to the Pskov-Pechery monastery and environs in 1937 and 1938.

In 1937 there was quite a group of scholars visiting the area. There was Professor Yelizaveta Mahler from Basle, who was going to record Russian folk songs in the Pskov area; Leonid Zurov, a writer and amateur archaeologist who had made a name for himself restoring a church in the monastery and was now carrying out an archaeological survey funded by Le Musée de l'Homme in Paris; and others from other countries. The Prague group included my friend Franz Dedič, who was an excellent photographer, and Irina Okuneva, an art history student.

When I arrived, I went to see the Father Superior, Agafon, early in the morning when I was told he could be found near his cell. I took with me the blessing of the Metropolitan of Estonia, permission from the police, permission from the Education Ministry, and permission from the Foreign Ministry. When Agafon appeared, I stepped forward for his blessing, he waved his hand over me, and I began to tell him what I had come about. As I did so, I was aware that practically all of the monks were craning out of their cells waiting to hear what Agafon would say. I finished. He looked at me, and said: 'I cannot show you anything in the monastery, as it is church property and your purposes are secular. You can walk around the monastery like everyone else, you can photograph what you like, but show you anything special I will not!'

I tried to reason with him, but he flew into a rage: 'We had people like you here from Paris and afterwards five things were missing! Your papers are worthless, I am the boss here. I am the Father Superior of the retreat and I don't care what people in Tallinn have written! You can come here with the police if you like, we'll shut the gates and defend ourselves!'

I stood there transfixed. 'But Fa – ' I began. He brushed me aside and swept out.

I thought over what I was going to do. Zurov had just arrived and suggested that our group join him on a trip around the Pechory district, ending up on the shores of Lake Pskov where he believed the Battle on the Ice had taken place. This would suit me very well, as it would give me time. I would do certain things to appease Agafon, and I would also be out of his hair for a few days. So Zurov and I quickly organized the excursion, and I wrote a letter to Agafon in which I explained why we had come, what we wanted to see, who had already given me permission to work in the monastery, but did not mention that he had refused me, merely that he might like to consider what time and terms would be acceptable to both parties.

The excursion around Pechory gave me a great deal. First, I really experienced this area in a different way, not as the tourist or aesthete who came here before, but as a researcher. There were things I simply needed to understand, for example the psychology of the peasants was particularly interesting, and had probably changed little since the sixteenth century. I was struck by their reaction to two things. The fact that I did not have a beard or moustache robbed me of authority in their eyes where religious art was concerned, icons especially. All the priests and Old Believers associated with icon-painting had beards, and all the Russian saints too, so I was at a disadvantage. Then when we visited the village of Kolomna we wanted to look inside the chapel, which was on a hill. Zurov and I went down to the village, leaving Kira Irtel, Zurov's companion, and Irina Okuneva, by the chapel. Zurov soon found the sexton, a lot of villagers came out, because it was an event having strangers come to see the chapel, and we all walked along talking and laughing. Suddenly some boys shouted: 'Look, look! Angels!' We looked, and could see that the chapel was silhouetted against the evening sky and the women were sitting either side of it in light dresses. 'Ah,' said Zurov. 'Those are our assistants.'

This had a devastating effect on the peasants' attitude towards us. In their terminology, we had brought 'wimmin' with us, i.e. we amused ourselves nightly with these companions, yet we were supposed to be studying icons. I should stress that we treated our companions like gentlemen, but the idea that they were our mistresses dogged us wherever we went. I realized that if one was going to do serious research here, from the peasants' point of view it was better if women were not involved. The peasants were happy with women recording songs or dances, they accepted Yelizaveta Mahler because she was a professor and liked the 'wimmin' to dance and sing for her, that was good. But involving women in church matters was bad.

Standing on the shores of Lake Pskov had a powerful impact on me. It was the border with the Soviet Union. Over there, in the blue haze, were our own people…but we couldn't go there! That was the emotional aspect, but whether the Battle on the Ice took place here was another matter. There was a gigantic boulder called the Raven's Rock, on which according to legend Alexander Nevsky had stood watching the battle. Zurov was convinced by this rock. I had my doubts.

We all returned to Pechory in excellent spirits. And now Zurov did me a great favour. He thought that Agafon could be influenced by people who were manifestly higher up than him and whom he respected, and it was decided that Baroness von Bűnting would act on my behalf. She was the widow of the last governor of Estland, Baron von Bűnting, and was greatly respected by the local people, including Agafon. She had a splendid house, slightly above the monastery, from which you could even see the monastery roofs. Dmitry Aleskeyevich Smirnov, the famous tenor, was also in the area. His wife had died and was buried in the catacombs of the monastery. He was very highly thought of by all the Russians at Pechory, and especially by the monks because he often sang solos in their choir. He had an immense following, even among the foreign tourists. So now I was introduced to the Baroness, it immediately transpired that we had friends in common, she knew Princess Yashvil, and she concluded that I was a person of her own circle, although I wasn't. She was very quick off the mark and said: 'Let's negotiate round my table: we'll invite Agafon to dinner.'

Which she did, along with Zurov, Smirnov and myself, and it went extremely well. Smirnov was a superb raconteur and charmed everyone. Not a word was said apropos of me. The first to leave was Agafon, and we all went up to him for his blessing. To me he said: 'Regarding your matter, come and see me at five tomorrow morning when I shall be celebrating in the catacomb church. We can discuss everything then.'

Extraordinary! I turned up next morning at this tiny underground church, the oldest one in the monastery, where the monks were buried and before that, in Muscovy times, many of the nobility who had perished in the Livonian War, and after the service Agafon arranged for me to start work.

My investigation proceeded along two lines. First, I had to look at all their icons. The monks continued to obstruct me, despite Agafon's promises, because they would not let us take the metal covers off the miracle-working icons. Dedič had nothing to photograph then, because these covers were enormous and the small holes for the faces were glazed with mica. I never did manage to photograph this group of icons. However, we did photograph many of the rest, and I also went through those kept in the attic. The result was negative: there was not a single icon-subject that could be a western innovation and I found no new compositions in the Pechery monastery's stock.

The second line was very important. I read and then started copying out the inventories, especially one of 1639. It had actually been compiled by outsiders, not monks but clerks under the supervision of boyars, the tsar's plenipotentiaries in Pskov, and therefore was more objective. The inventory of 1586 had been published long ago. I found some interesting information in the former, but I was startled to discover that everything I looked at showed there was no western influence in the icons here. The whole purpose of my research had gone! I did not tell anyone this, however, I just carried on photographing and thinking. Obviously, the hypothesis was wrong, but perhaps it had been over-influenced by my predecessors' approach. I needed to look more closely at my own material.

Suddenly I saw the answer. It was completely new. The nub of it was, which powers had set up and run the Pskov-Pechery monastery? Of course, I should have to double-check in printed sources in Prague, but my working hypothesis was the converse of before: at the Pskov-Pechery monastery, which initially arose as a spontaneous manifestation of religiosity in this area, in 1518-19 new forces came into play – Mikhail Misyur-Munekhin, the clerk of the Grand Duke, had been given the province to run after the amalgamation of Pskov with Muscovy in 1510. Here he encountered opposition to Moscow's ecclesiastical influence. Being a very clever man and a diplomat, and knowing the religious problems very well, Misyur-Munekhin decided to found a pro-Muscovy monastery on Pskov soil, and his choice fell on this one, which was then a very small monastery 'in an unknown place' as the chronicles put it. This 'unknown place' gradually developed as a pro-Moscow monastery. It was quite obvious, then, why there were no new religious icon-subjects in the monastery as such. They might occur beside it, in Pskov, in the possession of the Pskov painters' guilds, but there were none in the Muscovite base on Pskov's soil, nor could there be, because this monastery was traditionally conservative, that's what the secret was.

As soon as I understood this, the facts began to fall into place. I was making a very important discovery: I was providing the key to Muscovy's ecclesiastical policy in Pskov province. Clearly, my work was becoming broader than the original focus on icon provenance. This was the main achievement of that summer, during which I was on a creative high.

We also made a trip to Narva, Posad Chorny, and ancient Izborsk, accompanied by Father Aleksandr Kiselev, whom I had known since we were both in short trousers and who now had a church in Ivangorod.

In Narva my main object of interest was the Cathedral of the Transfiguration, which was in the courtyard of the very building that I had boarded in when I was at the Narva émigré high school. We quickly photographed the iconostasis, which was eighteenth century but had been heavily restored in the nineteenth and twentieth. Of the large icons that we found, only one attracted our attention, a St Nicholas the Miracle-Worker with scenes from his life. The locals considered this very old, from the sixteenth century. According to chronicles, when the Russians took Narva at the start of the Livonian War they found a fire blazing in the middle of the castle courtyard, where the inhabitants had thrown various things including Russian icons. Two were saved: a Virgin and Child ('Hodigitria') and a St Nicholas. The icon of St Nicholas in the Cathedral of the Transfiguration could not be the one in question, because of its appearance.

However, a Hodigitria that we found in Father Aleksandr's church after lunch interested me greatly, as it had a reputation for miracle-working. It was completely covered in metal. It was large – it came up to my shoulder – and when we first removed it from its case you could not make out much on it, as it was thick with dust and candle-soot. We placed it on a pedestal and got on with the other icons. About an hour and a half later, when I went over to it, I suddenly saw that it had 'got its breath back' as icon-painters say, and the outline of the mother and child was emerging from the dark background. This made a very strong impression on us. I immediately began cleaning the icon, using a recipe given me by Toll. We did not rub the surface, but the mixture broke down the soot and dust, which were soaked up in the cotton wool used to apply it. The icon should have been thoroughly cleaned including removing the dark layer of linseed oil, which we had only managed to wipe the surface of, but enough of its true colours could now be seen to realize that it was a wonderful piece of work from the very beginning of the sixteenth century or even the end of the fifteenth. And what struck me most was that it bore signs of burning. Some of these marks were doubtless from candles that had singed it, but the board was also inexplicably charred in places. I drew up a description of it there and then, measuring everything exactly, and I got the impression that this very icon had been described in the chronicles, i.e. it was the miracle-working Hodigitria saved from the castle. Father Aleksandr was overjoyed by this and said a short service and canticle before it.

From here we went to Posad Chorny on Lake Peipus. Most of the population were Old Believers of the Priestless sect, so there was no church, just a meeting-house. I was hugely amused by our reception in the Safronov household. Pimen Safronov was an icon-painter from here who was associated with our institute. His mother was a very agreeable elderly lady whose house was an intriguing mixture of old and new. She sat us down to lunch and served us all kinds of delicious things, especially fish, as Lake Peipus was full of them and they were first-class. I remarked in passing: 'I see that *you* are eating plainly, I mean with very plain utensils, but you have given your guests very smart ones.' It would be unthinkable in a Russian household to lay different plates, knives and forks like this. But she misunderstood my compliment, blushed, and said: 'Please forgive me, dear guests, we keep different sets because you are Nikonians, aren't you, and we aren't allowed to eat from those plates.' I nearly fell off my chair! The schism had started in the seventeenth century, over two hundred and fifty years ago, and suddenly, when she said 'Nikonians', it felt as though we were back there! It was as though we were from a different civilization. We tried not to aggravate things, of course, but I must say I was staggered by how long prejudices can last.

We returned to Pechory, where I witnessed a very interesting event. The monastery was named after the Assumption of the Blessed Virgin Mary and I was invited to a feast to celebrate this on 15 August. It followed a mass and was organized in a part of the gardens closed to the public. There were many local big-wigs there, as well as representatives of all kinds of Russian organizations, members of the Estonian parliament, Archbishop Nikolay of Narva, and Zurov. Never in my life have I seen so much vodka. A large number of tables had been set out, which were groaning with victuals, mainly fish, and vodka was supplied with all of it. Why there was so much, I do not understand. However moderately you drink vodka, it still has an effect, and within half an hour all the monks were pixillated, so much so that the reader – the monk required to stand in the midst of all these tables and read something edifying, what we could not tell, because everyone was talking at the top of their voice – crashed to the ground. He too had been drinking, probably on an empty stomach. I was terribly surprised at these goings-on. But people later explained to me that it happened only once a year and this time was special, as their bishop (who was teetotal) was retiring.

The youth in the Pechory area were generally anti the past and did not like all the visitors who were 'stopping us from developing'. In fact the basic boorishness that permeated peasant life surprised me in 1937. Whenever we stopped in a village, people would say to us bluntly: 'For God's sake don't talk to the local girls, or the lads could be jealous and carve you up.' I was sceptical about this, but Zurov said you really did have to be careful, as the *mores* were still close to the soil.

In a prosperous village where we stopped overnight during our trip, I went down to the well next morning to have a wash and shave. The well was on the land of a well-to-do peasant, a friend of Zurov's, but there was a road ran by it. I lathered up, I started shaving, then I looked down the road and saw a chap coming towards me. The weather was fine, here we were in a Russian village, with a Russian strolling along, I myself was young, healthy, happy…so I looked at him and smiled.

'Why you gawping?' he suddenly barked. 'I'll come over there and slash your face with that razor!'

I was really shocked. Of course, I didn't say anything to him, but when I told our host and Zurov, they both said that unfortunately that is how people carried on here. Even some of the monks were like it. I was once sitting outside the main church in the monastery when a monk came up to me who had been working in the garden. He too said: 'What d'you keep staring at me for? I'll whip your balls off with a sickle, then you'll stop staring!'

I don't remember his name, but I said: 'Father, what's the matter, what's got into you? Whoever forbade us to look at people, everyone looks at each other, that's what eyes are for!'

'Maybe they are, but it's not nice when they stare at you! You remember that, or you'll feel my sickle!'

This kind of crudeness could get you down, mainly because you had done nothing to provoke it. But I only mention it to complete the picture. On the whole, I had a wonderful time at Pechory. I learned much, I understood what were the main problems facing me, I called in for a few days to see my parents, of course, and then I hurried back to Prague.

In the winter of 1937/38 Toll invited me to write an article for the next issue of the *Seminarium Kondakovianum* and I chose as my title 'Ivan the Terrible and Icon-painting in the Sixteenth Century'. In the Soviet Union they were hopelessly exaggerating the role of Ivan in every area of culture, even icons. I realized that it would be some time before I could write a full-scale study of the penetration of West European subjects via Pskov, but I wanted to get this idea into print. In a special section of my article I voiced several thoughts on the subject, so as to secure the right to return to them in more detail later. I was beginning to understand that not many new things are said in the world of scholarship, so new ideas must be particularly valuable, and I had two: that the Pskov-Pechery Monastery was a channel of Muscovite policy in the Pskov region, and that the rest of the region offered opportunities for introducing West European elements, whence through Moscow they spread all over Rus.

The following year, 1938, I returned to Pechory and my father came over to stay with me for a while, as my mother had the year before. Together we were invited to the Assumption Day feast, as my father had sung for them in the choir and they immediately took to him. Again there was a lot of vodka – too much. We tried to avoid it, because he didn't like it and I was mindful of the fact that the previous year the local intelligentsia had tried to find out what this chap from Prague would be like in an inebriated condition. We managed to drink little at the main feast, but then unlike the previous year the monks started inviting us into their cells to try their home-made varieties. *Papa* and I visited two or three cells, in each of which we had one or two glasses. In the third cell *papa* dozed off, and I soon followed.

On this visit I worked like a Trojan in the monastery's library and archive and at copying out inventories by hand, which I was allowed to do at my digs. I had not finished, however, when I was called back to Prague because of the Sudetenland crisis. I went to Tallinn, saw my parents, and left the next day for Czechoslovakia via Poland.

7

The Future of the Kondakov Institute

It was a wonderful sunny, still September. Poland was steeped in an Indian summer. I changed trains in Warsaw and by the time I reached the Czech border I was the only person in my carriage. The Czech customsmen did not look at my luggage, and said that I was a brave man to be returning to Prague when everyone else was trying to run away from it.

I arrived, and hardly recognized the city. The station was covered with bags of earth that were meant to help protect public buildings in the event of a German air attack, there were similar bags in people's windows, which were also criss-crossed with sticky paper, and the streets were half empty. When I arrived at my flat, my neighbour gave me a letter from the landlady saying I must put myself in charge of fire and air-raid defence, and enclosing official instructions. I read these and was horrified: the shortest one said that when bombs fell their temperature would be 3000-3500 degrees Centigrade and you should go over to them, sprinkle sand on them, and then plunge them in a bucket of water! There were boxes of sand and pails of water everywhere.

I went to find my best friend, Kostya Gavrilov, and discovered that he was leaving by 30 September for Bremen. His father lived in Argentina and could see more clearly from there that Europe was heading for war, so he had arranged free passage for his son on a training ship of the Argentine Navy which was returning to Argentina via Africa and the South Atlantic. It was an enormous loss for me personally, but everyone understood that it was best for him to go. We corresponded for the rest of our lives, but he never returned to Europe and we never met again.

The situation at the Institute was dire. Some of its members wanted to move to Belgrade, and theoretically a new section had been set up there under the patronage of the Yugoslav Prince Regent, Paul. Some major Russian scholars, including Ostrogorsky, were there, and Rasovsky had also gone there, to set up this section on a proper legal basis as had been done in Prague. The problem was, though, that in Prague the Institute had been constituted as a Society, and there was no legal document dissolving this Society at the Prague end. Moreover, the Institute had begun with publications and we were closely linked to Prague's printers. When the idea of moving to Belgrade was discussed, I said I was very doubtful that the Institute could carry on there because the Yugoslavs did not have the printing technology needed. Then it was proposed keeping a base in Prague, where the Institute's publications would still be printed, and moving a part of it to Belgrade as no-one knew what historical upheavals were round the corner.

The Princess was categorically opposed to Belgrade and found it extraordinary to be contemplating, as Rasovsky, Toll and Ostrogorsky were, moving the whole library there without so much as a by-your-leave, transferring the publication stocks there, and so forth. She thought it was insulting: although Masaryk was no longer alive and Beneš was giving us no aid, Czechoslovakia had supported the Institute for many years and we could not just make off with everything like thieves.

On the whole, Toll agreed with her. But there was also a personal factor where he was concerned. His brother-in-law, Georgy Vernadsky, was living in the US, Toll's wife and daughter had joined him there, and Vernadsky was insisting that Toll go to Belgrade, whence Vernadsky could get him a visa to the US. The allocation of American visas from Czechoslovakia was already exhausted and it was assumed Toll would work at Yale as assistant to Professor Rostovtsev.

The Princess, whom I one hundred per cent supported, was right: a law had already been passed in Czechoslovakia banning the export of valuables, and our library was a very valuable object. Nor could our publications be illegally exported from the warehouse, or we would be prosecuted. This was a real possibility, because various people were watching us closely, for example Nikolay Okunev, a member of the Slavonic Institute, who was fiercely opposed to the Kondakov Institute and certainly did not want such a fine library to end up abroad. He himself had ambitions of becoming director or financial manager of the Kondakov.

I also had personal reasons for not wanting to go to Belgrade. I did not want to be even further from my parents, I did not know Serbian, it was not that easy to learn, and I would have no back-up there. Two factions had formed, pro and anti moving to Yugoslavia, and I belonged to the latter. The Institute's main operator in Belgrade would be Dmitry Rasovsky. Of course, the top scholar there was Ostrogorsky, but Rasovsky would be in day-to-day charge. And my relations with Rasovsky were already cool.

Rasovsky had gone off to Yugoslavia followed by Irina Okuneva, who it transpired was going to marry him. Of course, they did not need me there, because Irina could perfectly well do my job, and this would save the Institute money. So I should be thrown out. Rasovsky had already tried to do this two years earlier, but I had faced him down. I talked to the Princess and General Chernavin early in 1938 about the situation, he supported the Princess, and as chairman of the Institute's auditing commission he was outraged at the management's illegal actions. Meanwhile, I had been in Pechory and Toll had been called up.

He came to see me at the Institute in uniform and carrying a rifle. It was intriguing how swiftly being in the army suppresses a person's more individual side. He was still acting director, he was glad that I was back and already getting down to work, but he wasn't very interested in things; he merely said that he was arranging for our friend Petya Khmyrov to deliver some packing-cases that he, Toll, had ordered from him for despatching the library. Then he went back to his regiment.

Khmyrov turned up with his brilliantly made boxes for the books. He wanted to start packing them, but I said I could not sanction it, as I had no instructions from Toll and in any case, if I did start I would have to make a list of what was going. Petya was always very easy to persuade, and he and I went off to the nearest pub, where he gave a witty account of how lily-livered everyone in Prague was, how nobody understood anything, and how things were moving towards a real clash of arms, although for some reason he was sure this wouldn't happen, because at the last moment the Czechs would funk it. He did not have a high opinion of Czech courage.

It turned out more or less that way. On 30 September the Munich Agreement was signed, after which it transpired there would be no war, because the Czechs were surrendering the Sudentenland to Germany without a fight. This caused convulsions of popular anger, because tens of thousands of Czechs felt it was the end of their independent republic. They rushed to the presidential palace and demanded action. Syrovy was made acting CIC, but the general staff were glad that there was not going to be a fight because, as General Voytsekhovsky told me, in the circumstances it would be hopeless. Austria was already occupied by the Germans, i.e. Czechoslovakia had been outflanked in the west, and without French help no battle could last long. The city of Prague would probably have been razed as an example.

Toll 'shed his armour', as he expressed it, and became wholly civilian again. He said to me: 'I'm going to America. I've been told that the American Embassy in Belgrade has a visa for me. So I've got to go to Yugoslavia, possibly very soon, in a few weeks. Before then we must get all these books out.'

Looking him straight in the eye, I said: 'My dear Nikolay Petrovich, you have heard my point of view officially, now I repeat it: you cannot do this.'

'What can't I do?'

'Export valuables. We cannot export them, because they will be stopped.'

'That's all been taken care of. We shan't be exporting them, the Yugoslav Embassy will.'

We called on the Yugoslav ambassador, a tall, very affable man, with whom we conversed in Czech as we did not know Serbian and he could not speak Russian. He said that if we had two boxes he could take them. The two large boxes that Petya brought were duly packed with books. I wasn't there at the time, but when I got back the books were already crated up. Toll had whipped off the shelves what seemed to him valuable, and had not even noted down their titles. I was appalled, I protested, but he said I was being bureaucratic about it and now was not the time for bureaucracy, we had to get them out because either the Germans would take them all, or there would be a bloodbath in Prague and they would all be destroyed.

He loaded the crates onto a lorry and we delivered them to the Yugoslav Embassy, where the porter very grudgingly accepted them. Then Toll said that Petya could make as many boxes as were needed and I must gradually pack them all up.

I said: 'Nikolay Petrovich, you are disappearing, as all the senior members have, but what am I meant to be doing? No-one has said anything about me, no-one has wangled *me* a visa, so am I supposed to stay here?'

'Of course,' he replied. 'You must stay here to defend the property.'

'And how will I do that?'

'You will manage all the business here. This is the Institute's base, Belgrade is just a branch of it, all the business will be referred to Prague and you will send on to Belgrade what in your opinion should be sent, or you will act on your own initiative.'

'Fine. What powers will I have?'

'I'll give you all the powers you need.'

He took me to the bank and signed a document transferring all financial matters – the bank account, what we had in safes, and the keys to the safes – to me. 'Doctor Andreyev is the fully empowered representative of the Kondakov Institute in all financial matters,' it said. He also left me a document in which as acting chairman of the board of management he was temporarily transferring the day-to-day running of the Institute to me. This gave me some ground under my feet. Everything was to come into force on 1 January 1939 and Toll was leaving the month before.

Before he left, he went to see the Princess, who was very unhappy about what he was doing. They had a bit of a row and he was even quite rude to her, saying that she was too old to see things 'in their real light'. She said: 'But I can still see them in the light of honesty and conscience, whereas what you call realism is just sharp practice.'

Although they thought highly of each other, Toll was extremely put out and left her house huffing and puffing like a steam engine. He never met her again, whilst she was made quite ill by it because actually she was fond of him and understood that he thought he had done everything for the good of the Institute, but she believed he was wrong. She was supported by Chernavin, who came to see the Princess every day, and of course I shared her view. I showed them the documents Toll had given me, I said that the finances were now in my hands, the two crates of books were his affair, and no more library books would be going.

The first thing I did was to make my own audit of how much we had in the bank and how we stood with our printers. It was all very satisfactory, we had some money and lots more to come in from selling books, we had a lot of coal in our cellars, so I thought we could survive for a while yet. Our publications stock was still in Prague, although during my absence Toll had managed to send off some surplus copies. When I was able to read the minutes of the management meetings and so forth, I saw that there wasn't a word in them about it having been decided to send the library books abroad, and you couldn't possibly envisage the Institute being legally wound up as there was no mention of that anywhere.

A transfer of power had taken place, but we were still under threat from the Slavonic Institute, which thanks to Okunev suspected that we wanted to clear off to Yugoslavia with all our valuables. As I understood it, my principal task was to consolidate our position in terms of the law. What they did in Belgrade was their business, we could not influence anything there, but Prague was the base and everything here should be legally exact. We decided that since I was now managing the enterprise, I could not be a member of the auditing commission at the same time. I resigned from it, therefore, and E.I. Melnikov, my friend and colleague with whom I shared a room when first at the Kondakov Institute, took my place. The board of management now consisted of Princess Yashvil and myself, and the auditing commission was General Chernavin and Melnikov. This gave us some sort of legal framework.

It later turned out that a legal framework was vital for defending the Institute against not only the Czechs and then the Germans, but also against the Belgrade section, which absolutely refused to consider the situation on the ground here and upset everyone we had dealings with, whether lawyers or just people of common sense. I think this was not so much the fault of Ostrogorsky, who just wanted to wash his hands of us, as Rasovsky. The latter evidently wanted to cause me trouble personally, either by winding up the members of the Institute so much that they threw me out, or by making it impossible for me to manage the organization. Perhaps I am being over-suspicious, but sadly the situation was very tense and every letter that we received from Belgrade caused *terrible* stress.

Rasovsky might have succeeded in harming my position, but for two factors. First, the Institute was in the middle of publishing a monumental archaeological work that was on volume five or six. It was being printed in Prague under our supervision and Toll had handed all responsibility for it to me. The printing would not be complete before the middle of the summer, so no steps could be taken against me before then. Second, when Toll got to Belgrade and saw the state of things there, he wrote me a very interesting letter. 'Act as you see fit,' he said, 'and ignore everything Rasya (his contemptuous name for Rasovsky) writes you.' I think he was shocked not only by the absence of a typographical base for publishing in Belgrade, which we had been warning him about for eighteen months, but by the fact that the section was run by the husband and wife team to the exclusion of everyone else. Evidently he felt that they didn't

15. Nikolay Andreyev outside the Kondakov Institute.

even want to tell him everything, as he had already 'jumped off the bandwagon' and was leaving for America. So in a way he revised his instructions to me. And 'Rasya' really was writing us one piece of nonsense after another. None of it had the slightest basis in law.

That was the background at the beginning of 1939. Gradually, with the help of Melnikov, whom I paid to do certain things at the Institute, we worked out which books Toll had sent to Belgrade. All this information was declared secret, as I did not want trouble from the Slavonic Institute. When Okunev turned up and tried to investigate under the guise of using the library, I said to him: 'Bear in mind that some of the books were taken by Ostrogorsky personally the last time he was here.'

The behaviour of the Belgrade section was uncollegiate and even criminal, because they were putting us in the position of people who had broken the financial laws of the Czechoslovak government, which could have had unpleasant consequences including arrest and imprisonment. The auditors and a legal consultant I brought in were horrified. Toll had also advised me to consult Savitsky in some cases, as he was working at the Prague German University and was in a good position at that moment because of Germany's growing influence in the city. Also, Toll said, Savitsky was sincere and undoubtedly sympathetic towards the Institute, and if I approached him he would give me conscientious advice.

I spoke to Savitsky in February following the stupid letters that we were receiving from Belgrade and I explained the situation. He immediately took my side, and said that they were playing with fire. 'Be terribly careful how you reply,' he said, 'because your correspondence could be intercepted, copied, and charges brought against you for smuggling property out of the country.' This conversation proved very useful for the future. Savitsky now concerned himself with the problems of our Institute, and this had a number of positive consequences for both us and him.

8

The Nazi Occupation

We felt that the Germans would put political pressure on Prague, but we did not expect them actually to invade. This happened on 15 March 1939.

The evening before, my landlady had come running to me saying that there was a very strange announcement on the radio reminding everyone that Prague was an old German city. She was Czech and terribly indignant: 'But we are independent, our republic may be small, but it's independent.' I failed to console her by saying that perhaps it wasn't a very accurate broadcast. At six o'clock next morning she hammered on the doors of the Institute again (my flat was in the building) and told me: '*Pan Doktor*, they've just said that the Germans are not only entering the whole republic, but Prague itself.' I did not have a radio then, as I regarded it as a waste of time. I quickly dressed, shaved, grabbed an umbrella because it was raining, and ran towards the centre of Prague.

I got to Wenceslas Square at about 8.15. It was choked with people, most of them with umbrellas, and German troops were pouring across it. The Prague police were clearing a route for them, pushing back the crowds. There were armoured cars, followed by motorcyclists at low speed, and an endless stream of trucks with soldiers in the back wearing helmets and holding rifles. It was a demonstration of German might and they were heading for Hradčany (the Castle) where the appointed Protector of Prague, von Neurath, was to appear.

Everyone was deeply depressed by the feeling that this was the end of Czechoslovakia and its spell of freedom. The crowd sang the national anthem, people wept, one woman sprang out and spat at the troops, some phlegm landed on a soldier's cheek, but he did not even wipe it off, perhaps he did not notice it, and the woman melted into the crowd again. The troops passed, the crowd broke up, many people were crying as they walked along. There was a terrible, disorienting sense of impotence. How had all this come about? For twenty years we had worked shoulder to shoulder with France, and suddenly we had been betrayed. For twenty years we had been the bedrock of the Petite Entente, we had been trained to resist the German threat, and now that it had materialized not a shot had been fired, everyone had surrendered, and what lay ahead was unknown.

I went to the main post office and sent a postcard to my parents. I was amazed to see hulking great SS men strolling about, smiling sweetly and talking to Czechs in German, which all the Czechs had suddenly begun to speak fluently. Such a quick changeover shocked me, I had been so wrapped up in my own affairs that I hadn't noticed that German culture already existed in the Czech world. The Czechs knew how to adapt: their history had taught them to. At heart they were great nationalists in a small republic, not blameless in their dealings with their own minorities. But I understood: their behaviour now was caused by despair. We learned from various friends that during the night of 14 March a lot of Czech officers of the General Staff had flown out, including Czech Intelligence men.

The blossoming of Czech freedom was over, but it had been a beautiful phenomenon in so-called Versailles Europe. I could testify myself that in all the years I had lived in Czechoslovakia no-one had asked me about my political

beliefs, no-one had ever drawn any conclusions based on my approach to life.
I remember that until the Munich crisis you could find on all the newspaper
stands the Nazis' *Völkischer Beobachter* side by side with *Pravda*, to the
genuine surprise of the Soviet citizens who were visiting Czechoslovakia in
larger and larger numbers. You could buy newspapers from all over Europe –
Fascist, non-Fascist, whatever. And you could find everything in the bookshops
from the works of Stalin to the publications of Mussolini. The only exception
was *Mein Kampf*, which was banned in Czechoslovakia, and the Russian books
I mentioned earlier about the Russian gold supposedly seized by the Czech
Legions. Otherwise there was complete freedom, every kind of political party
existed, from the Fascists to the Communists, and they found expression both
in the press and the everyday activity of Czech citizens. Czechoslovakia was
undoubtedly a democratic country in the best sense of the word. There was also
great linguistic freedom, because it did not insist on Czech as the language of
its schools. You could find in them the languages of all the different minorities.

Sic transit gloria mundi. The Protector of Bohemia and Moravia, von Neurath,
was preparing to meet the leader of the German people, Adolf Hitler, at the
historic Hradčany. In the city squares, German military bands played marches,
sentimental songs and waltzes. The enormous building of the Petschek Bank
was taken over by the Gestapo, who were getting ready to purge the protectorate.
The newspapers published various decrees and a national association was
formed called *Národní souručenství* in which everyone vouched for everyone
else (the whole protectorate belonged to it), rather than having the despised
political parties. Our friend Prince Schwarzenberg's son was made one of the
youth leaders of the organization, which discussed what form of greeting to
adopt. They decided to introduce the Aryan salute raising the right arm. 'But
wouldn't it be more realistic to raise both arms,' Schwarzenberg interjected,
'as though surrendering?' This risqué joke was made behind closed doors, but
within an hour the whole of Prague was repeating it.

The Russian emigration was to be reorganized at a meeting to which basically
all Prague's Russians were invited. Apparently the Germans had been horrified
to discover that there were 131 Russian organizations! They said that a stop had
to be put to this liberal chaos, and in any case the basic principle of organizations
– electing a committee – had been abolished. Special plenipotentiaries were to
be appointed. By whom? At the meeting we were told that the Germans wanted
a united emigration and therefore only one political organization was being set
up here, as had already happened in Germany. It was to be called 'The Russian
Émigré Base'. The head of the entire Russian emigration in Greater Germany,
into which the protectorate had been incorporated, was Cavalry General Vasily

Biskupsky. He had been made a cavalry general by 'Tsar' Kirill in emigration, having once been an officer in the Imperial Guards.

A ceremony was held. The chairman of the United Committee of Russian Organizations in Prague, Prince Pyotr Dolgorukov, stepped forward and addressed General Biskupsky, entrusting him with care of the Russian Emigration, 'Which God Preserve'. It was a decent speech, reserved, concrete, free of flourishes. Dolgorukov emphasized that the emigration had existed here eighteen years and had many local interests which should be taken into account. Someone sitting near me said: 'He's the last Cadet cockerel, and already plucked!' Both parts of this remark were true: he was a Cadet cockerel, and events really had stripped him of his feathers.

General Biskupsky replied with a long speech that took us by surprise. First, he thanked the Prince for putting him in the picture about the local Russian colony, and for the trust placed in him, General Biskupsky, to whom was being transferred the destiny of the Russian émigrés in the Protectorate. This was said as though we had handed ourselves over to him voluntarily! Then he came to the point: 'I have to tell you that I am a monarchist. As a monarchist, I cannot be a Nazi, because the idea of monarchy and the idea of a Nazi state are incompatible. However, I personally am reconciled to Nazism by the fact that we have a common foe, communism. Therefore, as far as I could, I have supported the leader of the German people, Adolf Hitler.' This was a reference to the fact that in the twenties Biskupsky, who had made a lot of money on the Berlin property market, gave Hitler's movement a sum of German marks. It was a fairly token amount, I think, but Hitler remembered it.

Biskupsky continued: 'So you must not be surprised that I am not a Nazi or a member of the Russian National Socialist Workers Party (for there is a Russian section of this party). But I do support the leader of the great German Empire, who has a great future ahead of him, because this Reich is of course destined to defeat world communism, and then the Russian monarchy will be restored. I call upon you all to support the actions of Adolf Hitler, the leader of the German people and Third Reich, and if you don't wish to become Nazis, nobody is forcing you to.'

This speech amused us slightly – after all, the whole Gestapo leadership was sitting there in the front row! But now the head of the Russian Émigré Base was introduced. He was the leader of the local Nazi Party, one Konstantin Yefremov. He had started as a Russian taxi-driver in Prague, built up his own taxi firm apparently, and made a lot of money. I had never heard of him. I subsequently met him when I had to visit the 'Base', and he was always very polite. This was because he thought I had friends in high places. Yefremov's job was not an enviable one: he was under the second department of the Gestapo, which was responsible for the Russian emigration, and basically he had to grass to them on the Russian colony.

At the 'Base' there were always odd-looking young men hanging around – as someone put it, bouncers and stool-pigeons rolled in one. They were servile towards Yefremov, they stood up when he came into a room, and they virtually stood at attention when speaking to him. But I had the impression that the main player here was not Yefremov, and not these young people, but a certain A.A. Kanke. I think he was a Germanized Czech. He spoke fluent German, had lived in Russia, and was therefore considered a Russian émigré. At one time, according to himself, he had been secretary to Count Witte, who dictated his memoirs to him. This exalted him in his own estimation. I thought he was educated and very dangerous. He came to the Institute once or twice, I assume to find out who visited it and to sniff around. He too was convinced that I had very high-up German contacts and therefore treated me respectfully, even liked to make out that he and I were buddies, expressed amazement at how many girlfriends I had – every time he saw me on the street, he said, I had a different girl on my arm. I think Kanke survived everything, eluded the Bolsheviks, and ended up in West Germany. Yefremov was not so lucky: he was handed over to the Czechs, who hanged him with Heide, the head of the Gestapo's second department.

As soon as the Germans arrived, everyone had problems, the Kondakov Institute included. They announced that all institutions had to be re-registered. I wasn't quite sure whether we should do this: the Institute was not a Czech institution, nor was it Russian, it was more of an international institution with a special charter. It wasn't obvious who we should come under. The announcements said that the object of re-registration was to lump together similar institutions. This really frightened me, as it suggested we could be classified with the Slavonic Institute and Czech scholarly societies and end up being run by some obscure professor. I had to be very careful. I purposely missed the first re-registration, having decided that if they sent me a reminder I could always say that I hadn't understood it applied to us, because we weren't a Czech institution. Then it was announced that Russian émigré institutions would be re-registered, also with a view to lumping them in groups. At this point, I suddenly thought of asking my German pupil what we should do.

This pupil, Josef Dedio, was a gift from the gods. One day in March shortly after the invasion, I received a letter from Savitsky on the German University's headed paper (I kept it as a very important document, but I don't know whether it has survived in the Institute's archives). He wrote that he wanted to ask me to take on Herr Dedio as a student of Russian. Dedio was from Berlin, had a knowledge of Russian, but wanted to improve it. 'I think it would be in your and the general interest if you accepted him,' wrote Savitsky. Clearly Dedio was an important figure. I replied straightaway that I would be pleased to meet Herr Dedio to discuss his requirements, and a few days later I had a letter from him in German asking me to meet him at the Palace Hotel. This was a building that had previously housed the Russian Free University. It had been refurbished as a first-class hotel, and it had a first-class barber's shop on the ground floor called 'Vasilieff's'. During the war this became a kind of club: you could have a shave there and at the same time pick up lots of news from the Protectorate and abroad.

I was somewhat thrown when I arrived, as the hotel turned out to be packed with German military and SS men. Herr Dedio was short, stocky, and about fifty. I was very surprised to see that he had a perfectly spherical head – I had studied a bit of anthropology and knew that this was a feature of a particular European race. His ancestors, in fact, were Huguenots who had fled from France but become completely Germanized. Dedio spoke in pure literary German and was regarded as Germanness personified. His hero, apart from Adolf Hitler, about whom he never said a word, was Bismarck, about whom he chatted approvingly to me on several occasions.

He immediately appointed a time for the lessons and gave me an address where I could meet him. I later realized that this was in a block of flats confiscated from the Jews. He could speak Russian fairly well. He had been taken prisoner by the Russians during the First World War and his captivity – spent practically in Siberia – seemed to have agreed with him. He and his fellow-prisoners were put to work on the land, so essentially he was completely free, and I think he had some amorous adventures, because he was definitely indulgent towards Russians and loved Russia. He said it was because of this love that he was particularly opposed to Communism, which had turned this beautiful country into goodness knows what. He had witnessed the start of the revolution and told me that he could not for one second sympathize with such methods.

When I came for the second or third lesson, he opened the door and I stepped back with a gasp: before me stood an SS man in all the splendour of his officer's uniform. He was delighted with the effect and said: 'You must remember, not everything you see is for telling about.' I took this as a warning.

We went to various cafés and small restaurants and he kindly paid on top of my fee. On these occasions he was always in civvies. He was surprised once when the waiters immediately addressed him in German. 'Do I look that German?' he asked, inspecting his appearance, then said: 'Ah, I forgot to take my Party badge off.'

When his wife and children arrived, he moved to a bigger flat, where we always played chess, which he was extremely fond of. I must admit, after a stubborn defence and a few risky positions, I thought it was sensible to lose, as he was in a far more winning position in the world outside than me, a poor émigré.

Dedio explained to me that he worked on Russian matters, so I asked permission to discuss with him the problem of whether we should register. He was interested and asked to see the papers, which I had with me: the Institute's charter, the accounts, the membership list, and even a German translation of the charter which Karl Schwarzenberg and I had made. He read it all, asked me a number of questions, then came out with an aphorism: 'Why go to meet evil? It will come to you, if it wants to.' I gathered that we need not register. At a later lesson, he expressed a wish to dine with me at the Russian restaurant '*Ogonyok*'. Suddenly Konstantin Yefremov rose from one of the tables and came over to us, bowing deeply and mumbling compliments at Dedio in German. The latter said to him frostily: 'Ah, Yefremov, do you know Dr Andreyev?' – and motioned at me. Yefremov didn't, so Dedio introduced us. This kept Yefremov at a respectable distance from the Institute and me for the rest of the German period. He knew Dedio, because Dedio was an assistant to the head of the second department dealing with Russian affairs, and Dedio treated him contemptuously because he was just a subordinate. Yefremov, however, decided that there were mysterious links between us. This was the kind of illusion that determined the fates of people and institutions during the German occupation.

Another factor was Dr Morper.

One morning the bell at the Institute rang, then our caretaker Nalivkin appeared in the library with a frightened face and said: 'There's some German to see you.' I went out and in the vestibule I found a German infantryman holding his cap and staring raptly at the portrait of Kondakov hanging there. Before I could speak he launched into an encomium of Kondakov in the German high style, concluding with 'and I am delighted I could come here to pay my respects to such a great scholar'. In the last couple of years I had grown used to manifestations of mental instability, but I simply could not work out who this was. Then he turned to me, clicked his heels, and said: '*Ich bin aus München. Ich bin Doktor Morper.*'

He was an art historian/archaeologist who had been corresponding with the Institute for years, but we had never met him. I welcomed him warmly and ushered him into the library, where I was able to show him the box on the shelves containing all his offprints. He was very flattered. He explained that he was in Prague on official business: he had been seconded to the Protectorate from his regiment to work as an art historian in the administration's section for ancient monuments. He had arrived a week ago, got settled in, and come to find out, as he put it, whether he could help the Kondakov Institute in any way. He certainly could. He wrote a report which we never saw but which had a favourable effect on the relevant German authorities. All the institutions in the Protectorate, except the purely German ones, were under threat of being wound up. Thanks to Morper's report, which also reached Hamperl, the Dean of the German University who oversaw us, and thanks to Dedio, the Kondakov Institute was seen as doing useful scholarly work in a category of its own. Morper created good will towards us from the Protectorate administration, which dampened the desires of our fellow countrymen to get their hands on us. Yefremov did not dare attack me.

However, Professor Vladimir Ilin, who had been put in charge of the combined émigré organizations, did everything he could to make the Institute register and to bring it under his control. Ilin had been appointed by the Germans because he was acting Rector of the Russian Free University at the time. He lumped all the organizations together – except the Kondakov Institute. He did his utmost to corral us too, going so far as to summon me and try to frighten me by saying that our self-determination was infuriating the Gestapo and organs of surveillance. I smiled enigmatically at this and said that the organs of surveillance were informed and had given me certain assurances, whilst representatives of the cultural administration had visited us and told us to stay as we were. Ilin was enraged at this; he wasn't a Nazi but he was a megalomaniac, he was a typical demagogue, he wanted to control everyone. He managed to crush all resistance to himself, but he did not succeed where the Kondakov Institute was concerned. As is often the case, he ended up respecting me, because I never met him head on, I always played things down, reacted vaguely, told him that the money was not mine, it came from private sources, that even President Masaryk had helped us in a private capacity rather than as a man of state. Ilin even offered me the position of vice chairman of his association, but I continued to act dumb and would not budge. On the other hand, there was now no danger of an assault on us by Okunev at the Slavonic Institute, as Morper's protection was proof against all their intrigues.

So that is how it all turned out: quite unexpectedly we were safe and sound.

Nevertheless, I realized that if we were to avoid approaching the Protectorate or the Germans themselves for help, we must have our own money. We still had some funds, because I had economized, and if it hadn't been for the disgraceful action of the Belgrade people we would have been financially completely independent. For some time I had received no money from our Germans reps;

so I wrote to the main one, Otto Harrassowitz in Leipzig, reminding them that, as they had told us themselves, they were holding a large sum from the sales of our publications, and we would be grateful if they paid it to us. Suddenly we received a letter from them saying that a few months earlier they had transferred this money to Belgrade, as requested. This put us in a terrible position.

I decided that the only way out was to improve our position in the Protectorate. We could not publish anything, as we did not want to collaborate with the occupiers, but we could attempt to enlarge our collections. This would turn our small institute into a museum as well, which would attract general support and be very useful to us. I talked to Josef Girsa, who I think was the first Czechoslovak consul in Moscow after Czechoslovakia recognized the Soviet Union *de facto*. He had brought out in the diplomatic bag a large collection of Old Believer icons that had belonged to the Soldatenkov family, he kept them in his house, and lent us some for an exhibition in 1936. Now he was afraid that as part of the Germans' actions against diplomats he could be arrested and all his property confiscated. We therefore agreed to transfer his collection to the Kondakov Institute, exchanging letters that confirmed we had been given the Soldatenkovs' property to study.

The main step we took, however, was to find ourselves a patron in the person of Prince Karl Schwarzenberg. He offered us 50,000 Czech crowns, which was in those days a huge sum. 'We could enter this in the Institute's books,' he told me, 'as my life membership subscription.' He had large estates and several saw mills. For a number of reasons he did not want to attract the authorities' attention to his gift, so I received the money in notes, wrapped up in newspaper!

Once I had got it into the Institute's account we began to enlarge our premises at Slunná. Princess Yashvil had died in the summer of 1939 and to cut our costs we gave up our lease on the basement and I moved from a flat on the ground floor to the Institute's former kitchen and stockroom. Then in 1940 we also acquired the top of the building, knocked rooms through, and created an icon collection. The stockroom was moved to the attic, the old kitchen and stockroom became exhibition rooms, and another kitchen was converted into my accommodation, where the Institute occasionally held receptions.

At this point Professor Hamperl, Dean of the German University, received a denunciation of me from Belgrade written in very good German and signed by Ostrogorsky.

The gist of it was that it had come to their notice in Belgrade that the youngest member of the Institute was throwing his weight about and acting contrary to official provisions made for the Institute's future. Evidently, they said, I was

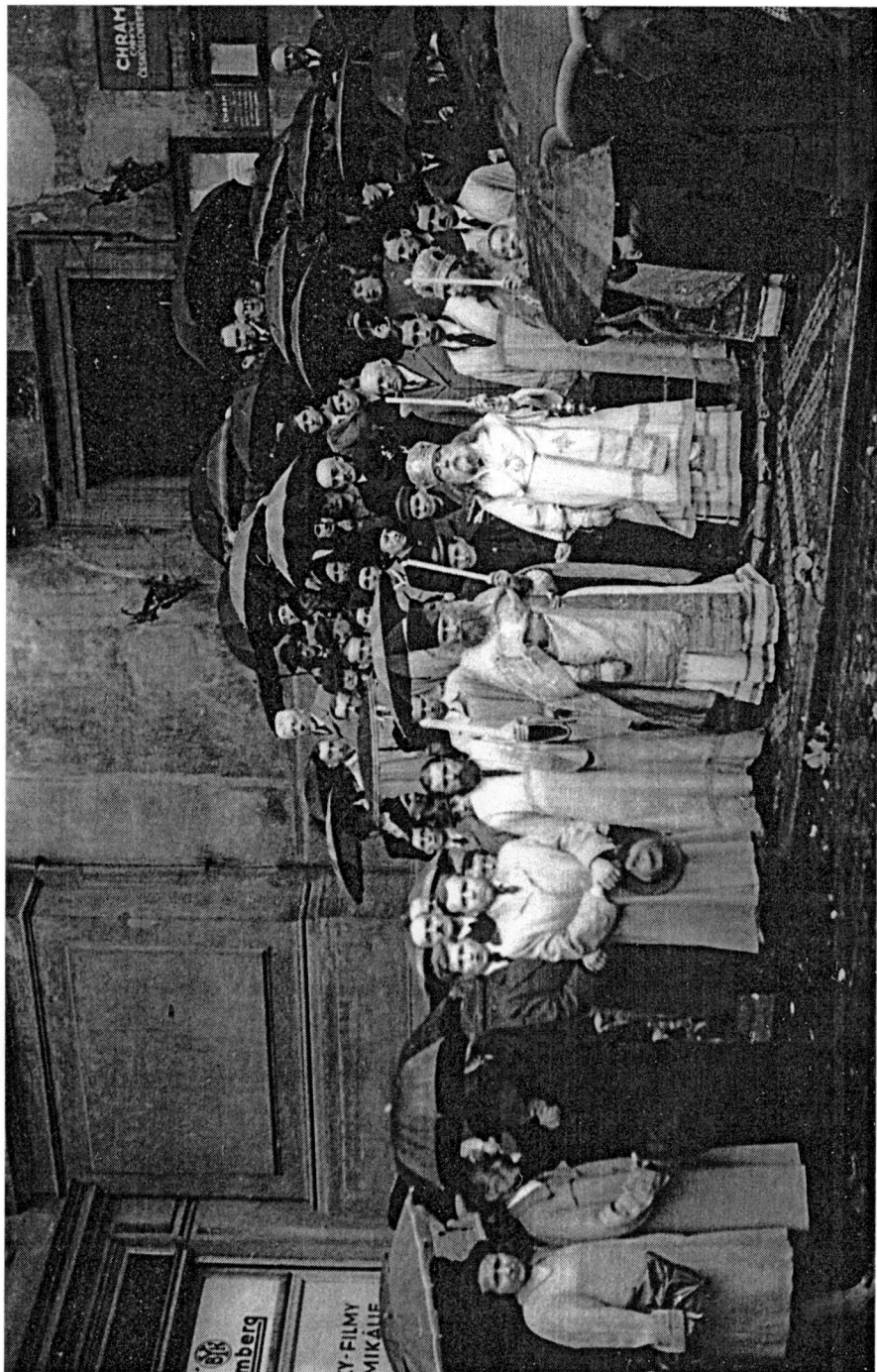

16.   Funeral of Princess Yashvil – 1939.

misinforming those people supervising my activity in Prague and they therefore deemed it necessary to draw attention to my behaviour as not conforming with the wishes of the Institute's scholarly members, who were based in Belgrade, were raising their voice in the person of their chairman Ostrogorsky, and dissociating themselves from my activity. I was a usurper and an opportunist and the policies I was pursuing disgusted all the members of the Institute.

Hamperl sent me this denunciation with a letter asking me to prepare answers and bring them with me to see him urgently. Fortunately, that very morning there was a meeting of the Institute's trustees, including Savitsky and Schwarzenberg. When I read them the denunciation they were speechless. Schwarzenberg held it up to the light as he suspected it was a Gestapo forgery. For how could a Byzantinist with a world reputation, a man who was considered my friend, Ostrogorsky, write such mendacious twaddle? He knew what Nazi Germany was like, yet he was inciting the German authorities to take action against me; at the very least to dismiss me.

I was so shattered I could not do anything. But the others felt we must act immediately. They drafted a reply, point by point, Schwarzenberg expressed it in elegant German, and it was typed up there and then. I don't remember it exactly, because I was beside myself – this was one of the saddest episodes of my life. Basically, they reminded people of the posts I had held at the Institute ever since being awarded a scholarship there, and said that since 1 January 1939 I held full powers from Dr Toll to manage everything, and had acted strictly in accordance with the orders issued by the Protectorate's government. Thus absolutely all my actions were legitimate; for instance, all financial decisions were made with the approval of the trustees. I had no personal ambitions whatsoever, simply the desire to keep the Institute going with all its collections, which we were now putting in order and registering, and naturally if there were any plans to publish things we would consult scholars in our Belgrade section first.

The next day I took the reply to Hamperl. He was in a terrible mood: usually he spoke to me in Russian, but this time he greeted me with 'Heil Hitler!' and addressed me very officially in German. He summoned a secretary to take down our conversation. This was very short, because as soon as he saw the letter he relaxed, brightened up, and said: 'I see. I'll let you know what we decide.' I bowed and left. Two days later he sent me a copy of his reply, which was splendid in the sense that it was short and businesslike. He wrote to Ostrogorsky that he had received his letter, discussed it, and found it disproven in every point. He also mentioned that the motion Ostrogorsky referred to calling for the transfer of the Institute abroad was not to be found in the Institute's minutes and there was not a word in them about the Institute being wound up. It was depressing to think that Russians close and apparently friendly to me had tried their hardest to put my head on the block and I had to be rescued by the Austrian Hamperl.

Unfortunately, at one of our subsequent meetings Hamperl made a suggestion that dismayed me: 'You know, I think we should give you a job at our German University, so as to make your financial and legal position more secure.'

All I could mumble was: 'I er um do not speak German well enough...'

'Perfectly well enough to teach Russian,' he countered. 'You have enough vocabulary and grammar to explain your examples. Your German is no worse than Savitsky's, he may use more words but he often makes elementary grammatical mistakes.'

To have accepted an appointment at the Nazis' German University after the dissolution of the Czechs' Charles University would have been monstrous and I was completely against it. However, this was only the thin end of the wedge. Three weeks later I had another letter from Hamperl, saying that the Rector's Office had decided to appoint a *Vorsitzender* to oversee the Institute, one Professor Weigand, a Byzantinist just transplanted to Prague from Munich.

When Weigand came to see the Institute, I made sure that Schwarzenberg was there, so that he could meet him – like all Germans, Weigand respected the aristocracy. He stayed for about half an hour, glanced at all our exhibits, and it was obvious that he did not understand much about Russian icon-painting. But he was very affable and told me I could carry on doing what I wanted, as long as I sent him a report every quarter. Evidently his appointment was a sinecure, although it could have been dangerous because previously we had been autonomous. He could have interfered or vetoed things. In fact he was very tactful.

The war was spreading, conflict broke out with Yugoslavia, and in the very first air-raid on Belgrade the branch of the Kondakov Institute there was destroyed by a bomb. Rasovsky and his wife were killed. We all shuddered – even more than when Belyayev had been killed in 1931. We saw in it a strange sign. They had used every means, fair and foul, to drag the Institute there, and now everything had been destroyed. News reached us that part of the library had survived, in a semi-charred condition, so we tried to contact Ostrogorsky, but it was impossible by post and in the end Hamperl arranged for the German military authorities in Belgrade to load the remains of the Institute's belongings onto army trucks and bring it back to Prague. Yet again I felt that there are decisions God takes which are beyond our understanding and which issue as tragic events; but taken they are and they determine the way our relationships on this planet develop. It was very depressing to go through this, but now other events were bearing down on us: we had to move to a new building because the Gestapo, which already occupied the neighbouring large houses, wanted ours too.

Out of all the alternatives offered, we chose the third floor of 6A Haštalská, Prague 1, and completely redecorated it. The Gestapo gave us a month, I think, to get it ready, but not everything was finished when we moved in. The result, though, was impressive and I must give Khmyrov credit for it. He had had to find the building materials and get round the ban on buying paint, which all meant dealing with the black market. He probably took commission from the workmen for this, and we also gave him extra, but it was worth it.

On 22 June 1941 Germany attacked the Soviet Union. By December the Russian generals I knew in Prague were concluding that the Germans had lost the first year of the war with Russia. Hitler himself now took command of the army and the struggle with Russia hotted up. She was holding out longer than any other country since the war began, and we realized that no more concessions would be made to Russian émigrés. In my case, to my great relief, this meant that Hamperl dropped the idea of making me a lecturer at the German University. But he also suggested that the Institute move into University premises. This idea appalled me, because it would mean a complete loss of independence and before long we would be swallowed up by the German University. I managed to parry it by saying that Schwarzenberg might think he had wasted all the money he had given us to develop our collections and recently move. Hamperl conceded this. But it made me think that the idea had been mooted because some people were expecting a deterioration in Nazi policy towards Russians generally, i.e. émigrés included. The bulk of the Russian emigration remained patriotic, it believed in Russia and not Greater Germany. Some Germans were beginning to see that sooner or later the Nazi authorities would hit at the emigration and therefore the Kondakov Institute too.

Paradoxically, the financial state of the Institute kept improving. This was because I had the bright idea of increasing sales of reproduction icons by using our colour plates. I went to Nejbert's printing works to discuss the technical details and he said it was possible. 'But what about the art paper?' I asked. 'We can't use worse paper for the reprints than the original run.' 'You've got vast stocks of paper.' 'Stocks?' I repeated, surprised. 'Didn't you know that?' he said, and showed me the figures: we still had several *tons* of paper of different kinds including art paper.

'Where did you get it all from?' I asked him.

'We've had it for years, ever since the Seminarium Kondakovianum was set up and we did our first jobs for them. All the paper was bought then and left in storage with us.'

'So you registered it all and now we have to ask permission?'

'No, we didn't register it, because it's your paper.'

I was sorry I hadn't registered it either, simply because I hadn't known of its existence.

'You don't have to ask permission for such small items,' he said. 'They might refuse. So we'll print them without asking. The Germans'll think that the Protectorate authorities gave their permission, and the Protectorate people will think that the Germans authorized it. They won't check with each other about such a small item.'

So that is what we decided to do, and we printed blown up versions of the popular Vladimir Mother of God and other icons. I also discovered that Nejbert had some coloured plates of ours that had never actually been used. I had some samples printed, showed them to the Committee of Management, and they decided that we should publish these too.

I sent out publicity about these reproductions all over Germany, and got a response from shops in Berlin, Dresden and Leipzig. The response from the Rhineland, however, was exceptional and we received orders for tens of thousands of copies of different icons. When the money came in from these sales, even after paying 33 per cent to the middle-man, we turned out to have made a huge profit and a colossal amount of money was accumulating in our account.

I informed the Committee of this and said that I didn't think we should hoard it. We were able to raise the salaries of all the Institute's staff to the normal levels of the Protectorate's cultural institutions, and I acquired a host of rare books for the Kondakov special collection. I even managed to buy a complete set of Greek texts needed to study Christianity, and some complete series that we had previously lacked. I received many positive letters about our publications from German firms and private individuals. I particularly remember one from a Catholic priest in the Rhineland, who wrote that when he looked at these reproductions of Russian icons he couldn't believe that Holy Russia was really dead.

In 1943 people active in the various Russian cultural organizations were invited to a talk at the Russian Nazi Party building by Baron Meller-Zakomelsky from Berlin. He was the son of the famous Baron Meller-Zakomelsky who had 'pacified' the Baltic States in the Russian Empire after the 1905 revolution. We were told on the invitation that it was important for us to be there as he would be talking about our future. A lot of people came and the front rows were full of Gestapo men in civvies. 'Melsky', as he signed his articles, was very intellectual-looking. He told us that as nationally-minded representatives of the emigration we should not only support German victory, which was 'assured', but contribute to it in areas that we knew best. He was referring to the sphere of ideas. Propaganda in Soviet Russia was crude, but highly developed, and gave the 'Jew-Communists' a powerful weapon (he prefixed many words with 'Jew' in imitation of Goebbels). He thought a Russian magazine should be founded that was not simple propaganda directed at the collective farmer or proletarian, but actually took 'Marxism and Judaism' apart. Prague, he thought, was heaven-sent to lead such a venture…

We inwardly groaned. Whereas the botanists and mathematicians amongst us would get away scot-free, we – historians, literary scholars, journalists – were trapped. What he was asking for was pro-Nazi writing. He announced that he would be glad to talk to us at his hotel and as we left the meeting we were handed personal invitations to do this. 'Good Lord,' I said to myself as I walked home, 'my only hope now is for a miracle.'

I turned up at the hotel on Wenceslas Square at the appointed hour to discover that the Baron was seeing us one at a time. The other person invited from the Institute was Savitsky.

Meller-Zakomelsky was very polite, he knew my Christian name and patronymic, and was very flattering about my journalistic skills. I could now bring them to bear, he suggested, on our common foe, the Communists. I should write something about Soviet literature, for instance show without pulling punches that all the leading Marxist critics were Jews and what a baleful influence they were having on the talents of Russian writers. I demurred by saying that I had stopped following Soviet literature in 1937 and was therefore out of date. Naturally, he said I could get up to date again by reading Soviet publications. I pointed out that this was impossible as they had been completely banned as soon as the war with the USSR started. He promised that I would be given special permission to read them, and could take a couple of years over it. I then decided to say that I was afraid to get involved in such a politically active magazine all the time my mother was 'in a zone that seemed not entirely safe'. 'Don't worry,' he said, 'we can bring your mother to Prague whenever you like' and he took down her details. Nothing came of either promise.

Savitsky was not so lucky. His lectures on Russia at the German University were wildly popular. Some of his pupils later rose very highly in the local Nazi

Party and Gestapo and retained great respect for him. I was told that his lectures got people so interested in Russia that it began to seem a positive country unlike everything they were used to hearing. All this stopped after Hitler attacked the USSR, and it was thought best by all concerned if Savitsky resigned his post. Immediately after, the Czech authorities made him headmaster of the Russian High School in Prague, where he did much good in maintaining a Russian cultural environment. Also, of course, he was an important member of the Kondakov Institute's board.

His interview with Melsky was a long one. He came straight to the Institute after it and looked green about the gills. 'You know, Nikolay Yefremovich,' he said to me, 'I think I have just signed my downfall.' Apparently he had told Melsky that their differences on the Russian question were irreconcilable. Melsky had once been a Eurasian himself and thought he would be able to argue Savitsky into writing a fierce article against Soviet economic management, with some anti-Semitism thrown in by Melsky. Savitsky told him that his, Melsky's, programme was aimed not at the good of Russia as a Eurasian entity, but against it, and from the viewpoint of a state waging war on the Soviet Union and therefore Eurasia. Melsky tried to convince him they must compromise in these difficult times, that Savitsky's views were utterly unacceptable during the conflict between communism and national socialism, but he would not report them to his German friends because he respected Savitsky so much. The latter could not resist telling Melsky that when the latter was a Eurasian his views were closer to the historical truth than they were now, and on that note they parted.

Ten weeks later Savitsky was dismissed as headmaster of the Russian High School. This was Meller-Zakomelsky's doing. Savitsky, like everyone else, then went onto the labour exchange. He was sent to local firms working for the German arms industry. Each time, they took one look at his stooping, intellectual figure, and rejected him. So he went back to the labour exchange. This continued for weeks – months. It had become a dangerous situation: he could be sent into the Reich, where he might disappear into the army of workers who had no rights, or even the slave-labourers. So I talked to Schwarzenberg and together we had words with a Czech colleague, who in turn talked to the labour exchange. He told them that Savitsky was a top academic who needed to be kept out of the Germans' sight. They decided to send him to cultural institutions, for instance a university department that needed a caretaker. But the qualifications needed to be a caretaker were not those that Savitsky had. Or he would be sent to a bank as a cleaner, but when the manager saw him he would say to him, 'I'm sorry, but we cannot have you amongst our unskilled labourers'. All this was done on purpose: eventually the labour exchange sent him to us, because we needed a workman to help in our book storeroom. We received him with open arms and told him that we would simply pay him a salary (our finances were excellent by then). But Savitsky was a man of principle and insisted on helping in the library. Evgeny Klimov, our icon-restorer, even painted a portrait of him stock-taking in the library.

At this precise time refugees from the Ukraine and Eastern Europe started pouring into Prague. Some of them liked coming to the Institute for a chat, and some of them were pro-German. I had at all costs to keep them away from Savitsky, because after his recent experiences he was particularly bitter about the Germans. Many times I said to him: 'Pyotr Nikolayevich, you must not say these things, you are asking for trouble.' But I later discovered that the reason nothing came of it was that his former students now in the Gestapo simply ignored the denunciations of him that they undoubtedly received.

Dedio told me that denunciations were rampant in the Russian community, and 'in your shoes I would not put too much faith in some of your academic colleagues'. After the war, when I met Dedio in West Germany, he said he had received many professorial denunciations of me, but not from the Kondakov Institute. He told me that he had twice read serious denunciations, the first being that I was a British spy. This surprised him very much. He said: 'I put you through an interrogation, but you didn't notice because we were playing chess.' The second was even worse: members of NTS were being arrested and the denouncer pointed at me as a major NTS ideologist. Again Dedio checked everything and dismissed it. Denunciations, then, must have rained on Savitsky.

In February 1945 I heard that Meller-Zakomelsky was back in Prague, and that the new police chief of the city was his personal friend. This chief had special powers, as they were expecting all kinds of disturbance, possibly even an uprising. When Melsky heard in March that Savitsky was working at the Kondakov Institute, he got the German authorities to investigate at the labour exchange. Here they demonstrated that he had been drafted to eighteen different organizations before we took him on to help inventory and pack books. The labour exchange people were not affected, but Savitsky was dismissed and goodness knows what the Nazis would have done with him if the German fronts had not started collapsing a month later and the Prague Uprising had not broken out.

This episode is an interesting illustration of life under the occupation. It may look as though we simply 'led the Germans by the nose'. In reality the stress was terrible. It took its toll on the health and nerves of Savitsky, his family, and all his friends. As was often the case in Nazi Germany, power groups collided. Melsky undoubtedly represented the Russian National Socialist group and,

17.   Dinner at the Kondakov Institute.
Khmyrov standing next to Nikolay Andreyev, Petr Savitsky looking round with Prince Karl Schwarzenberg on his right.

moreover, was affiliated to the Goebbels group, who gave him money to increase his propaganda. But we were under the wings of the local German organizations. Consequently Melsky and the police could not attack our Institute as that would antagonize other sources of authority. This coexistence of authorities in Nazi Germany was the only thing that enabled us to go on living, because it allowed *some* manoeuvrability.

Most of the population of the Protectorate seemed to adapt to the new order, which was utterly alien and essentially hostile to the traditions of the Czechoslovak Republic and the Russian emigration. This led to us cultivating two faces and two modes of behaviour. You put on one expression when there were Germans around, and another when you were alone with yourself or your friends. Outwardly there was complete obedience and even recognition of German superiority. People said as much in speeches and the press all the time. Simultaneously we were just counting the months until this cannibalistic regime would go. I strongly suspect that many, possibly most, Germans were in the same psychological predicament as ourselves.

The most popular form of disobedience was to buy on the black market everything that the Germans had officially banned. The black market sprang up as soon as rationing was introduced three weeks after 1 September 1939. It was kept going by the fact that Slovakia was still independent and contraband goods streamed across its border. The Germans had not planned for this, so they started arresting speculators and even executing them. But the idea of supplying the population with more than the norms set by the Nazis, lived on. For the first two years of the war I hardly needed rationing coupons, because most of the restaurants or cafeterias that I frequented knew me from before the war and served me and my friends food that was not on the menu, and without taking coupons from us. Gradually the consideration for that, i.e. the tip, got larger. The Germans must have realized something was up, but they did not react at all.

Someone told me that the boss of the Russian Émigré Base, Yefremov, occasionally entertained the Gestapo men of the second department, his bosses, in his own home, and each time gave them a Rabelaisian repast with endless drink. The drink did not surprise anyone, as you could get alcohol everywhere, it wasn't rationed. The interesting thing is that it never occurred to Heide, the head of the department, to ask Yefremov where he got such quantities of first-class meat. Obviously it was from the black market. This double standard – officialdom's one thing and we are another – was widespread in the Protectorate not only among Russians and Czechs but evidently Germans as well.

In 1943 a rumour flew round that wine cellars were going to be confiscated for the army. The black market was therefore flooded with excellent wines at very low prices. I also had a pupil who was the daughter or niece of a vintner. Like my other students, she paid me in kind. All the cupboards backstage at the Institute were therefore crammed with bottles. Mind you, it was quickly consumed, because there was nowhere to go in the evenings. If you went to the theatre you might walk into a police round-up, or the SS would be checking documents looking for agents dropped from British planes. A visit to the cinema was also rare, as the films were either old ones you had already seen several times, or new ones with a Nazi message. So I used to invite some friends round, pull out a couple of bottles of wine, and we would polish them off. They told me what they had heard on the radio and anti-German jokes.

The Czechs have always been masters of the anecdote. Here is one that I remember from the early war years. It is morning, dark, raining or sleeting, people are going to work on a packed tram, and they are in a terrible mood. Suddenly a little old lady says: 'And to think this is all the fault of one man!' A figure looms over her, turns back his lapel, and reveals the badge of the German secret police. 'Which man, grandma?' he asks, and the old lady says for all to hear: 'Khoorkheel!' (this was how the Czechs pronounced 'Churchill'). 'Khoorkheel, of course, who did *you* think?' There were even more anecdotes at the end of the war. For example, it is 1943, the Allies have bombed Berlin, and Hitler is walking over the ruins with some of his cronies. His face is as black as thunder, but suddenly he hears Goebbels chuckling behind him. He turns round and asks him why he is laughing. '*Mein Führer*,' Goebbels replies, 'I was just remembering that speech you gave ten years ago, in which you said, "Give me power over Germany and in ten years you won't recognize the place!"'

There were also, of course, many underground organizations in Czechoslovakia at this time; and I suddenly came under their surveillance. Apparently, some of their leaders were asking why we had not been closed down, or lumped with any Czech, Russian émigré or German organization. What were we doing in order to remain in this unique position in the Nazi state?

I had a very able student, a Czech girl, who was born in Vienna, moved to Czechoslovakia, and spoke fluent Czech, German and Russian. Let's call her Lenochka. On several occasions she helped me with the Institute's German correspondence, because we received a lot of letters, Schwarzenberg was not always around, and although I more or less knew German my written German was not flawless. Lenochka helped me a great deal and at some point we became intimate. She was a darling little blonde, slightly prone to sentimentality, and I was even afraid I had fallen in love with her. If she stayed overnight at the Institute, she always left early next morning firstly because she worked in some central office, secondly because she did not want to cause gossip in the Institute, whose other members turned up at nine.

One fine day, Lenochka announced: 'Nikolay, I've got to give you up.'

'Why? What have I done?'

'Nothing, I like you very much, I hope that after the war we can have a more definite relationship, but I've got to leave you now, because the organization says so.'

'What organization?'

She then explained that she was a member of an underground organization that had used her to find out everything about the Institute.

'Now I have found out everything and told them you are totally clear. We know everything about you and can see now why they are keeping you in a special position – they want to produce their little ace after the war, they want to be able to say, "Look, this Institute lasted all through the war, we never touched it". So you can relax now.'

I was relaxed, but livid. Although Lenochka swore to me that first she had become my girlfriend, and only then had the organization asked her to spy on me, I did not entirely believe her. Putting two and two together, I think that she was first given her mission, then decided that the best way to carry it out was to become my lover for a while.

As a precaution, not for myself but for the Institute, I did not keep a radio. Without a radio, I could not disseminate foreign news, which was an offence brutally punished. I was told the news every morning by those colleagues who had one. Gradually the forms of German control became more and more primitive, and an element of extreme cynicism crept in. One day in 1944 Prince Dolgorukov, who lived not far away, came to see me in an awful state. He said: 'Nikolay Yefremovich, I've come here simply to cry.' He told me that the son of some Czech friends of his had been arrested and executed – by guillotine. The Gestapo had sent them a bill, for their son's board and lodging in prison and 'a physical operation', i.e. the execution. 'This is what things have come to,' said Dolgorukov. As the whiff of German defeat grew stronger, their cruelty knew no bounds, especially after the assassination attempt on Hitler in 1944. They had systematically destroyed Czech society, from the officer class to every conceivable left-wing political group, and now they evidently had orders to spare no-one. The general mood in Prague became gloomier and gloomier.

Nevertheless, there is no doubt that for the émigré community the single most traumatic event of the war years was the attack on Russia.

It basically split us into two groups: 'defencists' and 'defeatists'. The 'defencists' believed that the attack on the Soviet Union by Nazi Germany meant that the emigration should suspend its own hostile actions towards the Soviet government and morally support it. Many of my friends fell into this category, including Savitsky. There were 'defencists' in all the centres of the Russian 'diaspora', as journalists liked to call it; for instance Mark Slonim, who wrote for a 'defencist' organ in Paris. The 'defeatists' believed that the Soviet Union and its Communist Party had to be smashed first, then they would see. This was the point of view of the émigré military organizations, monarchists, and to some extent NTS. The latter believed that they could take advantage of the German invasion to get onto Russian soil, where they thought they would have boundless opportunities. In 1940, before the attack, the general feeling was rather pro-German, and in many houses that I visited people said optimistically: 'I have a feeling we will soon be home.'

But then the war with Russia began, it proved more ferocious than any the Germans had encountered in the West, and the Soviet Army put up surprising resistance. People who had become interpreters in the invading army, mainly in the support units, returned to Prague on leave and described in a whisper the horrors not only of the Soviet regime but of the conduct of the occupying troops, their cruel treatment of Russian prisoners and the local population. The mood amongst us began to change radically. Russians, it transpired, had a very strong sense of the blood-tie – what we call patriotism. Under the surface, this began to well up amongst the émigrés. It was an interesting and complex phenomenon. You had to be very careful about it. I tried therefore to avoid visiting houses where I could be swathed in pro-Hitler nonsense or, at the other extreme, drenched in pro-Soviet euphoria. Both had lost touch with reality.

Was there a set of young people in Prague who were pro-Soviet, or were there blatantly pro-Soviet sentiments amongst the emigration at this time? I must say, I knew hardly any such people. There were Soviet citizens such as Professor Izyumov, who worked at the Russian Historical Archive, or V. Bulgakov, Lev Tolstoy's last amanuensis, but I did not know they were Soviet, this only emerged after the war with the Soviet Union began. They were not even arrested, they were interned in comfort and sat out the whole war in peace and quiet, without the Gestapo taking any action against them.

We first heard about Vlasov in 1943. Georgy Klimov visited Prague after accompanying Vlasov and some German officers as an interpreter to a mass gathering of Russian prisoners or *Ostarbeiter* near Pskov and Gatchina. Klimov was a fine raconteur and gave a vivid account of how Vlasov could handle a crowd – how he fired them up to join the struggle against Stalinism. To do this, Vlasov did not mince his words about the Germans either. For instance, when he asked his audience, 'Do you want to be slaves to the Germans?' tens of thousands roared back 'No!', which must have terrified the Germans present and hardly advanced his cause. However, Klimov suggested, since Vlasov, a former lieutenant-general and Soviet hero, was travelling about behind the German lines giving speeches like this, the Nazi leadership must be wanting to bring Russian forces into play.

General Voytsekhovsky listened to all this and expressed grave doubts that it could change the military situation. In his opinion the Third Reich had been in a deeply defensive state since the second half of 1943. New military creations such as Vlasov's were possible, he thought, but they could have had some effect only in 1941/42, when if they had been introduced in the east they would have repelled people from Bolshevism; now they were too late. After Vlasov's manifesto was launched in 1944, we saw thousands of his troops in German uniforms with the Russian national colours sewn on. Himmler allegedly promised Vlasov that he would form ten divisions from Russian prisoners-of-war, but Voytsekhovsky said: 'It's too late. By the time they've got them together and trained them, a year or eighteen months will have passed, and they'll be a drop in the ocean. The Germans should have done it earlier. Militarily, Vlasov's troops can't change anything, but the psychological effect they could have is a different matter.'

His analysis proved absolutely right.

9

Family Matters

The last time I had seen both of my parents was during my visit to Estonia in 1938. People still thought then that a world war could be averted. After I left, however, and the Germans marched into Prague, it became clear that the Baltic States would be annexed by the Soviet Union.

The Baranovs, friends of my parents who owned several houses in Tallinn, took this as their cue to leave for Italy. They offered my parents their main house, but my parents declined because it would have entailed too much responsibility. Then the Baranovs made the cottage next door available to them, they settled very comfortably there, and my father even became the Baranovs' property manager, collecting rent for them and sending it to them abroad whilst possible. All this happened in 1939 and I was able to keep in touch with them by post throughout 1940.

At this time many people left Estonia for Germany. Anyone who had the least drop of German blood in them declared themselves a *Volksdeutscher* and went. The Nazis recognized two categories of German: *Reichsdeutsche*, 'true' Germans who lived in Germany, and *Volksdeutsche*, who as in the Baltic States had lived for centuries under foreign rule and were now returning as *Volk*. The situation was extremely worrying, as no-one knew when the Soviets would march in and what they would do. Early in 1940 they were given military bases in Estonia. I mentioned the subject to Dedio and he said he advised anyone with German ancestry to leave. This ruled my parents out, of course, and they couldn't speak German anyway.

By now my father had finally stopped working for various ridiculous firms that used him mainly as manual labour, and under pressure from my mother and my own conversations with him in 1938 had agreed to concentrate on singing. He had always had trouble with Zyablik, the aggressive precentor of the St Nicholas choir, so he left that choir, to everyone's amazement as he had sung in it for twenty years, and took the post of precentor-psalm reader at the cemetery chapel. He wrote to me that it was a job that made you aware of the vanity of worldly things, because every day brought several corpses, several funeral services, or at least several readings over the body, if not actual special services. Of course, he said, it was sad, but he preferred the job because he was his own master. The church paid him something, and if it was a special service the dead person's relatives almost always gave him something, so he earned quite good money.

Whenever he was at odds with people around him, especially those in authority, he would say: 'Not a word will I utter!' – implying that there were many words he could utter if he had to. This habit became stronger with time. 'I consider it a sin to elaborate' was another formula that he had developed ever since his first brushes with Yanson and Andrushkevich. This became almost an *idée fixe* of his: he would behave politely, smile sweetly, and talk only of the weather. The number of people to whom this 'I consider it a sin to elaborate' applied, grew. It worried my mother, who used to say to him that this was not quite right, one should stand up for one's views. He answered: 'I have a very eloquent son, he'll stand up for my views when I am gone, and a very voluble wife, a famous speaker, she can also stand up for my views, whilst I…consider it a sin to elaborate.' My father possessed a precious quality: he accepted everything fate had thrown at him.

Now the Soviets took over Estonia completely. Tallinn was full of Soviet military and civilian personnel and lorries arrived with army song and dance ensembles, which made a certain impression on the populace. But the arrests also started – at first of individuals, then mass arrests. As my mother later described to me in detail, many people close to those at the top, or simply with a position in society, disappeared at this time, along with military figures who had not managed to get out. They arrested ministers and chiefs of police, and purged the Estonian security organs. When the Germans came, my old P.E. teacher, Vladimir Utekhin, was found executed by the Soviet 'organs' at a villa outside the town. Vladimir Novitsky, a journalist with whom I was very friendly, struck his interrogator with a stool, apparently, and this sealed his fate. Serafima Gorbachova, a prominent cultural figure, came home from a summer party in a light dress and high heels, was arrested in what she stood up in, and never seen again. Over 100,000 people were arrested or deported from Estonia at this time. How many survived and returned, we do not know.

My mother told me that many young émigré Russians in Estonia, and probably throughout the Baltic states, were hoodwinked by very experienced Soviet propagandists, who exploited their patriotic feelings. This did not surprise me, as their own elders had never made a serious effort to mould them. Those who were known to believe in something were removed immediately, of course. But many of the rest, even my friends, went off to serve the Soviet state. For instance, although her uncle had been shot by Stalin, Irina Krestinskaya agreed to work for the Soviets and because she could type and spoke German, Estonian and Russian she was taken on as a secretary in the secret police.

However, as a former girlfriend she still had a soft spot for me, and was fond of my parents. One day in 1941, when my father was at the cemetery church, she turned up at their house, was very subdued and hesitant, then suddenly said to my mother: 'Ekaterina Aleksandrovna, I want to tell you something, but it must remain between ourselves, because if it is found out I shall be in deep trouble. You see, I have been typing up the lists of people who are to be deported from here, and you are on one of them. It's not the first list, or the second, but the third, and you and Yefrem Nikolayevich are on it. So I advise you both to make up a parcel each, containing a change of underwear, a toothbrush, medicine if you are taking any, spare stockings, and handkerchieves. If you make up one bag, you could be separated and one of you won't have anything. Please don't give me away, will you?'

Of course, my mother assured her she would not, and that to begin with she wouldn't even mention it to my father. She got everything together, sowed the idea in my father's mind, and he always carried the parcel with him and wore an overcoat even in warm weather, just in case.

But one fine day Irina turned up happy and smiling and said: 'Ekaterina Aleksandrovna, I've come to tell you that the third list has been postponed, the front is collapsing so fast and there's such a shortage of transport that they can't even get out everyone on the first and second lists. So you are safe.'

Mama thanked her again, but left everything as it was.

Before long, there was no Soviet power left in Tallinn: the remains of it had loaded themselves on trains and were somewhere around Narva, or they had tried to get on the last vessels out of the harbour. The Estonian security forces immediately took charge, and very soon after that the German troops marched in. We know less about what the Germans did in the Baltic states than the Soviets, simply because no-one has given a detailed account of it, or no-one there actually knew. They rounded up the Soviet stooges and put them in prisoner-of-war camps, then they started hunting down Jews, who were also put in camps. There was a camp near Riga with a very bad reputation, and others. People spoke about these events under their breath. How the population as a whole survived, it is difficult even to imagine.

My parents got through this period because they had lived in Tallinn a long time. They had contacts, so even when they had no food coupons they could get enough to eat, and obviously they had laid in reserves. They were able to sit it out. Some Russian interpreters arrived with the Germans, including Valeryan Bibikov, a relative of General Baranov, and he moved into the latter's main house and started sending its remaining furniture out of the country. He also let my mother use his forces postal number, which enabled us to re-establish contact.

I had two letters from her, and then the sad news that my father had developed terrible pains and the doctor feared it was cancer. They asked me to send various powders for him, and a special sugar that he had to drink because he could not eat anything. I sent it all and to my amazement it got there. I even sent money. There were no banknotes circulating in Estonia, so I got permission to send them German marks, which apparently delighted my father so much that his pain subsided for two hours. He said to *mama*: 'Lord what happiness to have a son who cares for us.'

But nothing could save him and he died quite soon, I think in February 1942. It shames me that I can't remember the exact date. I have a poor memory for death dates generally, I simply don't consent to remember them because basically nothing changed, I continued to regard my father as existing in this world. Even to this day he has remained alive and dear to me, just as I saw him all my life and especially when we met for the last time in 1938 and walked together in the Katharinental Park.

His funeral, as my mother described it to me, was extraordinary. It was a very fine day, a huge number of people turned out, and the combined voices of all the Russian churches in Tallinn sang, making an enormous choir of almost a hundred people. Several Russian priests took the service – from the cemetery church, St Nicholas Church, and the Alexander Nevsky Cathedral – all of whom had known my father for many years, and litanies were sung at several points along the way. My parents lived in the Upper Town, opposite the Cathedral, and this is where the procession started from. My mother walked streaming tears of joy for my father, because he would have been so glad that everyone had come together to remember him, so many people, even those at whose relatives' funerals he had sung in the last couple of years at the cemetery church. It transpired that a multitude of people in Tallinn had respected my father as a leading light amongst the Russian singing fraternity, as a precentor who knew his job, and a devoted performer of Russian Orthodox church music. So he was laid in his grave to the sounds of a massed choir.

Later it even occurred to me that God had purposely saved my father from the many, many trials still to come. There is a limit to every man's endurance and to the sufferings that life has allotted him. I always think of my parents with great tenderness and I believe my father's influence on me was enormous, although he hardly 'instructed' me in anything and was always a gentle, yielding older friend. Now, as my own old age and death draw closer, I wish I could repeat many of my father's traits. Despite his mildness, he was a man of principle, he would not argue but he never acted against his convictions. He was totally kind and believed that any sort of peace is better than war or conflict. At the same time, he was a man of great personal courage.

In a strange way he was fatalistic. I always laughed when this came out, and said that that was the oriental streak in him, confirmation as it were of Savitsky's theory of Eurasia. But it was an optimistic fatalism: he believed that in the end everything is for the best. Whenever I protested, sometimes violently, that this was an impossible view to take, how could our expulsion from Russia, the death of several members of our family, and our twenty years in limbo be for the best, he would say: 'But it could have been worse! We might *all* have died, there were many times when I could have been arrested and shot, we could have been separated, but the Lord God kept us together. Perhaps what has happened to us is the best of all possible paths for us.'

This philosophy seemed disarmingly passive, but in fact my father was never passive. It was really a form of wisdom: he understood that it was not in his power to change the course of history and his own life, and this made it easier for him to think in terms of predestination, of the Lord God having already ordained things so.

Fate had been hard on him. It had not allowed him to recover the rights he had won in Russia. Of course, being abroad saved his life, gave him food and security, my parents had me with them, nobody separated us, and despite all the difficulties I received a higher education. All these were pluses, but abroad my father sank to the bottom socially. I understood that perfectly well, but I did not know what I could do about it. It was impossible to help from a distance, and I did not have the means to support my parents myself. So I am left with the feeling that I did not do all I could have done for my father – and would have shortly, as I did for my mother.

After my father died, my mother applied twice to join me in the Protectorate, but the German authorities turned her down. I tried from my end six times, but Dedio was no longer in Prague. A special office had been set up at the German police to take applications for relations to enter the Protectorate. They turned my applications down five times, supposedly because they did not fit the regulations. On the sixth occasion, they flung the application back, a policeman stuck his head through the hatch, and shouted: 'If you come here again I will arrest you! You know perfectly well that the Protectorate isn't for Russians!'

Nevertheless, *mama* came to Prague, and in an unexpected way. I had a friend called Zina Renning-Igenbergs, whom I had known since we were teenagers in Tallinn, she had always been nice to me, I had courted her slightly, and she was terribly fond of my mother. She had married a Latvian diplomat and was now living in Prague with him and their two children. In April 1944 I bumped into her on Charles Bridge and she asked after my parents. I explained that my father had died and I had failed to get *mama* out. Suddenly she offered to put my mother's name on an application she was making for her own parents to come to Prague. I could not believe my ears, and I must admit I did not attach great significance to her offer as I thought she was just trying to cheer me up. But she later explained to me that she had gone to the police office looking her blonde Aryan best, lectured them on how after *Heimat* and *Führer* the most important thing was *Mutter*, and an SS man there had agreed with her and accepted her whole application.

So one fine morning *mama* turned up at the Institute! She hadn't been able to send a telegram, as no-one knew when and where her train would arrive. We had even gone out to meet her the day before, but the train did not come in from the direction expected because the track had been bombed. I spent ages trying to find out when the train was arriving, but they said 'we don't know, maybe tomorrow morning, maybe later'. It did arrive in the morning, and the Czech family she travelled with brought her to us. She was in raptures. She immediately had a bath, but her clean clothes were in her luggage, which was brought round a few days later. So she wore one of my shirts. We took a photograph of her the same day wearing my shirt and a tie and they suited her no end. We registered her with the police, and her place of residence, of course, was my room, as there was no other accommodation.

In the nine or ten months that we spent together, *mama* succeeded in creating around her a remarkable spiritual centre, a focus of care and human kindness. She had the most varied friends, including Bishop Sergy and General Chernavin, and they were always coming to see her. I used to joke that it had become difficult living there because our room was always full of visitors. She felt herself wanted and totally accepted by the Russian colony. Everyone who met her was drawn by her magnetism.

Where the numerous candidates to be my wife were concerned, *mama* displayed her customary tact and wisdom. She even corresponded with some of them behind my back, and altogether cleared the air. At the moment, she felt, there were no serious candidates at all. The Czech girls were all very nice, but not really adapted to be the companions for life of a Russian academic. Some were married and *mama* considered it quite wrong to destroy someone else's family in order to create one's own. She was very cautious and preferred to wait and see rather than make snap judgements. One must admit, the war years were bad for women. There were a lot of them about and their currency became debased. The war produced a destructive licentiousness; but my mother's appearance on the scene made everyone pull themselves together, starting with me.

10

The Prague Uprising

The uprising has been described by many historians, so I shall confine myself to my personal, very narrow impressions. We did not know that the uprising was going to happen. There were just rumours that underground committees existed, one more left-wing, pro-Communist, another more 'national' but also with a major left-wing component and not excluding Czechoslovakia's older parties.

I still had no radio, but when *mama* arrived people often brought a radio in and listened to the news, which was necessary even because sometimes they broadcast air-raid warnings. At about twelve o'clock on the day we suddenly heard a hullabaloo on the radio followed by shooting, as though it were a play about a revolution, and then shouts of 'Help! Help!'. The civilian and military police, the right-wing elements that had mostly collaborated with the Germans, were apparently trying to seize the radio station, but were repulsed and the radio station called on the people of Prague to rise up, after which they immediately started broadcasting signals and appeals to someone outside Prague, never saying who exactly, just 'Prague calling, the uprising has started, please help us'. This went out in several languages. There was a commotion on the streets, and forces we had known nothing about swung into action. From the windows of the Institute we saw a German soldier walking along, suddenly gunfire was heard, some people rushed at him and knocked him down, a woman who had just walked into the Institute had hysterics because she could not bear violence, and this was how freedom began: with a rather small soldier being beaten up.

A few days earlier the acting 'protector', K.S. Frank, a former pharmacist from the Sudetenland and a brutal Nazi, had broadcast a speech in which he said that Prague was dear to both the Germans and the Czechs and must be saved. He had even implied that it should be declared an open city, so that the Allies would stop bombing it. His general message was that there was no need to stage an uprising, the city could be saved without carnage and destruction.

A young painter I knew, Misha Romberg, came to me and said that the Czechs were offering to put him in touch with partisan units outside Prague. 'Why not accept?' I replied. 'It doesn't mean you will become a partisan, but I think it would be sensible to find out what they are up to and what forces they have, as long as they don't ask too much of you.' Off he went. Three or four days later he turned up tired, pale, and terribly distressed. He had been outside Prague, in the forest, for the last few miles they had even blindfolded him, and he had found himself in a hut with Soviets – evidently Chekists – who were scathing about the Russian emigration. Romberg was convinced they were going to purge it ruthlessly. They proposed that Misha prove his loyalty by taking a suitcase full of explosives back to Prague and delivering it to a particular address. He did this at great risk to himself: if the Germans had caught him he would have been a dead man, and the explosives could have blown up anyway. All this had a ghastly effect on him, as he was a sensitive person and suddenly confronted with gruesome reality. He told me then that there would be a move against the Germans, but no-one knew until the last moment (because it was a secret) whether there would be an uprising. It began differently from how the pro-Soviet committee had assumed. Evidently the national committee tried to turn the situation in its favour by seizing the radio station first.

Misha put me in touch with someone and I was brought a rifle wrapped up to look like an easel. When I unpacked it, I discovered an old shot-gun with no cartridges. I was bemused: 'What do I want this for?' 'Ah,' they replied, 'you must have a weapon. Some nutcases might try to force their way in, so you just show them this gun and they'll take to their heels!' We put it in the storeroom, as it was obviously only decorative.

But just before the uprising Lenochka turned up from her 'organization' and a notice appeared on our doors with a Czech seal on it saying that the Institute was under the protection of the 'People's Militia'. Who the 'Militia' was, I don't know, nor who put the notice up, but it was on our doors when the uprising began. This was dangerous, because if the Germans had come to the building and seen it they would have raided us. Chance reigned. During the uprising I was concerned at the fact that in all the doorways down our street there were young people who, presumably to give themselves courage, kept firing off the various guns they had. It was dangerous to put your head out of the window, because at that moment they might start firing and hit you. I told everyone in the Institute not to stick their heads out. Basically everyone who was there stayed there, as it was impossible to go out.

Then we heard that the Germans were bombing the insurgent part of Prague and the population should take to the shelters. The building had a large crypt, so we all sat down there and were told to sleep there as well. I refused and slept upstairs on a sofa, fully dressed. The following day, a Saturday, someone came along and told us that things were going badly, the Germans were bringing in two SS divisions, who were already in the Pankrác district and whenever they came upon barricades they were shooting the whole male population without exception. On the other hand, the German troops were retreating across Prague, the uprising was a thorn in their side, and they had to keep clearing all these barricades in order to get their trucks through.

At about eleven in the morning a man turned up wearing an armband in the national colours. He told us that he was in charge of the national defence of a part of Prague, and ordered all the men to go onto the street and build barricades. This was our first contact with the insurgents' organization. I went outside and saw a crowd – he had been driving men out of all the houses and there were many from other districts of Prague. He had a directive to build a barricade between our street and Kozí square. This was the first time I had seen a barricade being built. Thanks to the quantity of people, it was done in a flash: they commandeered vehicles, turned them on their side, filled the metal rubbish bins with bits of broken pavement that they tore up, dragged all kinds of stuff from the yards. And the sides were kind of stepped. I said we shouldn't build a barricade that way. Everyone looked at me with respect and asked what I meant. I explained that if German soldiers came along, we had already provided them with the steps to climb over by – the side facing them ought to be sheer. Everyone agreed, and within five minutes I was being called 'the emissary from Moscow'. I myself had to do very little, because there were so many people there and after making my observation I was promoted to a commander. In forty minutes everything was ready: they had smashed the pavement to pieces and God knows how many years it lay around afterwards.

Now lots of people came along with rifles and revolvers and guarded the barricade. Suddenly those on top shouted that some German armoured cars were approaching. Two of them emerged from a side street. Everyone sent up a shout and scrambled off the barricades. The armoured cars opened fire. The first shot hit the corner of the building which the right end of our barricade abutted, and this corner collapsed like playing cards. The second shot was aimed at the base of the barricade, which was blown to smithereens. The defenders of the barricade now exhibited amazing athletic ability. After the first shot, I discovered I was pressed against the wall of a house three blocks away. After the second, I was already inside our own building and running down into the cellar. It was a personal record: I had never run so fast in my life!

The street was empty. One of the armoured cars drove off, the other stayed at the corner of the side-street and then began to turn round. This proved its undoing. In our building lived a Frenchman who had escaped from a prisoner-of-war camp. He had got a German anti-tank gun, and all the buildings in the street were linked by underground passages to help during air-raids. The Frenchman came out by the collapsed corner of the house, fired at the armoured car, and hit it. It caught fire, the German soldiers scrambled out, and ran off. Hurrah, victory! But it was fraught with unpleasant consequences: the Germans could send in several armoured cars to retaliate and clear our barricade altogether. It was a nasty situation.

Suddenly news started coming in on the radio that interested us greatly, particularly me. Units under General Vlasov, the Vlasov who at a ceremony in November 1944 was proclaimed Germany's principal ally, had come to Prague's rescue. One of his divisions had turned its guns against the Germans and we were told his men were fighting the SS. Vlasov's First Division, which was armed with the latest automatic weapons, was winning. They took great pleasure in flattening two SS divisions and halting their progress to Prague. According to the radio, joyful crowds were welcoming them everywhere as Prague's saviours.

Vlasov's representatives went to talk to the Czechs' revolutionary-military committee. But the committee soon announced that they could not reach agreement and Vlasov's units, which had saved certain districts of the city from the SS, were withdrawing. I realized why, but the Czechs, of course, did not. Vlasov's people were anti-Stalin, whereas the committee, if not pro-Soviet, was at least not anti-Soviet, so the two could not see eye to eye.

We were surrounded. The long street leading from Staroměstské square had barricades across it, but these were now manned by German soldiers, who had set up machine-guns on them and were periodically raking the street. At the other end were the armoured cars, based at SS headquarters in the old Law Faculty by the river, and the Germans controlled everything. What was happening in the square itself, we did not know, but we could see a terrible fire raging there and hear shooting.

There was also a barricade across our street, Haštalská, and it had been manned by our people. Suddenly we received instructions to leave this district one by one. That was easily said, but where were we to go? We certainly had to leave the district where we had taken part in building the barricades, especially as everyone had noticed I was a foreigner and even an 'emissary from Moscow'. *Mama* had already made up a bag for me, which I wore on my back, and now I was just trying to judge when was the moment to run across the long street with the machine-guns.

Beyond it was Prague 2, which was safe – there were no German checkpoints there and you could escape into other districts. As always in such cases, the mob had either evaporated or decided to go back to the Germans. I had already heard people saying that there were 'Russians all over the place' who had 'incited' them. I went into the alleyway next to our building, stood there, and contemplated rushing across. Every so often the Germans would fire their machine-guns, and immediately afterwards I could run for it – it would take them two or three seconds before they could fire again.

Whether this plan would have worked, or whether I would have been riddled with bullets, I do not know, but whilst I was standing there ruminating the loudspeakers suddenly sprang into life. They announced that a ceasefire had been negotiated between the Czechoslovak revolutionary-military committee and the German military command. It would start at six o'clock and end at midnight. In those six hours we were to take down the barricades and let the German columns through without resistance. The German divisions that were trying to get as far away as possible and surrender to the Allies rather than the Soviets, would then be able to cross Prague without fighting.

The Soviet troops, which by the end of the uprising were quite a long way from Prague, did not save the city, basically the Czechs were saved by Vlasov's First Division, which entered Prague on the evening of 5 May and in a battle on 6 May routed the two SS divisions that were trying to restore order in Prague. Not having reached agreement with the revolutionary-military committee, Vlasov's First Division also departed westwards on 7 May.

I immediately went back home, took the bag off, and lay down to rest. Sleep is a wonderful thing: I drifted off at about eight in the evening, and at about four in the morning *mama* woke me to say they were bombing again. I lifted my head from the pillow and could tell she was wrong. She had a bit of a complex about air-raids, ever since she experienced them in Tallinn when the Soviets bombed the lower town, where fortunately she did not live. After that, she panicked whenever she heard anything resembling bombing. But what I heard now was not falling bombs and explosions, but the terrible scrunching of metal on stone, and I very soon realized that it was Soviet T-34 tanks entering the city at high speed. It was the army of General Rybalko, the future marshal of the tank force. They had broken through the German defences in the Erzgebirge and were attempting at top speed to take Prague, drive through it, and cut off the retreating German forces, who were trying to reach the Americans before they were caught. The only German resistance left in Prague was some SS units in the former Law Faculty, who had refused all negotiations. Whenever they were addressed through loudspeakers they answered with German battle songs and bullets. They were destroyed by several point-blank shots from Soviet tanks and this put an end to German rule in Prague presumably for ever.

Actually we did not hear about this until later; we heard the salvoes, but knew no more. It was a restless night for me and at about half past five I was awoken by violent ringing and knocking on the Institute front door. I was sleeping fully clothed, so I ran to open it and found a crowd of people from the flats above us, who had put excessive faith in me ever since the rumour that I was an emissary from Moscow and specialist in building barricades. 'Pan Doktor, what are we to do?' they cried. 'The Americans haven't entered Prague, the Soviets are coming in, and we've got no red flags to hang out!'

I immediately suggested using the Nazi flag. We cut out the middle – the white circle with the swastika in – and made two not very big red flags out of the remainder, which we promptly hung out on our middle balcony. I washed and shaved, ate something, and rushed off to see what was happening on Staroměstské square. Mama stayed at home, after making me promise to be careful.

The streets were packed with people brought out, like me, by the rumble of tanks and the shooting at the Law Faculty. I emerged onto the square. Prague had really deteriorated during the war. From being a beautiful, clean, well looked-after and very prosperous capital city it had become a battered town with charred buildings all over the place after the uprising. Almost all of the town hall was gutted, and the famous clock with its procession of apostles and figure of death with his scythe had been destroyed. On the other hand, everyone suddenly felt a weight lifted: it was the end of an era, to hell with the Germans now, we would have to see what the Soviets would do, but at least they were brother Slavs.

A Soviet T-34 drew up next to St Nicholas church, its commander stuck his head out of the turret, and shouted: 'Anyone speak Russian?' The Czechs did not, and just shouted, '*Nazdar! Nazdar!*' ('Hurrah!'). I immediately noted the difference in cultures: when the Germans had arrived in 1939 I saw massive SS men smiling like boa-constrictors at the little Czechs around them, who all spoke excellent German. Here was the friendly Soviet Army, and no-one, alas, spoke Russian. 'Well doesn't *anyone* speak Russian?' he cried in hope, and horror that they might not. I owned up.

'Where am I then?' he asked. 'What place is this?'

'It's Prague, comrade commander, and you're on Staroměstské square.'

'On a square, in Prague...' he repeated, and let fly some choice obscenities about both. He was meant to be at some small place outside Prague, he told me, so which way was that? Fortunately I knew, I explained to him, he disappeared back into the turret, turned the tank round, and thundered off. Now the troops came in, followed in many places by dance and song ensembles in the back of lorries. Then carloads of officers arrived. Prague was the intersection of three fronts: the right flank of Marshal Malinovsky's Balkan front, the central thrust of General Yeremenko's front (the defender of Stalingrad), and Marshal Konev's forces coming from Germany via Berlin and Dresden. It was being particularly thoroughly dealt with from every quarter.

After seeing all this, I went home and took my first step towards adapting to the new circumstances. It was clear that we had become part of the Soviet sphere of influence. So I took down the official portraits of Hitler and Hacha which in the German tradition had hung in our office.

A fortnight before the uprising I had been on a routine visit to Nejbert's printing works. As I was leaving, he suddenly gave me a long cardboard tube with the ends carefully sealed. 'A present for you,' he said. 'Don't open it until you are alone in your room.'

When I did, I gasped: it contained two freshly-printed, official-sized portraits, one of Beneš, the Czechoslovak president, and one of Stalin. If the Germans had known Nejbert was printing these, he could have been shot on the spot. I was surprised at how much he hated the Germans and welcomed the coming of the Soviets. After all, he was a typical entrepreneur really, a cautious financial operator. Every so often, however, he let drop something pro-Soviet in his conversation. I had even dared point out to him that if Czechoslovakia became Soviet he would probably have to say goodbye to his business, which was a surrogate wife and children to him. 'No no I won't, *pan Doktor*, because they are my brother Slavs.' This was typical of the Czechs' mentality at the time:

on the rebound from Nazism they had begun to idealize Soviet soldiers and the Soviet system.

But I had been very pleased with Nejbert's present, I didn't show it to anyone, I sealed it up again, and put it in the same place as the shot-gun. Now I produced these two portraits and put them up where the other two had been.

The bell never stopped ringing at the Institute as people came to re-establish contact after the anxious days of the uprising. Personally I tried not to go far beyond the confines of the Institute, as it was chaotic out there. There was no public transport and I didn't think it wise to set off on long trips across Prague, because I was constantly afraid that something was going to happen to the Institute. The notice was still hanging on our doors saying we were under the protection of the 'People's Militia', and Lenochka had promised to revisit us, but she was now terribly busy translating documents, as her 'organization' had taken over various German institutions.

When I went for a walk through the city with my mother, I was totally appalled and revolted by the mob. Summary 'justice' was being meted out wherever you looked. The corpses of people hanged by the mob dangled from the lamp-posts. Who they were and why they had been hanged, nobody knew. We came out near Smetana Hall and there was a huge amount of traffic, Soviet trucks were going by all the time full of army dancers and singers, cars with Soviet staff officers, there were crowds of people out walking, it was terribly hot, overpowering even. And there were men attending to people whose mouths had been gagged with rags and had nooses round their necks: these too were going to be hanged from the lamp-posts. They stared with deranged eyes at their executioners, who exchanged jokes, smoked, spat on the ground, were in no hurry at all. It stunned me: there was no hatred here, nothing, just downright sadism, with groups of small boys standing by watching. The bodies on two lamp-posts had a notice above them saying TRAITORS, but who were these traitors? Who condemned them? Why were they hanged without trial, without judicial investigation, without proper sentences being passed? I tried to distract *mama*'s attention, I kept thinking she would faint, or rush to free them and get into trouble. It was a terrifying and sickening spectacle.

As we walked on, we saw other things. People were taking down a barricade. They were barefoot, their hair was hacked about, their clothes were in shreds, there were men and women together, and round them were standing Czechs with 'Revolutionary Guard' on their armbands, spitting at them. The people were clearly terribly thirsty, they were getting heatstroke, some of them kept saying, 'Water, a drink!', but the 'Guards' just swore at them: 'Get on with it you bastards, traitors!' Some people in the crowd told me that these were

German collaborators and narks, girls who had gone out with German soldiers…
Maybe they had, but I was shocked at the absence of any process of law: we
had just risen up against German tyranny, the sadists in the Gestapo, and what
were we doing? Perpetrating these things publicly, without a court or proper
investigation, and calling it 'the people's wrath'! Fortunately it was stopped
by two Soviet soldiers. They watched, they knew the heat was overpowering,
nearly 90 degrees Fahrenheit, that people were dropping from thirst, and
suddenly they were angry and shouted to the one in charge to give them some
water. He looked at his liberator-allies in amazement, but they effed and blinded
at him to give these people something to drink and in five minutes buckets of
water were brought.

Those who had fought their way here, genuinely risking their lives rather than
cowering like jackals whilst the Germans were in control and then coming out
to murder and hang people as they saw fit, were also clearly disgusted. Within
two days an order from the Russian general in charge of Prague was posted up
everywhere: 'Down weapons and stop taking the law into your own hands.'
And everything stopped! The most striking feature of the mob is that it fears
the least threat of the whip. I had come to hate this mob with all my soul. I had
come across it many times before, but never in such numbers as in Prague after
the thrice unnecessary uprising.

Later I thought: why was the uprising staged? Why were so many monuments
destroyed? Why did young people die on the totally unnecessary barricades?
What was it all for? For the kudos? Were they wanting to send some message
to Beneš's incoming government? The uprising took place and the uprising was
bloody; a lot of people died for nothing. So did many of Vlasov's men. It was
obviously they who had saved Prague from the Germans, who had enabled the
revolutionary-military committee to negotiate with the German Command, yet
three days later the official line was everywhere that Prague had been liberated
by General Rybalko's tanks. TASS's telegrams were sheer fantasy. The Soviet
troops were given a rousing welcome, but it still was not they who had saved
the place. The Germans had already stopped fighting when Rybalko arrived and
finished off the SS's hornet's nest with a few rounds from his T-34s.

The Czechs had always had a sense of humour, but I don't recall a single joke
about the uprising. Evidently it was too dirty a business for humour.

In the wake of the Soviet Army came the arrests. Units formed by no-one
knows whom started arresting Czechs who had worked with the Germans.
Meanwhile the Soviet security organs, i.e. military counter-intelligence or
SMERSH ('Death to Spies'), which was particularly thick on the ground in
Prague since three fronts met here, started arresting émigré Russians in particular.

As those in the know told me later, these units in the three fronts vied with each other to arrest the most.

Curious to relate, the general mood amongst the inhabitants both Russian and Czech, their sympathies towards the Soviet soldiers, began to wane when it was discovered how fond they were of watches. They tried to buy them or purloin them. One of my friends and his wife could not wait for their heroes to come and liberate them. When they arrived, the couple invited the first sergeant or tank commander they came across to lunch, they gave him vodka and what have you, he ate his fill, lit up a cigarette, told them a few tales, then said: 'What's that watch you're wearing? Show me!' The host showed him. Then he said: 'And what's that clock there?' The latter was an alarm-clock or something, and the hostess was also wearing a wrist-watch. 'What do you do if your watch breaks down?' he said to his host. 'Oh, I've got a couple of spares.' 'In that case,' said the soldier, 'thank you very much, I'll take this wrist-watch for the memory.' The host thought he was joking, but he wasn't. This really upset my friend. The watch was a good one, it had cost a lot of money, and he began to refer to the Soviet troops as 'looters'. I objected: 'Stop generalizing. One of them was a looter, but the Soviet Army as a whole doesn't rob the population, they're our allies...'

Things like this lowered the army's standing. The Soviet troops treated Czech women too loosely. They often drove girls around on their T-34s. Many apartments were occupied by soldiers who filled them with shouting, screaming, plundered alcohol and Czech girls. The Czech men did not like that. It was the usual story as with any army.

11

Arrested

By Summer St Nicholas Day, 22 May 1945, almost all the prominent members of the émigré community in Prague were either in custody or had done a spell in the clutches of the Soviet 'organs'. I had so far slipped through the net. Someone who had been released expressed their surprise: 'What, haven't you been arrested yet? Strange!'

I was always on the move trying to find out what institutions were being set up in the Czechoslovak Republic that could take the Institute under their wing. Prince Karl Schwarzenberg put me in touch with his younger brother Frantiszek, who worked in the Foreign Ministry. I thought it would be better for the Institute not to be under the aegis of the Interior Ministry or the Ministry of Education, because it was not a Czech organization but an international one. Frantiszek Schwarzenberg agreed, and promised me every assistance. We arranged that I would come to the FM on 23 May, by which time he would have spoken to various advisers about how best to bring the Institute under the FM's patronage. I went home well pleased with this, but I found *mama* and Nalivkin, the institute porter, waiting for me in a terrible state.

Whilst I was out, a Czech of suspicious appearance had turned up with a Soviet soldier carrying a submachine-gun. The soldier, a half-literate lad, wanted to know where I was. I wasn't there, so my mother asked: 'What do you need him for?'

'I've got to take him to my superiors.'

'And where are your superiors?'

'Where they know best.'

My mother suddenly went right up to him and asked sternly: 'Have you got a warrant?'

This threw him completely. He probably didn't even know what a warrant was.

'You haven't?' said my mother. 'You could cop it then for acting out of hand: do you know what kind of an institution this is?'

'Er, I...my superiors – ' he mumbled, and left taking the Czech with him.

My mother felt we should vacate the building immediately. We packed a day case and went straight to our doctor's, Lidiya Yakubova. Nalivkin went home, after hanging a notice on the Institute doors saying it was closed until 23rd.

We celebrated Summer St Nicholas at Yakubova's and heard a simply incredible number of sad stories of how the Russian colony was being gone through by the 'organs'. Droves of former members of NTS and other youth organizations such as the Scouts had been arrested and disappeared, as had all the members of the Warriors League. Taxi-drivers, who were listed as Russian Nazis, not because they really were, but because otherwise they would have lost their licences, also disappeared. Many teachers had been arrested. The remaining colony was holding its breath. What would happen next? The prospects looked grim.

On 23 May I dropped my mother off at the Institute around nine o'clock and went on to meet Schwarzenberg at the FM. He had held his preliminary talks and gave me a summary of what to say if tackled by the Soviet or Czech authorities. He said that it would be another two or three days before the file could be presented to the deputy minister, but the advisers he had spoken to agreed with us. He had even written a memorandum explaining point by point why the Kondakov Institute had been accepted by various committees, and a statement apparently from the Institute explaining why we sought patronage. I was relieved and set off home again.

Outside the Institute were two enormous covered trucks with benches in the back and on their sides the words IN THE FOOTSTEPS OF VICTORY – GLORY TO THE HEROES OF THE SOVIET ARMY and THE DONBASS MINERS GREET THEIR VICTORIOUS ARMY. People were milling around and there were several passenger cars as well. I went into the Institute and found its office full of people. A happy smiling Nalivkin said to me: 'There's a whole group arrived, they want you to show them Prague, they're miners from the Donbass, and the officers here have brought you presents from the generals.'

About ten officers led by a colonel were sitting talking to my mother. When he saw me, the colonel exclaimed: 'Ah, comrade tour guide! We've brought you two dozen bottles of captured brandy from the generals you showed round Prague last week, and a bag of buckwheat kasha for your mother, she told them she hadn't eaten any for years. They said to thank you very much.'

I was touched. He said it came from the headquarters of this front and that they hoped I would also agree to show Prague to these Donbass miners. I said, 'Of course! We'll show them everything. But first let's try this captured brandy, shall we?'

We opened some bottles, brought some glasses, relaxed even more, and the officers started recalling their experiences and telling stories. Then there was a ring at the front door.

Nalivkin went to open it, came back, and said: 'It's for you.'

I went out into the corridor and saw a young man whose face was vaguely familiar, a first lieutenant standing next to him, and a soldier behind them with a submachine-gun. The lieutenant checked who I was, then said: 'I wonder if you could come with me, my superiors want a word with you.'

'How long are your superiors likely to detain me?' I asked.

'Twenty or thirty minutes.'

'Would you mind if I did something else first?'

'What's that?'

'Officers have just come from front headquarters with some Donbass miners who are doing a tour in the footsteps of victory, and the officers have asked me to show the miners round Prague.'

'I am afraid,' the lieutenant said, 'that you will have to come and have a word with my superiors first.'

'I really don't know...' I replied, and opened the door into the office where the colonel was sitting.

The colonel had driven the Germans out of my mother's home town of Torzhok, was telling her all about it, and she was getting quite excited as she recognized different parts of the town. I said to him: 'Comrade colonel, you want me to go off with the miners, but there's someone else here who wants me to go with him.'

'What? Who?' said the colonel. 'Tell him to come in here.'

The first lieutenant went in and the colonel said to him: 'First lieutenant, a group of miners has been sent here by front HQ and we are asking comrade Andreyev, who has already distinguished himself as a guide showing Prague to our generals, to do the same for us and the miners.'

The lieutenant stepped forward and said only one word. I had never heard it before, so I did not understand it, but I realized later that it was: 'SMERSH.'

The climate in the room changed instantly. The colonel crumpled, the officers clammed up, and looking at his watch the colonel said: 'Perhaps we should first go and have a meal, and come round for our comrade guide afterwards.'

And they all disappeared, forever, and, of course, no-one ever-ever came round with Donbass miners 'in the footsteps of victory' again.

I went out into the corridor, the lieutenant followed me, and the young man and guard stood by the doors.

'It won't take long, we can even walk there,' said the lieutenant.

Everything he said was a lie.

I was about to put on my mac, when he – first lieutenant Vorontsov as I later discovered – suddenly said: 'In your shoes I think I would put on a heavier coat. One minute it's raining, the next minute it's sunny, you'll be cold in just a mac.'

Of course, he was warning me. As he played with me like a cat with a mouse he already knew I was a doomed man and would never come back. But I did not ponder what he said, I decided that maybe he was right, the weather really was changeable, so I put on my thick woollen coat, which served me well in the years to come – as clothing, blanket, bedding and pillow. Then we left.

Mama kissed me, said something to Vorontsov, and he saluted politely and reassured her. I walked first, followed by Vorontsov, then the young man, and then the man with the gun. The procession slowly descended the stairs and people looked at me in amazement because they thought I had been an emissary from Moscow! Now the emissary was being led away like so many others. No-one, of course, understood that an era was passing with me and basically the Kondakov Institute was finished. There is something ignominious about being escorted along a busy street full of friendly folk as though you are a criminal. Frankly, when the Soviet Army arrived we found it strangely impossible to get on the same wavelength as the people in it, however sincerely we wished to. One reason was that you couldn't help fearing one day a degrading procession like this, under arrest.

To my surprise there was no vehicle. It started to drizzle several times, and Vorontsov had been right to suggest I take my overcoat. After a fairly long walk, we came out on the embankment. Vorontsov went into a building that had two sentries outside, stayed there about twenty minutes, then emerged and said the man in charge had left and we had to go somewhere else, after which we came out on a wide street that had lots of military vehicles coming and going on it. He stopped one of the trucks, we climbed in, and were taken to the Barrandovská district. We got out and when the truck lumbered off we found ourselves before a tall Cossack – an NCO in a round fur hat. He had a pair of bay horses and a tarantass. The horses were unharnessed and the Cossack was walking round them with a knowledgeable air.

Vorontsov said: 'You stay with him, we've got to pick up someone else in the city.' And off they went.

The Cossack was quite amiable. He suggested that we have a meal, as he had some lard, eggs and vodka. He sent me into a nearby house to ask them to cook us a pan of fried eggs, and the Czechs made a good job of it: eight eggs and some excellent bread. To my surprise, I was hungry. Then the Cossack said: 'You do what you like, but I'm having a nap' – and he got into the back of the tarantass and left the horses dozing on their feet. Previous to this he and I had had a rather amusing conversation about these horses. I had said to him: 'Not bad steeds, and it's a fine tarantass! Have you come all the way from the Kuban with a cavalry detachment?' 'Goodness no,' he replied. 'We took the horses and cart off a lord of the manor in Hungary!'

Basically I could have run for it at this point. I had my documents on me, and I knew this part of Prague fairly well. But I decided it wasn't worth it: I had no transport, and no guarantee that I wouldn't bump into Vorontsov and his machine-gunner somewhere. Also, I realized that I would be quickly caught and then, probably, they would treat me worse.

I always carried a piece of paper and an envelope with me, so I took them out
now and wrote my mother a letter, saying simply that we'd just had something to
eat, that I hadn't seen any 'superiors' yet, that we were proceeding to somewhere
else, and that she shouldn't worry. I had no stamps, but they had probably
stopped being sold anyway, so I addressed the envelope, sauntered over to the
corner, and posted it as it was.

Unfortunately, I couldn't get to sleep. It was nine o'clock before Vorontsov
turned up with his machine-gunner, the pale boy, and a brunette who turned out
to be a Hungarian Jewess recently released from a German concentration camp.
They wanted to use her as an interpreter, but when they turned up at her flat
she wouldn't let them in. She rang the city commandant's office and they sent
officers over to arrest Vorontsov and his machine-gunner: there was a terrible
rumpus between two different arms of the Soviet Army! Vorontsov had enjoyed
it tremendously. 'Fine girl,' he said. 'Put up a fine fight.' But in the end they
convinced her they weren't going to harm her. Our bays were put in the shafts
of the tarantass, the Cossack and I sat on the box, Vorontsov and the little Jewess
sat on the main seat, and facing them sat the gunman and the pale-faced youth.

Endless wastelands and fences jogged by, patrolled by armed Czechs and
Soviet sentries. We passed Germans – you could see them behind the fence –
ragged, unshaven, in civvies, herded here after their arrest. Then we came out
on a main road that ran along the Vltava towards Zbraslav castle. I had been a
trustee of a Russian museum in this castle, and knew the district well.

It was now dusk, and the poplars along the banks of the river were fabulously
beautiful in the moonlight. Whole German divisions were encamped on the
banks, they were already asleep, here and there sentries could be seen, and every
so often they would fire a few bursts from their machine-guns, obviously to
keep their spirits up. It was an interesting sight: thousands upon thousands
of German soldiers, and they had all surrendered. So this is what it meant to
have no will to fight whilst still possessing enormous potential force. The army
was no longer operating as a fighting organization. We kept going, we left the
districts I knew behind, and came out on the road to Sazava, which the Czech
population had been evicted from to make way for units of the SS. The Soviet
special forces, i.e. SMERSH, had taken over the same buildings here.

We drove through Czech villages twinkling with happy lights, past well-to-do
houses, everything was as peaceful as in Prague, and the general feeling was:
thank God, the war's finished, there is no longer this cursèd darkness over the
land! But for us, the arrested ones, a new darkness was beginning, complete
darkness was descending over our lives.

12

With 'SMERSH' on the Malinovsky Front

We rode up to a barrier that was evidently left over from the SS era, and halted. A searchlight immediately came on at the side, scanned us, and went out.

'Friends, friends!' shouted the driver.

'Pass!'

The barrier rose and we trotted on.

'Home at last,' said the driver jauntily.

The concept 'home' is relative; personally my heart sank even further. The moon was wavering over buildings floodlit with electric light, and we had stopped in front of a fairly large one with two sentries patrolling its perimeter.

Now a new character appeared, sergeant-major Romanov. He was to take me to my night lodging. He had the face of a Skopets (member of a self-castrated sect) and I had always been afraid of these fellows because I'd read that they were extremely cruel and used in the East as torturers. We set off along a path that was less and less well-lit, but I sensed that somewhere nearby was a large space with horses on, because I heard the occasional whinny and munching of equine jaws. I concluded we were at the SMERSH unit in some division of the Kuban Cossacks.

Romanov was walking beside me and would occasionally say: 'Careful you don't stumble, the ground dips here', and a couple of times he even supported me by the elbow, which seemed inappropriate, given that I was SMERSH's prisoner! Somewhere lilac and bird cherry were wafting their fragrance into the night. Eventually we arrived at another floodlit house. Romanov told me to wait outside, and went in.

Painful notes on an accordion were issuing from the house. Somebody was trying to play a tune. They would start reasonably enough, falter, and suddenly stop. This happened over and over again. It was as though the accordion was being put through one bout of torture after another.

Romanov came back and said: 'Please follow me.' I went up some steps into the house and we entered a large room with two beds, a wardrobe, a table, and several chairs, on one of which sat a lieutenant with his uniform open at the neck. He was still tormenting the accordion. Romanov and I watched him in silence. He said nothing and made yet another unsuccessful attempt at the tune. Then he looked at me and said:

'Do you drink vodka?'

'Yes, I do.'

'Well I haven't got any.'

He resumed his playing. Romanov and I just stood there. After a while, the lieutenant said: 'Romanov, go and get some er...' – and jiggled an imaginary glass in the air. Romanov nodded.

The lieutenant carried on playing, ignoring me completely.

Eventually Romanov appeared with a decanter full of red liquid and a small glass. The lieutenant laid aside his accordion, filled the glass with red liquid, handed it to me, and said: 'Drink that.'

I looked at the red liquid, the lieutenant, and Romanov, and concluded that they were trying to drug me, after which they would probably torture me. So I suddenly said very definitely: 'I'm not drinking on my own.'

The lieutenant looked me in the eyes and I could see that he understood why I was refusing. He smirked, and said: 'Romanov, bring some more mugs.' Romanov came back with a cup and a cracked glass. These were filled up with the red liquid, the lieutenant proposed a toast 'to victory', and we all knocked it back.

I nearly keeled over: it was vodka made from pure spirit and raspberry jam. The lieutenant explained that there was a shortage of real vodka, it had been supplied during wartime, but banned as soon as the war finished. 'However,' he said, 'we came across some surgical spirit in a German transport we took. Well, you can't drink spirit neat, so we got hold of some raspberry jam and brewed it up with that!'

Romanov brought us something to eat with the vodka: tasty cold chops, good bread, and even a gherkin.

I must confess I had not expected my first day in SMERSH's clutches to end this way. I drank with gusto and, of course, got tipsy like my companions. Soon all three of us were singing songs and the lieutenant kept trying to accompany us on the accordion, but alas he had no ear for music. We sang army songs – Soviet, pre-revolutionary and Cossack – practically with our arms round each other. In those days I knew lots of songs, although never the whole text, but my companions didn't either; for drunken purposes you just had to know the tune and a few words. I don't remember how it all ended, but I woke up next morning underneath my coat on one of the beds with a diabolical hangover. I dare not move my head. I hadn't woken spontaneously, someone had come in and bellowed: 'Comrade lieutenant, wake up!'

I saw before me another great big Cossack NCO, who said: 'As you ordered, comrade lieutenant, the mowers were sent out to cut fodder for the horses.'

'Right,' the lieutenant croaked. 'I remember.'

'Well I have to report, comrade lieutenant, that the military commandant's men have arrested them all!'

'That I did not order,' said the lieutenant in a sepulchral voice, although he was obviously sobering up and his voice clearing.

'Well I have to report,' continued the Coassack, 'that they were scything as authorized, and had mown enough, when these blasted Czechs went and told one of the commandant's patrols that they were mowing good hay.'

'What kind of hay *were* they mowing?'

'Well, good hay of course, we can't give the horses bad hay, can we? They saw some good hay, so they cut it!'

'And?'

'And as I said! The patrol comes along and shouts: "You, blah-de-blah, are disobeying an order of the Commander-in-Chief of the front – you must not mow hay without the consent of the local military commandant and that has to be agreed with the Czech authorities, which you riffraff haven't done!" So the sergeant who was with the mowers said: "Do you want the horses to drop dead whilst you appoint a committee?" "I don't know anything about that," says the patrol-leader, "but I'm putting you in jankers!" – and he arrested the lot of them.'

'How many mowers were there?'

'Seven, as you ordered.'

'But' – the lieutenant moved to a chair, his hangover was evidently subsiding – 'I did not order them to mow in such a way as to get arrested. I ordered them to mow on the sly, co-vertly!.. All right, I'll come and sort it out...'

First, however, he went and got the same decanter, which had been refilled, and said to me: 'I expect your head's as foggy as mine, so let's have a drop to freshen up.'

We did have a drop, and sure enough the excruciating pain in my head instantly vanished and I could think and move normally again.

It was seven o'clock in the morning and you could hear Kuban Cossacks and their horses on the move everywhere. Romanov brought me soap and a towel, I had a wash, then he said: 'I'll take you to have breakfast with the officers.'

The second of the two floors of the house was the officers' quarters and there I had a delicious breakfast. Later that day I made the acquaintance of their first-rate cook, a true Soviet *zhulik* (rogue) who under his shirt had fourteen watches up each arm.

At supper Savitsky appeared. It was the third or fourth time he had been arrested and I was shocked by his pallor, anxiety, and phoney talk. For instance, we were eating soup within the officers' hearing and he said: 'I haven't eaten soup like this for twenty years!', as though he were praising the Soviet system rather than the cook. Or he said: 'I looked at the field-newspaper today. Some very penetrating thoughts there!', when there was no thought in it at all, it was pure agitprop and even the officers understood that.

Obviously he was terribly frightened. Walking afterwards in the garden, I asked him how things were and he said: 'Very difficult. They keep asking me about the 1920s, which I no longer remember.' I realized that they must be interrogating him about his illegal trips to the Soviet Union, when he took part in conferences organized around Moscow by people who were supposedly Eurasians. According to émigré sources they were actually staged by 'TREST', which worked for the Soviet political police, and many of the Chekists who knew about them perished in the purges. Obviously the first people to arrest him hadn't known about these things. Now they had received instructions from the centre and that's why they had arrested him a fourth time. They wanted to check up on someone in their own *apparat*, or to fill in some details that they lacked because the Chekists in question had been liquidated.

It also transpired that Savitsky was obsessed with the fact that he had been wrong to think the upsurge of Soviet patriotism during the war was a sign of the regime 'evolving'. As a scholar, it was extremely unpleasant for him to experience his mistake in the flesh and see before him people like myself whom he regarded as unwitting victims of misapprehensions about the nature and development of Soviet power. He told me that his interrogator had refused to believe that Savitsky's pro-Soviet wartime poems were really by Savitsky, until he suggested that Savitsky write one about the Soviet cavalry divisions driving the Germans out of Odessa, and Savitsky obliged.

We walked about for three-quarters of an hour, then Savitsky said he had to go and make some written statements. I myself was getting more and more nervous. Even the banter from my friend the cook no longer lifted my spirits. I kept thinking of what was going to happen to me. The day was declining in the west, and the cook came along and offered me some supper. I didn't want any, but he said: 'Stop thinking all the time! Care killed the cat! Come and try this pie I've made, I'll give you some supper in the kitchen' – and he did. It was a marvellous pie, I ate it up despite being so stressed, and it was a good thing I did. At about seven o'clock Romanov came and told me that his superior wanted to talk to me. We went off to the main building.

But we did not go in. Romanov entrusted me to a guard with a submachine-gun who made me sit on a tree stump for two hours. Around nine o'clock I was led into a spacious office with a desk in it, behind which sat a major, who said: 'Andreyev, Nikolay Yefremovich?' I confirmed it and he told me to sit down.

He was dark, closely shaven, about twenty-seven, and as he talked he raised his voice more and more.

He had long wanted, he said, to fish me out and see what kind of a bloke I was, and now at last he had me before him. There were open enemies, who fight with weapons in their hands and visors up, and he, the major, was prepared to respect such enemies. But there were other, devious enemies, who lurk in the shadows and corners. These were scorpions who sting others, infect them, drive them mad, and do battle with the Soviet state. We ideologists, he said, sit in the bushes and prod them to fight. This view amazed me: as far as I knew, I had never been one of these 'scorpions'.

I tried to object, but the more I did the more he shouted. He said he had been watching me for ages. He came out with some nonsense about knowing every inch of my dastardly soul and even claimed that if he had come across me in wartime I would simply have been liquidated as vermin. Fortunately for me, the war was over and Soviet justice was now distinguishing degrees of dastardliness. By the look of it, mine was rather high and my prospects were poor. For instance, it was obvious that I was associated with the SRs.

'Did you know any SRs?' he asked.

'Plenty.'

'You see! And do you know what the SRs were trying to achieve?'

'Of course I do' – and I summarized their programme.

'There, you even know their programme, you worked in SR organizations, you can't wriggle out of it.'

I didn't wriggle, I told him that I had never been an SR, no-one suggested it to me, and I had contributed to the SR magazine *Volya Rossii* simply because it published young critics.

'Are you trying to tell me that the editor of *Volya Rossii* fell for your blue eyes and had no political ulterior motive? And never asked you what you believed in? Don't come that codswallop with me, you were associated with the SRs all right. And with other factions, especially the fascists.'

This really did amaze me. He now started reviling fascism and me as an ideologue of it. I was horrified, and in one of his pauses managed to say: 'Will you please tell me when I added one iota to the ideology of fascism? When and what did I ever say on this subject?'

'You tell *me*,' he answered, 'what you said and what you contributed to fascism!', and ranted away again.

It emerged that the fascists he particularly disliked were NTS, who had worked closely with Himmler, sneaked onto Soviet territory, and attempted to poison the pure minds of Soviet youth with stupid ideas. And I had played an extremely important part in this because I had supplied the ideas. At this point I lost my self-control and told him this was sheer fantasy.

'Do you deny, then, that you knew NTS people?'

'Of course I knew them! They were people of my generation and I spent hours arguing with Kirill Vergun, for example, because I did not share their views.'

'Yes, but you visited them even when Kirill Vergun wasn't there.'

'Kirill wasn't, but I went to their house very often for personal reasons.'

'Don't try to fool me, your affair with Vergun's sister was just a smokescreen for your ideological link with the organization.'

This really got under my skin.

'Listen, comrade major, not even the most depraved imagination could have foreseen that you and the Soviet organs would be here in Czechoslovakia. So there was no need for me to conceal my relations with any organizations whatsoever. Everyone could interest themselves in politics openly. Lots of political parties were of interest to me, and I received invitations from many parties to join them, but didn't.'

This was a sticking-point between us for some time, but eventually he said: 'You deny everything, as though you were a good little boy who never did anything wrong and who should be patted on the head. If you say that you're not a monarchist, or a fascist, a Nazi, what are you ideologically?'

Completely frustrated, I came out with a formula which suddenly brought things down to earth: 'What am I? I am a representative of the liberal intelligentsia, and as Lenin said, you'll get nothing out of them!'

The reference to Lenin had an unusual effect on the major. He stopped in his tracks and said: 'Exactly, exactly!', and questioned me no further on the subject. Perhaps this formula had reminded him that as a historian I might know Lenin better than he did, and he adopted it himself just in case. It produced a kind of block in his brain – Lenin's authority had been turned to my advantage. Nevertheless he said: 'Yes, but in your case the liberal intelligentsia has sold itself out to vile non-liberal ideas.' And he was off again accusing me of having ideologically skivvied for Nazism and all forms of fascism, in which he included NTS although he always mentioned it separately.

He shouted for two hours, the session was all crescendo, and by the end of it Goebbels himself would have envied me the mendacity I was accused of. Only abject penitence could save me. And all the time, we smoked – he like a chimney, I when he offered me one. I was smoking for the first time in my life, because accepting or not accepting a *papirosa* from him was like the last act of freedom left to me. The smoke at least hid his face from me for a moment, as he ranted on.

'You are a sinister figure!' he hollered. 'You are steeped in villainy and have poisoned the weak, you are a snake in the grass!'

'Comrade guards major,' I said, 'I see that you regard me as an enemy of the people, so why bother with this conversation at all?'

He flung himself back in his chair, stared at me, and in a terribly tired voice said: 'An enemy of the people? Don't be ridiculous!' – and he got up and walked out. It was ten to midnight. A sergeant entered to take his place, threw the windows wide open to let the smoke billow out, and the wonderful May air of Bohemia, full of lilac and bird cherry, poured in.

The sergeant immediately asked me if I was thirsty, and gave me a glass of water. Then he began telling me about his military career, how he had been shell-shocked in the battles around Perekop, after that he couldn't continue in active service, but was good enough for the 'organs'. His chatter was a great relief, he was relating simple things in simple human language and was evidently pleased that he had survived this terrible, bloody war – had only been shell-shocked. He was quite kind, I sensed no hostility in him towards me, and he was pleased I listened to him carefully and even asked one or two questions.

The major was away for almost an hour, because this was when they had their evening meal. The organs' day followed Stalin's: they began work late, after ten in the morning, but were in session until about four the next morning, with a 'dead hour' after lunch when Stalin was taking his nap. Supper was between about 11.45 p.m. and 1.15 a.m., when Stalin had his. But I discovered all this later.

The major re-started our conversation in a different key. He stopped shouting and accusing me of something, asked for my passport and other documents, wrote their details on a separate sheet, then asked me about my activity in Prague: when I had arrived, where I had studied, what degrees I had taken, what I had done at the Institute, what was my political biography. I told him I had no political biography. He stopped me:

'If I am not mistaken, you are a doctor of philosophy?

'Yes – '

'So how can you say that you're a man without a political biography? The very statement is political! I shall ask you again, then: what is your political biography?'

With difficulty, I ascertained that he wanted to know how I came to be in Prague, who I hobnobbed with, which political organizations I knew, where I was invited to give talks, and why I declined. We thus passed the time without excesses until about four in the morning. He kept stressing that I was close to the SRs and other organizations, and said: 'Here's a job for you. Write up your political biography for me tomorrow, then I'll call you.'

I asked him what was going to happen to the Kondakov Institute. Why had they taken me away from it? I explained that the Institute was in a very difficult position, and if I wasn't there the whole thing could fall apart. He thought for a moment and said: 'The fate of the Kondakov Institute does not fall within my competency. I'm merely trying to establish your political profile. Let's see what you write, then we'll draw our conclusions.' On that we parted. I was taken back to my room by a sentry, and fell fast asleep.

I spent most of the next day writing. I was now excluded from officer company when I had my meals. Although I still had the same food as them, it was given to me by the cook in the kitchen, which actually suited me better.

To my surprise, a table had been set up in the room I slept in, and I saw the lieutenant and a sergeant major eating there with a couple of German women, then they went off somewhere altogether. I asked the cook where they might have gone.

'To the bath-house of course.'

'What bath-house?'

'We've set up a Russian *banya* here.'

'And where do the girls come from?'

'They're prisoners. They've been fed, I gave them some grub, because the German girls are hungry, and our men also need a meal before getting to work on them, so now they've gone off to the *banya* for a good time.'

I was shocked.

'And what happens to the girls afterwards?'

'Back to prison.'

The commander's 'wife' too, it transpired, was a girl he had fancied and according to the cook he would 'wine, dine and bed her for a while, then pass her on to another unit whilst he found a fresh one.' It reminded me of a brothel.

The next morning at about eleven I was called to the major. As soon as I entered the familiar office, he looked at me and said: 'What's this drivel you've written me?' – and threw it all at my feet. It was terribly reminiscent of the way the German police had thrown my passport and application for my mother's visa at me. 'What do you think you're writing?' he continued. 'What the f— do I want your thoughts and feelings for? I'm not interested in them!'

'But comrade guards major,' I said, 'you told me you were interested in my political biography, I told you I didn't have one, you insisted I did, so I have described for you my attitude to politics, from which it's clear that in accordance with my political views I didn't do anything and wasn't a member of any organization.'

'I'm not interested! I don't want the rubbish!'

'You must explain to me then what you do want.'

In the end, it turned out that he wanted through me to discover the history of the various political actors and organizations that I had encountered in Prague; whom I knew in what organization; what meetings I had attended; who had invited me to join an organization, and why I hadn't.

This list interested him, it seems, not so much as a description of my activities as material for evaluating the people I would mention and their organizations. It was a mammoth task and took me another two days to write. When he summoned me again he did not mention my personal biography, but said:

'Basically, I don't see what your *corpus delicti* is, but you have a lot of black marks against you.'

'What marks, comrade guards major?'

'You've known some ve-ry suspicious people.'

When I expressed astonishment at this, he pulled out my manuscript and holding it disdainfully between his thumb and forefinger said:

'But you knew them all – Countess Panina, Prince Dolgorukov, Milyukov, a whole swarm of SRs, Denikin, etcetera etcetera. A collection of counter-revolutionaries, of the Soviet Union's bitterest enemies! Don't you think each one of them is a blot on your biography?'

I didn't, but it was better to say nothing.

'Nevertheless, this is what I will do. Today or tomorrow you and I will go and have a look at your Institute.'

I was very pleased.

The next evening we set out in a very smelly truck fuelled by German wood-petrol. We were joined by Savitsky, whom I had not seen since our walk. The major sat in the cabin next to the driver, Savitsky and I sat in the back on benches, guarded by two machine-gunners, and were not allowed to talk to each other. He was dropped off near his home, said goodbye, and disappeared into the darkness. A day or two later he was arrested for a fifth time, deported to Russia, and began his long passage through concentration camps and logging brigades.

In front of the Kondakov Institute, I was surprised to see, there was a sentry. He was caught unawares by the major and my armed guard, and said: 'Your pass please, major sir.'

'What pass?'

'Commandant's orders: we are only allowed to let people into the Institute with comrade Andreyeva's permission.'

The major raised his eyebrows at me and said: 'And where is "comrade Andreyeva"?'

'Inside the building.'

'Well go and tell her we're here.'

The sentry hesitated, then said: 'All right, sir, go in.'

My guard stayed with the sentry, and we walked along the corridor to my room. *Mama* was having tea there with one of my former students, Eva. You can imagine the reunion of mother and son. She invited everyone to the table, the major consented, a bottle of the captured brandy was opened and poured out for everyone, even my guard was called in, and then we talked.

The major said that from his point of view no offence had been committed, so after looking round the Institute he would process my release tomorrow. He couldn't leave me here overnight, but I would return tomorrow. He went to look at the other rooms, the icon galleries, the library, he inspected everything, noted the portraits of Stalin and Beneš, but said nothing. Evidently the Institute seemed to him respectable, as it did to everyone. He told my mother: 'I can understand you being worried about him.' *Mama* confirmed that my disappearance had caused panic, that people did not know what to do, and were waiting for me to come back. The major behaved well, but, just in case, I asked my mother to give me some toothpaste and a brush, a towel and a change of underwear. I was used to not believing the major, and it struck me as odd that he was able to let Savitsky go, but not me. However, he saluted my mother and said I would be back around seven tomorrow evening. Off we went.

I slept in the usual room, and next morning everyone seemed to know (presumably from my guard) that I was being released today and going to Prague. So they all asked me to get them vodka there and send it to them!

At eleven o'clock we – myself and another prisoner – were told we were leaving. We were packed into a passenger vehicle with the major in front and two armed guards behind. Suddenly I noticed we were not taking a turning to Prague, but somewhere else. We drove about thirty miles and arrived at an enormous country estate with a large house in it and a courtyard crammed with military vehicles. It seems to have been the SMERSH headquarters of this army, or even the entire front. The major left us in the car, where we were given some excellent chicken soup and observed the Soviet *mores* around us.

An official dinner was in progress. It had started at about 1.30 and reached its apogee at 3.30 with shouts of 'Hurrah! Long life the great Stalin! Hurrah!', when they were drinking toasts. Then the regimental band struck up with a hymn to Stalin and the Soviet national anthem. 'What happens now?' I asked someone. 'After dinner they give them their directives.' Directives were given out until seven in the evening, when the major reappeared, came over to the car, and said: 'Have they fed you?' 'Yes.' 'Any complaints?' 'No.' 'Let's go then.' And we set off the way we had come. 'You'll have to go to Prague tomorrow,' said the major. 'I haven't got any transport for you today, the meeting just now was unscheduled, I didn't know about it when I was at your institute.'

Early next morning I was loaded into a lorry with several other prisoners, who were not Russian, and a different major, who had a sadistic reputation. We drove across Charles Square in Prague and stopped outside a large building which under the Germans had been a hotel or a house for officers. The non-Russians were unloaded and led off in one direction, the major went off in another. I was called out and yet another major, completely unknown to me, said: 'Follow me.' I said to him: 'Comrade major, I was told I was going to be released now.' 'Maybe you are, but we've got some formalities to complete. Come on.'

We went into the building, and I saw that I had jumped from the frying-pan into the fire. My interrogator-major had deceived me one hundred per cent, because I was now one of an enormous number of arrested persons being processed, mainly Russian émigrés and many of them people I knew. I tried to speak to the new major, but he said: 'Later, later, just sit here and say nothing, we'll sort it all out in a minute, you can see how things are.' I certainly could: I had been completely conned.

Obviously I had fetched up in the general remand centre for émigrés. There were scores if not hundreds of them here. I saw Sergey Postnikov, once a prospective member of the SR central committee, with his enormous mane of grey hair and flowing patriarchal beard. He seemed much older than he was, and the soldiers called him *papasha* ('pop') and treated him well. Every so often he would buttonhole one of them: 'I say, young man, you couldn't bring me some tea, could you?' 'Of course I could, pop, of course!' And he would be brought 'Chekist tea', i.e. very strong and sweet.

Postnikov was gloomy about the future for Russian émigrés. 'What surprises me most,' he said, 'is that the secret police go about things the same way as they did before the revolution. But at least we knew then what we were in prison for and for how long, now we haven't a clue.'

I found Prince Konstantin Chkheidze, a leading Eurasian, equally pessimistic. He kept telling whoever would listen how he had been tricked into compiling a collection of his 'anti-Soviet' utterances – his own 'admission of guilt'. Evidently this was beginning to affect his reason.

Another person there was Professor Marakuyev, once the director of RACI and thanks to whom I had been able to enter Czechoslovakia in the first place. He smiled wanly, looked at me for a while, and suddenly said: 'I remember you when you were a lad, when you came to my study – a young lad with clear eyes. That was seventeen years ago!' He too was gloomy, and said he saw no chances for the emigration: even if we were not packed off to do hard labour that killed us, we would die of stress.

There were lots of members of the Engineers Union there, but I noticed that this remand centre did not have any of the most eminent members of the colony or leading political figures. So these had already been removed or were being held separately, or were being 'played with' like Savitsky.

The general agitation and stress got to me too. I suddenly lost my sang froid, I got edgy, which is not a good thing in such circumstances. I simply could not sit still, I walked around every floor of the building, but the top one was under guard and we weren't allowed up there. Who was being kept there I don't know. There were some other rooms we weren't allowed into, although we could see who was in them. There were plenty of rooms and they all had beds and bedside tables, the lavatories were civilized, there was hot and cold water, and everything worked. Some of the guards were laid-back and the room that I was put in with Postnikov had a liberal regime.

Outside the weather was glorious, there was the softest light blue sky without a cloud in it, as though the heavenly ocean was calling you to lie down in the long grass somewhere and just stare into infinity.

The building had lots of large windows, whose middle and bottom parts were boarded up. To jump out you would have had to tear these boards off, which would have made a lot of noise. Alas, three hours after I arrived, in the middle of a heat wave, an NCO came along with two soldiers and started boarding up the tops of the windows as well. We were horrified, but to all our questions and indignant comments he replied: 'The order's to block 'em off, it's not my fault if it's hot. Be thankful we haven't had time to fit peaks on them as well' (i.e. the wooden flaps above the windows outside, which in Soviet prisons create a permanent state of semi-darkness). He was unbending and we realized he was acting on instructions from the top.

What I could not bear was the thought that my mother had been deceived. She had waited for me yesterday, she was waiting for me today, and hadn't had a word. I couldn't send her any kind of signal even though the Institute was five minutes' walk away. Now I reached a fateful juncture, a mood that is very dangerous for people in prison awaiting sentence, the start of their psychological collapse. It had been summed up by my Prague friend, the very talented poet Vyacheslav Lebedev, who wrote: 'And now to me *my* fate is dearer/Than any others' tragic fate'. To hell with the fact that so many other people are in here, if only *I* could get out. An unpleasant moment... But it made me remember Lebedev, his experiences in the Civil War, his attitude to communism, his principled stand during the uprising, and this brought me relief, the anxiety was lifted from my heart, and I thought: I must get a grip on myself and stop going dotty like most of the people here who have fallen in the soup and don't know how they are going to get out alive.

I woke up next day very early. They even had showers here, so I took a shower, shaved carefully, and tried to spruce myself up. After a perfunctory breakfast, I set off to look for the 'new major', and found him. He had a slightly square face with sheep eyes and not much hair. 'Ah yes, I remember you,' he said, 'I'll just have a look at your papers.' He asked me my surname again, went off somewhere, then came back and said he'd passed on my papers and I'd soon be told what was happening. So there was a chance. Suddenly they might release me.

About three hours passed and I was drinking some soup with bits of macaroni in it, when the 'new major' came up to me and told me: 'Go to the room over there.' I went, and found another major and a captain sitting in it. 'Nikolay Yefremovich?' asked the major. 'Yes.' 'One of yours, captain. Go with him,' he said to me, 'he'll process you.' I still entertained the mad thought that they would 'process' me into freedom. I went out with the captain, we were joined by an engineer and two guards with submachine-guns, and the whole procession set off across Charles Square to a building where I knew courts were held, not that I had ever been there. We entered and at first were left downstairs whilst the captain went off, then he called us upstairs to a room where he sat down behind a desk and we before him.

The captain began by taking the engineer's papers, filling out a questionnaire, and checking with him the dates and details of his education and employment. From time to time he consulted documents in a file in front of him. Like most people in the remand centre, the engineer was in a state of paralysed consciousness. He didn't know what he was saying and kept trying to get over that he had always sympathized with Soviet power. The captain even interrupted his writing and they had a conversation which I remember:

'I see,' said the captain. 'You sympathized with Soviet power. In what way?'

'I, er, always went to see Soviet films.'

'Where did you see Soviet films?'

'Before the Germans came, when Soviet films were shown in Czech cinemas, I always went to see them.'

'Well,' said the captain ironically, 'and did you like the films?'

The poor engineer replied: 'Yes indeed! I really admired the Soviet actors.'

'Talented folk, aren't they?'

'Oh yes, very, I have always considered Russian art progressive.'

'Yes…' said the captain, 'I'm glad you've always thought that.'

This ridiculous dialogue, in which the captain was obviously making fun of the terrified engineer, went on for about ten minutes, but it was followed by one that was quite interesting. The engineer had been in the White Army and then joined the Warriors League. In 1941, when the Germans attacked the Soviet Union, General von Lampe, the president of the WL at the time, offered Hitler the League's assistance, but Hitler turned it down saying that he did not need the help of non-Germans.

'You see,' said the engineer, 'he wouldn't take us because we were hoping for a Soviet victory.'

'Your organization was pro-Soviet, then?' asked the captain.

'It was an organization of Russian patriots.'

'What were the aims of the organization?'

'To preserve the cadres of the Russian national army.'

'What for?'

'So that the basis of the Russian Army would – '

The engineer fell silent, but the captain continued:

'You mean that after the fall of Soviet power these would form the cadres of the Russian Army, right?'

'I'm not totally sure, but maybe that is what our leaders thought.'

'Ah, the leaders. And you thought differently? Did you express your opinion?'

'I was just small fry, I couldn't object!'

'So you didn't express an opinion, but you did pay your subscription?

'Yes.'

'And you thereby supported the thinking of your leaders?'

'But we were all obliged to pay, because we were in the regiments together.'

'However when Hitler declined the assistance of the Warriors League and you began to sympathize with Soviet victories, you stopped paying your membership subscription?'

'Frankly, it never occurred to me.'

'It didn't? So you continued to support an organization which in the event of Soviet power collapsing would form the cadres of a new national Russian Army, correct?'

The poor engineer did not know what to say.

'Don't give me that flannel,' said the captain.

He called a guard, who took the engineer over to a little door in the wall, through which they disappeared. The captain then 'processed' me and we did the same. The door, it turned out, communicated directly with a prison. A sergeant was standing there, who checked off my details on a sheet given him by the guard, and said: 'Well, where am I to put you? Let's try number nine...' The most interesting thing was that I was still carrying a small brief-case with my toothpaste and a change of underclothes in, and no-one had looked in it once. He unlocked cell nine and said: 'Go in and make yourself at home.'

I did, and my heart sank completely. During the Czechoslovak Republic criminals had been kept here, but the Nazis added politicals. There was something still naïve and nineteenth-century about the place: you first entered an 'ante-cell' formed by a partition with a doorway, and in the 'ante-cell' stood the *parasha* (lavatory bucket), which stank appropriately and poisoned the air and your soul.

Two steps and you were in the cell proper, which was fairly spacious and held five. Beneath the windows there were plank-beds with mattresses. The latter were filthy. The window was very elongated, impossible to squeeze through, but it allowed you a glimpse of the tower at the entrance to Charles Square, and we could see the clock face and hear the chimes. This was a link with the living world. There were four other people in this cell and they jumped up and introduced themselves. I was immediately plunged into doubt about my own future, as my cell-mates were so obviously doomed.

There was a German whom the 'organs' accused of working for the Gestapo, which he denied. There was a Ukrainian from the so-called Ukrainian insurgent army active in Galicia/the Carpathians. There were two Russians of about twenty-three who had been in the Red Army, been captured, and because of the starvation in the camps had joined the 'labour battalions' that worked for the German Army. Someone had said to them 'Come with us and we'll give you some grub', so they went. They had no ideological reasons for doing it, but that was irrelevant to the Soviet authorities and they were obviously heading for the camps, the question being for how long. All of them were fearful to behold:

their hair was overgrown, they were unshaven, they were mentally exhausted, their underclothes were filthy, and their mattresses made me want to throw up.

I sat down on the floor completely drained. I was appalled at the thought of what was going to happen to me. Half an hour later the bolts scraped and the sergeant reappeared. He looked at me and said words for which I am so grateful to him: 'Now why are you losing your morale, Andreyev? You're not the first man to be in prison, or the last. When you get out, you'll forget all about it!'

This strange statement was like balm to me. He was right: I might get out of prison! 'Come on,' he added, 'I'll give you a clean mattress.' And he and I stepped out of the cell, which he carefully relocked, and went along the passage to his desk, he opened one of the doors in the wall, and it contained clean mattresses stuffed with straw. I put my mattress along the wall where I had been sitting, and could now get some sleep. How little a man needs! Thanks to the sergeant, I had recovered my spirits. I hadn't been charged with anything; I hadn't been convicted; the first major said he couldn't see any *corpus delicti*; so maybe they would still let me go! But my fellow-prisoners had *no* hope left.

Prison began to seem better than it was. No-one touched us, we weren't summoned for interrogation, we could sleep for as long as we liked, and the food was excellent, with a lot of fresh bread. It is possible that this was all intended as propaganda to offset the impression of the bulk of the prison, which was occupied by Czechs. What went on there was unbelievable: beatings, terrible cries of pain, Gestapo-like drills, near-starvation rations. We were taken out for ten to fifteen minutes exercise every day in a part of the yard – the larger area was for the Czechs – and we were usually accompanied by a middle-aged Ukrainian soldier who strongly disapproved of what was done on the Czech side. The prisoners were taken out with no clothes on, made to do exercises in this state, and humiliated. He said to me: 'You know, men are beasts, they treat each other like beasts!' He did not know that he was repeating a truth known since Roman times: *homo homini lupus est* was being remembered in the torture chambers of the Czechoslovak Republic.

A couple of days after I arrived, I was suddenly summoned to 'the office'. Sitting there was another major, a Georgian. He was a very polite man. He asked me to sit down, offered me cigarettes, then said: 'I need your help. I've received a few letters in Czech. You couldn't translate them in pencil in the margins for me, could you?' I did this, and even offered to reply to them for him in Czech. He laughed and said: 'No, that's not necessary, my bosses won't understand what I'm saying to these people, we'll reply to them in Russian – then they can have the trouble of translating them.' He kindly offered me some Chekist tea with a huge quantity of granulated sugar in it. He was even sympathetic towards me, knew my file, and asked me how I had found things, living here 'in Europe'. At one point I said to him:

'Comrade major, I'd like to find out why I'm being held here. They actually told me I would be released.'

'So they did,' he replied, 'and you probably will be, but when? You must be patient.'

I said that if this continued it would wreck a lot of things – not just my professional life but the public activities I was engaged in.

'I know,' he said. 'But there's nothing can be done. We are only keeping you in prison, remember, we're not investigating your case.'

I saw what he meant. There was a telephone on his desk, so I said: 'Couldn't I just ring to say that I'm all right and in Prague?'

'No. In the first place you're not allowed to because you're under arrest, and secondly it's an internal line.'

'So what do you advise me to do?'

'Sit tight. You must take a leaf out of the orientals' book: when they don't know what to do, they just sit and wait.'

This reminded me of my father, who always used to say: 'If you don't know what to do, don't do anything, just wait.'

On the fifth day, at a quarter to twelve when we were just looking forward to a nice lunch, the locks rattled and an unknown sergeant came in. He asked which one was me, and said: 'Bring your things.' I had my things – my coat and my briefcase – with me, was ready in a trice, and followed him out thinking I was being taken to the Georgian again to translate letters. But as I stepped into the corridor, I could see that it was something else. I was surrounded by Prague Russians, most of whom I knew. It was a case of democratic even-handedness: it didn't matter who you were, you ended up in a Soviet gaol. 'Defencists' and 'defeatists', supporters of Hitler and opponents, were now all together, all had been shorn and shaved by the NKVD.

Someone uttered the dreaded word *etap* ('transportation to camp'). At the time, I did not know its ominous meaning for an arrested person. Savitsky later wrote to me that he had seen a man drop dead with fright on hearing the word. But we didn't understand this at the time, and for me the word *etap* just meant that we were being taken somewhere. So the hope by which I had lived these few days, namely that since I hadn't committed an offence I would be released, was fading. I did not have time to register who was there exactly, but they were all familiar faces, most of them with stubble, but some of them had already been shaved like me; I'd been shaved in the morning and that's why I had assumed I was going to the Georgian, because for some reason he always summoned me on shaving days.

The order was bellowed: 'Listen for your name and move when you hear it!' They started shouting out names forming the first detachment, which we saw being led off and loaded into a vehicle. Then they called out the second detachment, which I was in, and we all went outside and were surrounded by guards with submachine-guns as though they expected a riot. About twenty prisoners and five guards got into a truck with a tarpaulin cover. A major or captain in field dress was standing by our vehicle, then got in next to the driver. The tarpaulin was pulled down so that we couldn't be seen from the street, or see the street ourselves, and we were off.

Judging by the sounds, we were going through the centre of Prague, at first slowly then accelerating. People soon discovered where they could see through cracks in the tarpaulin, and worked out which direction we were travelling in. After half an hour they said that we were going towards the Sudentenland. But we did not turn eastwards, towards the Polish border, we seemed to have entered Germany. Finally, they announced that we must be heading for Dresden.

Part IV: Western Europe

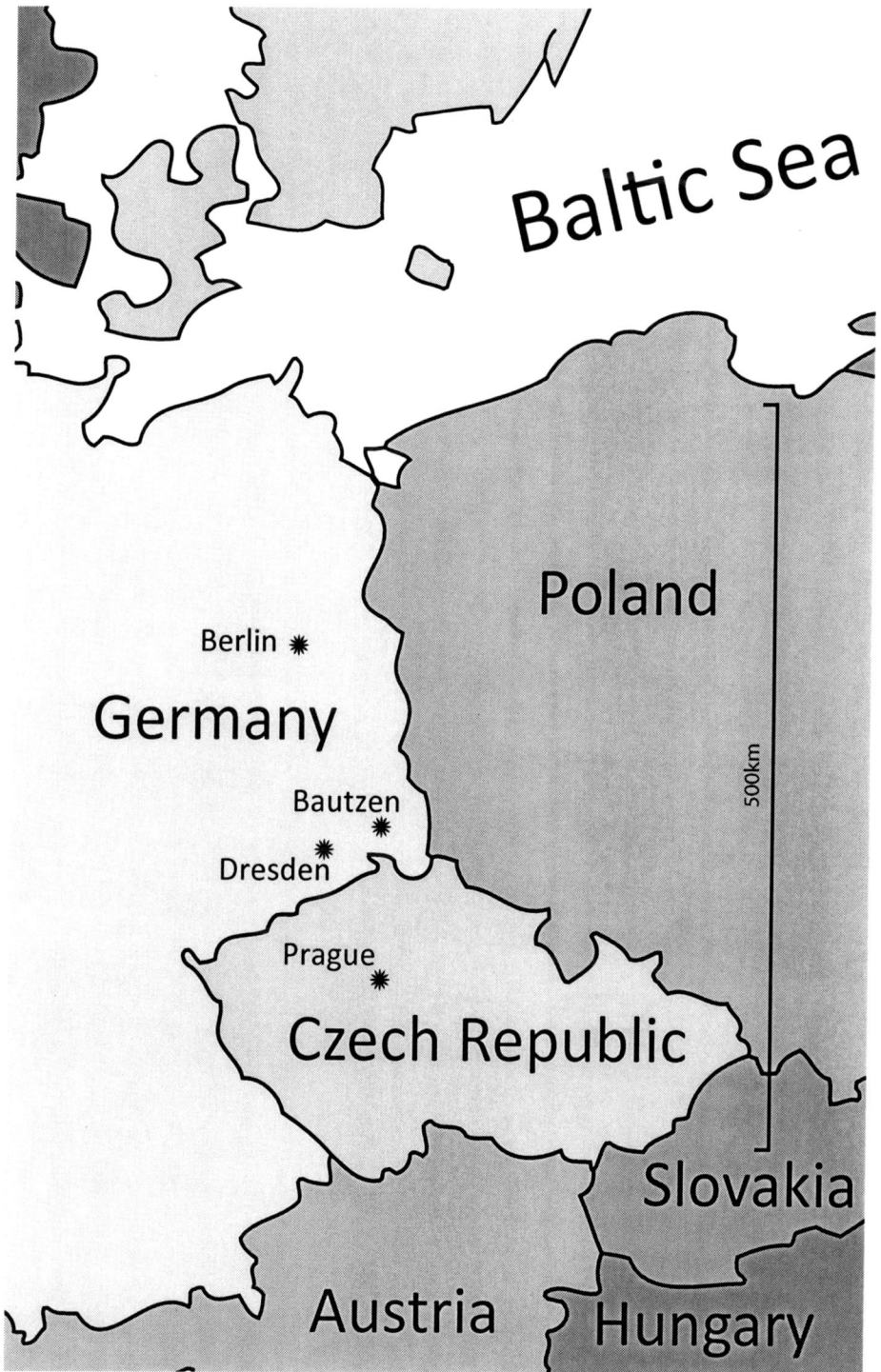

Map 5. Germany and Czechoslovakia.

1

Bautzen

There were several people I knew in the back of the truck, but the centre of attention was Boris Sedakov, whom I greatly respected and with whom I had had many chats in the past. He was a former Moscow barrister, a very clever, well-read, critically thinking man who was one of the driving forces of the 'Peasant Russia' party.

We talked under our breath.

'Mark my words,' he said, 'you will get out; not soon, but you will. I, however, will not, so remember what I'm going to say to you, because you may be the last person I can tell what happened. As you know, I had firmly decided to avoid the Soviet troops even before the uprising began. I therefore made for the West. I was right, but I should have left earlier, so that the Americans found me already living there.'

Sedakov had realized that either the Germans would drown the uprising in blood, or the Soviet Army would extend its patronage to Prague. The Vlasov interlude prevented the Germans from butchering Prague, and Sedakov got as far as the American zone. 'This was where I made my mistake,' he said. 'I should have laid low in a Czech house and moved into the zone at night, but I decided to do everything legally. I was tired, and I thought the Americans would have interpreters.'

He went up to the Americans checking documents at the gate, a lieutenant looked at his papers, didn't understand anything because Sedakov had a Nansen passport, and asked him: 'Nazi or democrat?' Sedakov replied 'Democrat'. 'Ah,' said the lieutenant, and pointed to the left. Sedakov went to the left, but this was where the Soviet gate was. The Soviets saw him and shouted: 'Halt, who goes there? Where are you going? That's the Americans there! Follow us!' And they led him off. They looked at his papers, wrote down his name, and decided that he was 'attempting to cross without permission from the Soviet to the American zone' – an offence. He was kept in a cellar run by SMERSH and sat there for almost a fortnight.

Suddenly he was called for interrogation. His interrogator, a major, stood up as Sedakov entered, said: 'I'm so pleased to meet you!', and shook his hand. Sedakov was bemused, but the major sat him down and exclaimed, 'Goodness, what a state you're in! How did that happen?' – and called an NCO, gave him orders, and within ten minutes Sedakov had been shaved, had his hair cut, put in a hot bath, and given clean linen. When he reappeared before the major, the latter said: 'That's better. I expect you are hungry?' 'Well, I…' said Sedakov, and was brought a first-rate breakfast and a glass of 'Chekist tea'. After that, the major offered him a cigarette. Sedakov did not smoke, but he took one for sheer joy. The major said:

'I am delighted to see you. Do you know who I am?' 'No.'

The major gave him his name and explained: 'I'm from Moscow. I'm the officer who has been shadowing "Peasant Russia" in recent years. I've got all the gen on you. If you are rested now, let's have a chat.'

They chatted for three days and all that time, as Sedakov put it, he lived like a prince. He was nourished and pampered, was shaved once a day, and from morning to night he conversed with the major, who displayed such a superb knowledge of 'Peasant Russia' that he remembered some events in its and Sedakov's life better than he did himself! It is interesting that he had flown to Prague, gone to Sedakov's flat, and even slept in his study on the very settee Sedakov had recently slept on, as the latter's wife and son had left for the provinces long before the uprising. 'I slept there,' the major said, 'so as to get an idea of your psychology.' Clearly this was one of the Soviet Sherlock Holmeses' 'techniques'. Sedakov chuckled: 'He looked at my books...but all the books that were any good had already been taken off to the sticks. When I told him this, he was a bit deflated.'

They also talked about me, since my article 'Culture in Exile' had been published in *Znamya Rossii* ('Russia's Banner'), the last magazine 'Peasant Russia' produced. The major surmised that all the items signed 'N.A.' or 'N. A-v' were by me, but Sedakov explained to him that I'd had nothing to do with 'Peasant Russia', I'd simply made a guest appearance in an issue devoted to culture, and the initials stood for Nikolay Antipov, who really was one of their contributors. 'They'll let you go,' Sedakov repeated, and asked me to pass on everything he had told me to his wife and son when I got out. I memorized his wife's address and when I got out I sent her a postcard, but there was no response.

We were approaching Dresden. Like all Russians, our guards were emotional people, not intellectual, and they put everything they saw into exclamations: 'Cor, it's been bombed to pieces!' 'Ruins and more ruins!' 'Look at that for a miracle: two buildings still standing, one's a prison, what's the other?' 'A Russian church! That's in one piece, too!' Subsequently, in Berlin, people told me that it really was regarded as a miracle. The whole city of Dresden had been flattened, but the Russian church and the prison had survived. Why? What was the historical irony in that?

We spent the night in that prison, which was all iron inside like the ones you see in American films, and there was even a flush toilet in every cell. However, ten of us were crammed in a cell designed for a maximum of two, and again we were given nothing to eat. Either we had been given no supper in Prague because they wanted to starve us a bit, or it was part of a typical Soviet fiddle – the food was signed out, but since we were leaving no-one would know it hadn't been cooked and the prison staff would whip it. In Dresden at noon the next day another *etap* was announced and we all groaned, because again we were being taken away from a meal. So they gave us a bowl of thin cabbage soup each, and off we set again.

Our group remained the same: twenty of us, including a woman. We drove eastwards, towards Poland, and began to fret. The Soviet guards did not know where we were going either. But we had some connoisseurs of the German landscape among us and they worked out that we were en route to Bautzen, thirty miles from Dresden.

At three in the afternoon we drew up in front of some massive gates and towers. It was like a fortress. Officially it was 'Special Camp Number 4 of the Occupying Forces', which may have been designed to fool the Allies that it wasn't a concentration camp. In fact it took 7000 people and was currently full.

We were ordered to form up in fours, we were marched through the gates, which were slammed shut behind us, and we gasped: before us was an enormous parade ground, green, with a grid of dead-straight pathways on it just wide enough for four people. They led to five multi-storeyed blocks in red brick with bars at every window. Inside, hordes of people with long hair and bony arms rushed to the windows to watch us silently from above as we walked in shock along the paths, following an NCO. 'My God, where have we ended up?' many of us muttered. At this moment the girl suddenly said firmly and clearly: 'Don't lose your heads. Courage!' This brisk admonition did make us pull ourselves together.

The vast majority of the prisoners – thousands – were Germans, there were about 120 Russians, and amongst these the Prague group predominated. We were marched to block three, the girl was hived off, and we were put five to a cell. From the German notices on the walls it was clear that the prison had been used for young offenders, one to a cell.

For the first time, they inspected my briefcase. It contained a torch that *mama* had put in, which could shine in four different colours. The soldiers and sergeant forgot everything and grabbed it. 'Don't be offended,' the sergeant said, 'we're taking it because you're not allowed to have it, but I'll give you some tobacco in exchange.' And he brought me a pile of tobacco leaves, a sheet of *Pravda*, and some matches. So my torch immediately did everyone else in the cell a good turn, because I didn't smoke but they did. Again I experienced the basis of Soviet existence: *blat* (you scratch my back and I'll scratch yours). Two days later I had another instance. A lance-sergeant came into our cell, saw my splendid yellow leather briefcase, and said: 'I'll swap you that.'

'For what?' I asked.

'What you like. You seem short of underclothes, so I'll get you a change, and I can give you a loaf of bread and some tobacco.'

'But what do you want a briefcase for? And what am I going to do without one?'

'I'll get you a briefcase, a German one, but it won't be as posh as that.'

'But why do you want it?' I insisted.

'Well, it's superb leather, I want to make myself a pair of shoes out of it!'

I sensed that if I didn't agree I would make an enemy, so I relented and he brought me the underclothes, a loaf of bread, a huge pile of tobacco leaves, a black briefcase which I still have, and even a nice shirt. Thus *blat* relations were established with the lance-sergeant as with the sergeant, and we did each other favours.

At first it was boring in this prison. They got us up very early, because everything was run according to Moscow Time: when we got up it was six in the morning in Moscow, but in Bautzen it was three, pitch black, and the stars were still out. Very soon they put up latrines along the pathways. You were taken out there in the morning, performed, came back to your cell, and were locked up for the night at six p.m., i.e. nine Moscow Time.

But soon there were interesting developments. Bogolepov, the sergeant-major in charge of the stores, shouted through our spy-hole: 'Have you got any engineers in there?' 'Yes!' we answered. 'There's something up with my refrigeration unit,' he said. 'Can you fix it?' 'We'll have to have a look at it!' we said.

Three quarters of an hour later he returned with permission to take Zelyony, Batrakov and Pivovarov from our cell, and they fixed it. Bogolepov rewarded them on the spot and they came back laden with all kinds of food, even sausage. After that, Bogolepov and his superiors took a shine to our engineers. The electricity plant had been got going again by a German engineer called Knüpfer, but there were lots of other things that needed doing, for instance most of the windows in the prison had no glass in them and autumn was on its way. The authorities suddenly decided, therefore, to create a team comprising all the engineers, all of our cell, and me. A lieutenant came along and said to me: 'They say you're a doctor of philosophy.'

'Yes.'

'So can you write big?'

'Big?'

'Yes. We're getting together a work-team and you'll have to write the notices for them, and they've got to be *big*!'

Big it would be, then. We were given two splendid rooms: one for Shcherbachev, leader of the team, and one for four of us, with actual bunks to put our matresses on, blankets, running water, flush toilets, and even a shower. Not so much a prison, more a holiday resort!

We immediately had to find skilled workmen, because we were told to form three forces – a foundry, a joinery, and an electrical workshop. Obviously, we had to find them among the Germans, and for this purpose I and others designed a questionnaire. We found about 300 qualified workers, which would be more than enough to get the workshops going and make the various things needed to put windows in and extend the electricity to the furthest blocks. We got on with it.

We had been treated specially, yet we were the first to start stealing. It is amazing how the socialist system corrupts people. We had been given our own beds, but our rations hadn't been increased. It was obvious that they weren't giving us all they should, but using it for their own *blat*. On the other hand, Bogolepov needed the engineers' help all the time, so he started 'feeding them up' to keep in with them. The first day that we went out as a work-team Pivovarov spotted a large potato field inside the prison. No-one was working on it, so he dug up a cauldron-full and boiled them for us. This was a great luxury. Pivovarov often dug them up, and when I said to him, 'One day you're going to get caught – you can be seen from the commandant's office', he said, 'So what, we'll have had some meals out of it.'

On New Year's Eve (which wasn't, of course, officially celebrated) Pivovarov and Batrakov suddenly said to me: 'Would you like to come to supper?' 'Supper?' 'Yes, in the room where the engineers live, after our official evening meal, the management'll be doing their own thing, so no-one will come round to check us.' Our whole work-team went, the other Russians couldn't be invited because they were locked up in their cells, but we could walk about in the block, and even within the prison, because we were assumed to be on 'work-team' business.

The meal was fantastic – for a start, it included alcohol. This was *sivukha*, raw vodka, moonshine with a strong smell, but quite drinkable. Then there was a piece of meat, not very big, but still meat, and fried potatoes, and sweet kasha of almost the very best. We drank two bottles and got tipsy. I said: 'Thank you very much! Now let us in on the secret: where did all this come from?' We had already noticed that Pivovarov and Batrakov enjoyed special status – they occasionally had *Droog* cigarettes, the occupying army's ration made from good tobacco. And they always had plenty of bread and had acquired good suits, presumably by barter. What was going on?

What they told us filled me with admiration and horror. After they had become buddies with Bogolepov and he'd given them the bread to swap for suits, he suddenly said: 'Comrade engineers, as you can see there's a shortage of vodka, and everyone would like some. Do you think you could make a small distillery, which we could set up in the coal cellars of the electricity plant? The only person who goes there is Knüpfer, and he's one of us.' So they did, and the moonshine was bottled by Bogolepov, and every morning as he left the camp to fetch milk from the prison dairy he would take these bottles with him, and when he returned after lunch he would bring them back as though from the Germans outside, and sell them to the officers. The latter felt that if alcohol had been found that was a good thing, where it came from they didn't care, and they'd prefer not to know.

Things went on like this for three months, by which time the officers had provided Bogolepov with quite an income. He himself didn't drink, and from time to time he would give a half-bottle to the NCO who controlled the entrance-exit point, and others, just to keep them sweet too. I was flabbergasted by the enterprise of our engineers, and especially Bogolepov, but I was also worried. None of us in this prison had been charged with anything; but if this were found out it could trigger a massive case against all the Russian émigrés. I was afraid they could get us on many counts: embezzlement of socialist property, morally corrupting the Soviet armed forces, exploiting the trust placed in us as a work-team – the list would be endless. The next day, when we'd slept everything off, I had a serious talk with Zelyony, who I think was the most restrained of the engineers. I outlined for him the kind of trial that this illicit moonshine production could lead to, and he understood entirely. The fact is, the Soviet and émigré ways of looking at things often did not coincide, and what from the émigré standpoint seemed a joke was treated extremely seriously by Soviet people and vice versa. I said that I thought the only way out was gradually to wind it down, to tell Bogolepov that the apparatus had broken and they couldn't get the part, then to dismantle the distillery so that it couldn't be found as a unit. Zelyony agreed, and by February 'Operation Moonshine' was over.

On a couple of occasions we witnessed parcels from relations being distributed to the German prisoners. Usually the relations came to the prison gates. How they knew where their loved ones were, I don't know, but they usually came to the right place, gave in their parcels, these were left to accumulate, then handed out at particular times. Those who got them were in seventh heaven, the others envious. After the second occasion we grumbled amongst ourselves: why doesn't anyone send us Russians parcels, why don't our relations know where we are?

The only person who could look at our files and addresses, and see that we were not a Hydra of counter-revolution and hadn't collaborated with the Germans, was the captain in charge of the records section. He occasionally visited our team office. He liked a game of chess, and it was always possible to slip in some request to him whilst playing. So we sowed in his mind the idea 'If the Germans received parcels, why can't we?'

By profession he was an oil-man, and he told us that he hadn't joined the 'organs' voluntarily, he'd been drafted into them when war broke out. His attitude to them and all of us was cynical, although he didn't seem to have anything actually against us.

Eventually the captain informed Shcherbachev that all the Prague Russians should write letters immediately and give them to him, the captain. He was going to Czechoslovakia next day and would post them from that side of the border, because Germany was occupied and virtually cut off from the rest of the world. I penned one of the most mendacious letters of my life, because I knew the 'organs' would read it first. I blathered about working hard, being 're-educated', and God knows what. But I added that if anyone was coming to see me I would very much like to have some garlic; a reference to the fact that we had few fresh vegetables and were in need of vitamins. The captain borrowed a car and was gone for three days.

Several weeks later I was sitting in our office when someone rushed in and said: 'You've got a visitor!' I bolted out and saw that several people from Prague had arrived, including Olga Doskářová to see me. She explained that *mama* had got my letter, but because she was an émigrée she wouldn't be able to get a visa, so it was decided to declare Olga my official fiancée. She had travelled for two days in terrible conditions and it was wonderful to see her. She had brought from *mama* a small icon and psalter, both of which I still have, plus some garlic, socks, underwear, and warm clothing, which would be very useful as winter was just round the corner. The visitors were able to stay two hours, during which we scribbled down notes for them to take, without asking permission, and above all were able to tell them how things were. I stressed that none of us had been indicted, so there was hope that sooner or later we would get out. Olga told me that my mother had stood on the Institute's balcony for two days waiting for me to return as the major had promised. I explained that this may not have been his fault: new factors may have intervened. She said that Prague was in chaos, no-one was doing anything, all the more or less prominent people had been arrested, and no work was going on at the Institute. Finally, Olga and I kissed, I asked her to look after *mama*, and above all to keep *mama*'s spirits up.

We never received any more visits, but this was a fillip. Every so often a rumour went round that the engineers were being taken back to Prague, or that the Germans would be amnestied on particular Soviet anniversaries. Nothing ever came of these rumours, but I think that they were planted by the authorities partly to bolster prisoner morale. Batrakov and Pivovarov were absolutely convinced that they were going to Prague and made two suitcases with false sides and bottoms which they packed with wedding rings, watch chains, gold and silver that they had swapped for food and so forth with the Germans and were intending to take out with them 'to make their fortune'. But this was as dangerous as building a radio and listening to foreign broadcasts, which other engineers were doing. I tried to reason with them, but to no avail. Our team was obviously beginning to fall apart. Some of the engineers hated Shcherbachev, because he tried to lord it over them. Pivovarov once punched a German in the face because he hadn't done something properly, and this shocked us deeply. Then an old Kalmyk of whom we were very fond died of illness and a broken heart. We weren't allowed to bury him, but were told to construct a metal box on wheels in which his body was taken to a crossroads outside the camp, and he was buried there. It appalled us. Zelyony had made a headstone for him, but we were ordered to take it back to the camp, so the grave was unmarked.

Gradually I began to be gnawed by anxiety. I felt that I had to precipitate a change in my situation, but I couldn't see how. This was probably the background to a dream I had which seemed to me prophetic and filled me with fresh hope.

In my dream I was sitting at my desk in the work-team office, which was on the first floor of a two-storey barrack. The ground floor held building materials and we didn't go there. Ten steps led up from it to our floor, which was basically one long storeroom, but if you turned sharp left at the top of the stairs you were in our office. Sitting there, I suddenly heard someone enter the barrack and start very slowly and heavily to mount the stairs. And I knew that if this person turned to go into the office and saw me, I was finished. I felt this with every fibre of my being, and I could hear him getting closer and closer, now he was at the top on the tenth step, and...the footsteps receded. I shouted out in my sleep, 'Thank God! He didn't see me!', and my cry woke Zelyony. He shook me and said: 'Nikolay Yefremovich, wake up, you're having a nightmare!' I did wake up, I recounted the dream to him, and he laughed: 'You must have eaten too much at supper!'

I turned over, went back to sleep, and the dream continued. This time I was in the storeroom, where there was a gangway down the middle with paths off it to the shelves. I was standing by a shelf close to the gangway, when I suddenly heard someone coming down the gangway towards me. And again I knew that if this person turned to me, I was finished, but if they missed me I would regain my liberty. I peered out and saw something white approaching, akin to the ghost of the Queen of Spades in Tchaikovsky's opera. This Queen of Spades seemed to symbolize death to me, and suddenly I realized I knew her: it was Mrs Matsova, who had once been a soloist at the Mariinsky opera house, lived on the same street as us in Tallinn, and visited us in Prague. Would she spot me? She didn't, she walked past, and melted into the depths of the barrack. Again I shouted, 'Thank God, I'm going to live!' I started weeping in my sleep, again Zelyony woke me up, again I told him what I'd seen, and he said: 'Yes, you really must have overeaten!'

This dream bucked me up. Together with the prayers that I said secretly every evening – secretly because I did not expect others to understand my feelings – it suddenly gave me a sort of confidence. Not that the news now was good. There were rumours about people being transported eastwards. Knüpfer told us that trains had arrived from the east with goods vans whose floors were deep in human excrement; so they had been used to transport prisoners. We got on well with the soldiers in the camp, most of whom had been drafted into the 'organs' because they had been injured or wounded in action, and they told us that demobilization was underway and would definitely affect us. Either we would be freed, or we would be taken eastwards. Something, it seemed, was just about to happen.

One day I was sitting alone in the office when the captain suddenly appeared and as usual offered me a game of chess. I played a robust opening, which made him think, but then he found the right moves and won. 'Hm,' I thought, 'why don't I have a chat with him?'

'Citizen captain,' I said, 'may I ask you something?' And I told him how I had been arrested, how the first major had said he couldn't see an indictable offence, but that I had 'black marks' against my name, etcetera, and I asked the captain if he would check this in the records. He said he would, and he did! About three days later he called again for a game and said: 'I had a look, and you're right. You've got a clean slate, they simply didn't manage to process your release in time. I'll see to it that you get sent to Dresden, that's the only place where they can do it, we can't release anyone here, but I can draw their attention to you. Don't mention it to anyone yet, in case Dresden doesn't react.'

I thought he must be lying like everyone else. Ten days later, a sergeant-major suddenly comes to our room and says: 'Get ready to leave tomorrow for Dresden. The captain's just rung and told me to warn you. Be ready by half past ten.'

It caused a furore. But as always, things turned out differently: they came for me at nine-fifteen. This wasn't such a bad thing, because everyone who wanted to give me their address and write illicit notes for me to take – they all recommended I hide them in my socks or shoes to get them through – was too late. I already knew my room-mates' addresses by heart, of course.

I think it was the eighth of May, International Women's Day, because the sergeant-major said: 'Scrubbers Day's a lucky day for you, you're getting out!' They all seemed to think I was being released, but I didn't, although I was encouraged: the captain had moved my case on. I didn't see him and couldn't even thank him. At the same time, I was perturbed: perhaps they were just going to investigate further, in which case I might be cleared and released, but I might not. I might get longer!

It was an emotional farewell. By nine-thirty I was at the gates, no-one searched me, in fact they gave me a larger piece of bread than usual, some cooked meat, and other food. Yet another half-ton truck was waiting. An unfamiliar lieutenant got in beside the driver and I sat in the back with an elderly German and a guard with a submachine-gun.

We set off very slowly towards Dresden. The roads were covered with snowdrifts and obviously saw little traffic. The lieutenant, the driver and the guard decided to shoot for partridges along the way, and bagged half a dozen. We stopped to stretch our legs and the lieutenant told me some of his war experiences whilst I took a bite of my provisions. One incident made me shudder.

He was escorting a group of prisoners somewhere in Central Russia during or after the war, when he discovered that two were missing – they'd escaped. 'Well,' he told me, 'according to regs I was responsible, I could have been topped for guarding them badly. So we nabbed two peasants who were coming along the road, they kicked up a shindy, so we said to 'em: "One squeak from you and you'll get these revolvers in your head." So they shut up.' I said to him: 'But that was illegal!' 'Ye-s, but I'd delivered the prisoners, now they could sort it out…'

I was horrified and even looked at him warily. 'My God,' I thought, 'he's shooting these partridges and all of a sudden he's going to finish us off and say we were escaping.' Fortunately the driver was a decent chap and I knew the guard, so we ought to get to Dresden all right.

It took us five hours. The outskirts were less demolished than the centre, but there was snow everywhere, the streets hadn't been cleared, and the general impression was very dilapidated. Wherever you looked there were placards celebrating Red Army Day.

2

Imprisoned at Dresden

The 'Remand Centre of the Investigative Section of the Occupying Forces Administration' where I was detained consisted of two villas and a courtyard. My cell was designed for about a dozen people and when I arrived there was only one person in it, a German. But it was underground and the air was stagnant and foul.

Contrary to expectations, my stay here proved long and debilitating. The day after I arrived I was interrogated by a colonel in a building down the street. He was middle-aged, relaxed, and even told me his name, which I promptly forgot. He gave me to understand that he had worked in the 'organs' since the days of the GPU, i.e. had survived all the changes of power. He had all my papers and asked some fundamental questions. How, for instance, did I explain that the different émigré political groups had 'proposed' to me so often? I said that I thought they all wanted to have their own historian – there weren't enough arts people in the emigration, so someone who knew Russian history and could write was useful; but I wasn't flattered by their approaches because I knew that if I joined their organization I would have to give up my academic work. He then started asking me in detail about my relations with NTS...

After that, I was taken to a different floor of the same building twice a day to write my 'political biography' under guard. For the first couple of days I wrote fast, then I put the brake on, to drag it out. On the fourth day they didn't call me, another two days passed, then suddenly I was told to shave and was taken to the colonel, who told me that 'the general' wanted to see me.

The colonel and I went to another building surrounded by sentries and entered a hall with a large table at one end and about forty officers standing round the walls. At first we stood at one end of the table. The general entered, sat down at the other end, motioned to the colonel, and the latter told me to sit.

The general opened his mouth and I discovered he was a true proletarian: he stressed words in the wrong place and used ungrammatical forms.

'Do you know where you are?' he asked.

I said I didn't.

'You are with Soviet Military Intelligence.'

This was a lie, but he continued:

'We want to build a profile of you so we can decide if to send you to the Soviet Union as a citizen with full rights, or leave you abroad to get on with your profession as before. What would you like to do?'

'Citizen General,' I replied, 'the decision is in your hands, I shall be glad to return to my mother country, which I hardly know because I've been abroad since I was a child, but if you recognize that I must work here, then I shall attempt to vindicate the confidence placed in me and work as I did before.'

The colonel wrote all this down.

'Do you know many languages?' asked the general.

'No.'

'Which ones do you know?'

'Russian, of course, German, Czech, Estonian, and I can read French, Serbian and Bulgarian.'

'There, you see, you know loads!'

He grinned triumphantly and the officers with him.

'Is what you wrote in your biography true, that you never opposed the Soviet Union in an organized fashion?'

'I have never been a member of any émigré organization.'

'We will verify that and decide about you. Have you any complaints?'

'No, Citizen General, the Soviet security organs have done me no wrong, excepting, of course, that I should like to get out as soon as possible.'

'An understandable desire,' said the general.

The conversation lasted about twenty-five minutes. He obviously knew the contents of my chats with the colonel, but I couldn't work out why he had dragged me before all these officers. I expected things to move fast now, but the phrase 'we will verify that' was ominous.

I went back to the cellar, where there were soon five of us and suddenly another seven, including a Russian German. I sensed that he was a stool-pigeon put there for my benefit. He was always coming out with anti-Soviet diatribes, so I defended all things Soviet. He was in the cell for five or six weeks, then vanished. The cells were cold and stuffy, we were not taken out for exercise, and the boredom was excruciating. To make matters worse, they kept changing the staff.

The senior warder was sergeant Smirnov. He used to shout: 'I've got a testimonial from Beria himself! For me, killing a man's like swatting a fly!' A terrible thing to say, but he was popular with the inmates – he was considered 'fair'. He would let us all out in the morning to queue to use the WC rather than the *parasha*. At first there was a whole telephone directory in this lavatory, then they started giving you two pages each. He was also fair with the food and never stole any for himself.

A more complicated case was another sergeant, who had a whole iconostasis of medals on his chest. He had been a crack shot during the war, but was wounded. He was edgy, brutal, and loathed the prisoners. The doors to our cells were like gigantic gates, with iron bars across them – you'd think they were keeping elephants or rhinoceroses in there – and when he opened them in the morning he would swear filthily. He had the disgusting habit of creeping up to the cell door and spying on us through the hole. However, after a few months I recognized the clink of his medals as he crept along, and could warn everyone. If they were lying around, sewing, or playing chess with pieces made of dough, they would quickly sit on their bunks looking innocent. He was difficult and unpleasant to talk to. I asked him once what he had got his medals for, but he was uncommunicative.

Then suddenly we became closer. The prisoners were eating particularly badly at this time. Either food was being kept back, or people were too lazy to distribute it properly. They gave us pearl barley that had no fat in it, so it formed a solid mass in your stomach. After a couple of days I had pains everywhere, couldn't eat this 'pearl' any longer, and went over to bread. The sergeant noticed this and asked me why. 'My guts won't take it,' I told him. He looked at me, thought, and said: 'If you don't eat, you'll snuff it.' I said nothing. After a while, they brought us 'pearl' again, and again I didn't eat it. 'Not eating it?' he said. 'No.' 'Then you'll snuff it.' At this point I exploded. 'Snuff it, snuff it – we're all going to snuff it! It's just a matter of time, some sooner, some later!' I refused it a third time, too. 'What a mule,' he said. 'You won't get far on bread.' I said nothing.

The next day during the 'dead hour' when Comrade Stalin was resting and all the 'organs' in the Soviet Union and its occupied territories with him, the bolts suddenly scraped back, the enormous keys ground in the locks, and our iron gates opened. The sergeant was there and said: 'Andreyev, come here.' I assumed it was to interpret in an adjoining cell, as I did when the official interpreter wasn't immediately available. But he said: 'Sit down, I've brought you something to eat.' Then he turned round and left.

I looked, and saw two covered mess-tins. I took the cover off the first one and...my God! It contained the most fragrant 'soldier's *shchi*' (cabbage soup) with meat in and good bread to go with it, and the second contained properly 'greased' pearl *kasha* with pork scratchings. I consumed them and felt a different person. I could put up with my hardships a bit longer. I mulled over what a good man this unpleasant sergeant was. He may have done it because I was one of the few Russians there and showed an interest in his medals, but I think that what really influenced him was my saying that we were all going to snuff it. When he came back, I thanked him. He said: 'Eaten and forgotten. Don't say a word.'

At Easter 1946 the following happened.

The most tedious days in prison are Sundays. There's no work, no transport, no new arrivals. As the soldiers used to joke, you just 'sunbathe'. We were sunbathing, then, in the cellar, when the bolts scraped back and Vaska, the warden on duty, came in. This remand centre had one liberal feature: when a warden or someone came in on official business, he shouted 'Stand up!', but if it wasn't official he didn't. So Vaska came in and said: 'Andreyev, do you know what day it is?'

'Yes. Sunday.'

'Right. But which Sunday?'

'I don't know.'

'Are you Russian Orthodox?'

The question took me aback. Generally no-one asked me about my faith, so I replied cautiously: 'I was baptized.'

'Well today is Easter Day!' he cried. 'Come on, let's exchange the Easter kiss!' And to the astonishment of the whole cell, where there were now about fourteen Germans, he suddenly kissed me three times on the cheeks. What the Germans thought, I do not know. I said to him: 'Are you a believer?!'

'Well... I'm a fisherman from Astrakhan, at school of course we were told God doesn't exist, priests thought him up, but my grannie said: "Don't you believe it, grandson, God does exist." And when I was called up, the most terrifying thing was going into battle, especially getting up off the ground and advancing in the attack. So I used to say: "Listen, is there anyone up there? If there is, have mercy on me!" And He did! Whenever I went into attack I said that, and I'm alive. I was just a bit concussed, so I got drafted into the 'organs' as a guard. But my gran was right, God does exist...'

I was touched by his childlike faith. He said: 'You're Orthodox, today's Easter, I'm going to treat you. Only don't let the Jerries have any! Give them your helping for supper, but don't give them this.'

He brought along a Russian salad with potatoes, gherkins, beetroot and even spring onions, plus a plateful of good bread, and said: 'Don't eat it in your cell, their mouths'll water.'

So I ate it sitting at a little table in the corridor, then he brought me some light German beer, but I wasn't used to the taste.

'Drink it,' Vaska said. 'Christ is risen!'

I drank it and felt good all over.

They continued to summon me to write long replies to their questions, and occasionally the questions were repeated, presumably to test me. Sometimes I was asked to explain details, for example what 'Tatyana Day' was,[1] how it was celebrated in Prague (there was an all-night ball), who organized it, and how we used the occasion to winkle money out of rich Czechs for our publications. They asked me to write down everything I knew about the Prague Russian History Society, which they erroneously suggested was a political organization, and then about the Russian Free University. I wrote a whole report on this – after all, I'd lectured there and been a member of its research association. I tried to give an honest, factual account of the emigration's cultural work. I haven't a clue where it all went and whether it was taken into consideration, but if they don't destroy their archives it will one day enable historians to reconstruct what went on in the Prague emigration's cultural life.

I was also occasionally summoned to translate documents. The first time this happened a major who was new to me came along and said: 'Remember, you don't know anything about these documents and you won't even say anything to anyone in this building about them. Only the general and I know about them.

---

1   Tatyana Day is 25th January and was celebrated as a students' day, a holiday which dated from the founding of Moscow University in 1775.

We are trusting you. It will be in your interests to stay mum!' Naturally, I did what I was told. I subsequently discovered that this major was the Party organizer in the place.

When I translated documents, I was given what I termed 'general's dinners'; excellent, high-calory meals on the general's orders. And some of the documents were particularly interesting. They had got their hands on the papers of a Czech agent who had worked in the Far East, Manchuria, and the West. These were his reports and contained lots of political rumours. The major's bosses were so interested in the ones about President Beneš and critical remarks he had made about Soviet policy, that they sent the major to check my work by getting me to retranslate *viva voce* whilst he followed my written version. 'Remember what I said about your interests,' he repeated.

Despite this translation work, I continued to languish in the stuffy cellar. Sometimes we were not taken outside for a week. When at last we were, for the first five minutes I felt drunk from the fresh air.

To make matters worse, the Crimean Tartar who was the 'commandant' of the remand centre came by some German handcuffs and decided to put them on people being taken to interrogation. It was nasty: the guards jerked your hands behind your back, put these tight handcuffs on, and you were soon in pain. Moreover, there were no buttons on your trousers and you had lost weight, so they started to fall down and there was nothing you could do to stop them. You had to walk about a hundred yards along the public pavement before you turned into the yard, and as soon as you appeared, with two submachine-gunners behind you, all the ordinary passers-by scattered. I walked along with my trousers slithering down and the guards making ribald comments.

The second time this happened, I was going to see the 'new' major. He looked at my trousers and the handcuffs and said: 'What's this pantomime?' I replied: 'You must ask your subordinates – it's their doing.' 'Well I didn't think it was yours.' He asked me various questions, then stirred things up. The orderlies told us that the Tartar got bawled into the ground for 'displaying inappropriate initiative', because 'this isn't the Gestapo'. The handcuffs were taken away from him and he lived in fear that he had 'exceeded his powers'. A typical paradox of Soviet life: on the one hand the desire to be tough, as Comrade Stalin teaches, and on the other a terror of overstepping the line.

Another officer, also Andreyev, but fortunately for both of us no relation, was very sympathetic towards me and always said that one should fight for one's rights. 'How,' I said, 'if you're in a cell?' 'You can tell your interrogator.' 'I haven't even got one, it's always someone different going through what I have written.' 'Tell them then.' As it happened, this was a time when the prisoners' food was being stolen, so I took this man's advice and when one of the majors interviewing me asked, 'How are things?', as though I could have the time of my life in their cellars, I said: 'The same as usual, but the meals are much worse.' He was interested. 'Why is that?' 'That's your department,' I replied. 'I'm just saying that they've got worse.' 'How, exactly?' 'Our supper's disappeared.' 'Disappeared?!' 'Instead of supper we get coffee with nothing in it.' 'Hm...I don't recall the allowance being changed. Tell me when this happened.' He took down the details and the result was extraordinary. One of the warders had teamed up with the cook, or the cook's assistant, and abolished our supper so that they could give their numerous German girlfriends something to eat. Next morning the warder turned up in a nearby cell without his belt, stripped of his epaulettes, and scared to death.

My case was gathering speed, then suddenly stopped dead: in March 1946 Churchill delivered his Fulton speech about the 'Iron Curtain'. It had a far bigger impact on the Soviet leadership than Churchill or the other western leaders imagined. As prisoners we immediately experienced this: whereas the 'organs' had behaved more or less politely so far, now they started arresting en masse. The Cold War was setting in. Large groups of Germans started arriving at the prison, and the cells were soon overcrowded. We had twenty-six in ours. There were not enough bunks and some people had to sleep on the floor. The food immediately deteriorated, the guards got rougher, and our cases were shelved. We were not taken out, so we became listless and depressed in the fetid air. Sanitary conditions outside the prison were poor and on one occasion a large brown rat appeared and started gnawing, or sharpening its teeth on, the bars.

But these developments brought a constant stream of interesting people. As soon as a new group arrived, we asked them what they could do to amuse us. One of them was Saxony's chess champion and I played him and beat him. I think it was a fluke: he was feeling low, so he fancied forgetting himself in chess, but then he felt even lower. He wouldn't play a second game in case he lost again.

Another German, a painter and former museum director, could tell fortunes. When my time came, he took one look at my hand and said, 'Your father died of cancer'; which was true. Then he said: 'What is happening to you now is an episode, it's not important. You will get out, forget it, get on with your profession, but in a different way from before. You will never return to the place that you think about all the time now, you will go across water, you will marry, you will have children...' – and so on. Naturally, by 'water' I understood

'Atlantic Ocean' and it all seemed so unlikely that I thought to myself, 'The
damned Jerry, he's just trying to calm my nerves.' But a couple of days later I
asked him to read my palm again and he said exactly the same, which he could
not have remembered because he had told at least a dozen people's fortune since.

This shook me. I told him he had a remarkable ability. He liked this, we
became friends, and over the week that he spent in prison being interrogated
he taught me how to tell fortunes using cards and palmistry. Word soon got
round that I could do this and soldiers came to me to find out when they would
be demobbed! The cards don't tell you exact dates, but these people still gave
me a helping of bread, or a packet of tobacco and some *Pravda* cigarette-paper,
which I shared with the cell.

However, I had a case that became rather tricky. A big brawny man, Russian,
was put in our cell, who had been driver to a colonel. The latter had told him
to drive to various places on illicit business and to make sure the milometer
always tallied with where they were meant to have been. As part of the 'organs"
investigation of the colonel, they were now trying to get the driver to tell them
where he had driven his boss, and he was refusing. He was getting more and
more desperate. I didn't know how to console him, so like a fool I offered to tell
his fortune with cards.

The future looked rosy for him: there would be unexpected joy, some news,
a birth perhaps, of a son perhaps, then a long journey, pleasant reunions, and all
the signs were that he was going to be demobbed and no harm would come of
him. He listened, frowned, and said: 'Do you offer a guarantee?'

'No, no.'

'You don't guarantee your own predictions?! I'll smash your face in!'

I looked at his fists and could see that a blow from one of them and I would
be leaving the 'remand centre' in a box.

'Don't worry,' I said to him. 'So far everything I've foretold has come true.'
'I believe you,' he replied, 'but I'm giving you a deadline: if what you say hasn't
happened within a fortnight, I'll pulp your face.'

He was called for interrogation nearly every day and after a week of this
he asked me to tell his fortune again. The cards came out the same again, in a
slightly different order, and I said to him: 'You're going to be demobbed.' 'Oh
yes, into a concentration camp! They're already saying I've had it easy here,
that – ' and he was off. For the first four days of the following week he was
called out, then for two days he wasn't. 'Tomorrow will be a fortnight since I

came to this cell,' he told me, 'and if there's no good news tomorrow you're done for!' He then mentioned that he had once been a professional boxer...

When morning came, he asked me for a third time to tell his fortune, which came out the same, and I was just explaining this when a warder came in and said to him: 'You – interrogation!' He got up, swore heartily at me, and showed me his fist: 'When I return, you'll get this!'

An hour passed, two, three, and he still wasn't back. Supper came, still no sign of him. I was worried. Supper was being taken round by a sergeant I knew, however, and he suddenly said to me: 'A big hug for you from the driver – the boxer! You were right, he's been demobbed; not only that, he's had a letter from home and his wife's produced a son.'

'How did they manage that, on the air-waves?!'

'No, no, she used to work in Dresden, he met her, seduced her, they got married, she was demobbed and sent home, now she's had the boy. Here's some cigarettes for you from the driver.'

I was enormously relieved that this Hercules with the terrible temper had gone out of my life. It was my cue to pack in the fortune-telling. I suspected that it would eventually come to the attention of the bosses that 'Andreyev is practising white magic' and I'd graduate to a concentration camp. The funny thing is, though, that it was so popular; everyone from privates to officers believed in it. Yet this was an army of materialists, inspired by materialistic ideology!

Someone I had endless conversations with was the exception that proves the rule. He had been in the last class to graduate from the Mikhaylovskoye Artillery Academy before the February Revolution, had been sucked into the Red Army, put in charge of a battery, and sent to Poland during the Civil War, where he came close to defecting on horseback. He didn't, however, and made quite a successful career for himself in the Soviet Army, even joining the Party, but being expelled from it in 1922 for 'domestic degeneracy' – he had twice lent his wife an army pony and trap to do some shopping. Not being in the Party probably helped him survive, and in 1939, though once a Tsarist officer, he was promoted to colonel. He was very informative on the rise of Marshal Voronov, with whom he had worked, the popularity of various commanders, and the modernization of the Army. During the Second World War he had commanded the artillery in one of Timoshenko's armies. They had been surrounded, the Germans kept taking masses of prisoners, but the command group of about thirty men kept withdrawing eastwards, and this colonel knew that they had eventually made it because he saw their names in the lists of those decorated. He, however, had been ill, had lagged behind, and been captured in a wood where he had fallen asleep from exhaustion. But when the Germans discovered he had learned German at the Academy, instead of sending him to a camp they employed him as an interpreter in the Ukraine. Of course, they were pushed out of there, and he ended up in Germany. Here too his luck held. The invading Soviet Army treated him well, took him on as an interpreter, sent back a favourable report on him, and he even wrote to Marshal Voronov. Then the day before he was due to return to Russia, SMERSH turned up and he was grabbed by Captain Pugachov, who was interrogating him here.

Pugachov was coarse and abrupt. He accused the colonel of being a traitor: he had 'purposely' dropped behind, 'purposely' surrendered to the Germans, 'purposely' worked for them as an interpreter (although actually he had worked for the self-governing Ukrainians). The colonel's prospects were dire. He argued with Pugachov but the latter stuck to his line, shouted at him, and several times the colonel came back to our cell looking sick. In his view, if you were being questioned by anyone lower than a major, things were bad; it meant that your fate was already decided and it was just a question of drawing up the charge, which was sometimes very long and devious. When Pugachov handed over to a lieutenant, then, a chill ran down the colonel's spine. He argued point after point for a fortnight with this lieutenant, but the document they produced was devastating: the colonel was a traitor and a scoundrel, an 'intellectual' scoundrel who had known what he was doing.

'I don't agree to the charge,' said the colonel.

'Yes you do, you and I drafted it together. Just sign it. You can argue with the public prosecutor later.'

This was a trick, because if you had signed the investigative file the prosecutor wouldn't ask you anything further. So, the colonel told me, he took the pen and wrote: 'Everything in this statement is a lie intended to discredit me. I did not mean any of this and I did not do what I am charged with.' The lieutenant was aghast. At that time SMERSH regarded an investigative statement as a sacred document. It could be altered, but not destroyed. It would have to be kept as it was, therefore, for subsequent alteration, and the lieutenant would be blasted by his superiors. The colonel was sure that he would now be handed over to a new interrogator, who would use physical force. He lived with us for another three weeks without being called out, then one day he was taken away with others on *etap*. After sharing a cell with him for ten months, I was very sorry to see him go. I feared for him.

Later in life I used to say that prison was a second university to me. I learned things there about the human mind that I had not grasped before when living in comfort. I respected myself more, because I discovered I wasn't as cowardly and easily frightened as I thought before I was arrested. Furthermore I had seen the Soviet Union and the Soviet system not from a study, or at diplomatic receptions with vodka and caviar, but from below, as a man with no rights in a 'remand centre'. Its symbol for me would always be a prison, Bautzen, with its bastion-like walls, its watch-towers manned by machine-gunners day and night, and its security strip of about two metres of smooth sand all around the inside of the walls, just as an even wider one ran round the borders of the whole of the USSR.

Sometimes we went to the big prison in Dresden to help out. For instance, I was given the job of ladling out soup to prisoners at meal-times. We were taken there in black Marias packed to bursting. On one occasion there were some young boys with us, including Russians. I was particularly struck by one of ten or eleven, who looked so sad.

'What is the matter, son?' I asked him.

'They've taken my mother and father away.'

'Why have they done that?'

'We were heading for somewhere in a cart, we were trying to get away, now they've taken them and we've lost each other for ever,' he said, brimming with tears.

I felt so sorry for him, and he reminded me of my own childhood. But the worst was still to come. When we arrived at the prison various workers and guards came out to look at them, followed by warders and their wives, and one of the latter said to her husband: 'The poor darlings, they'll come to grief in prison, they'll die!' I stared at the scene mesmerized: it was all regarded as a normal occurrence, none of the Russians lifted a finger, the Germans didn't understand what was going on, and the little boy was beside himself with grief. I thought, whatever they write for their jubilees, victories and leaders' birthdays, the system set up in our country is a sorry sight and this little boy reduces all the achievements of the Russian Revolution to naught, just as Dostoyevsky says that no end can justify a child's tear.[2]

The life of the remand centre continued as before. New prisoners kept arriving, others left on *etap*, whilst I remained and felt my energy and hope

---

2   This is a reference to a point in Dostoyevsky's novel *The Brothers Karamazov* where Ivan
      rejects a divine harmony which costs a single tear of a child.

fading. I was called for questioning less and less often, but I was very frightened when a captain who took over put down in my record that I had been a Russian Nazi. I had to insist he change it. 'Well, that's what your friends at another of our centres are saying about you!' I explained that I had always categorically rejected Nazism, but another interrogator confirmed that some Prague Russian Nazis were saying I had been a Nazi lecturer. Fortunately they described me as having a beard and glasses, which I have never had, but the incident frightened me because it could have led to me leaving on *etap* too.

Suddenly, however, there was a change. One day after the dead hour all the bolts and locks flew open and a general walked into the cell. I just had time to leap up and shout to the others: '*Aufstehen!*'

He was young, unknown to me, and accompanied by his own interpreter. He immediately sent the warders out and asked each person two questions: 'When were you arrested and when were you last interrogated?' He was clearly surprised that I'd been arrested in 1945 and it was now 1947 – all the others were newcomers. He had presumably been sent to speed things up because the prisons were getting choked. When he asked me if I had any complaints, I said merely that I'd been told back in 1945 that I'd be released, and I still hadn't been. This was risky: they could say there was nothing to prove I should be released. But I was desperate. I was beginning to get medical problems from this cellar that remained with me for life, and I had no strength left, physical or otherwise.

I think the general's visit probably helped me by forcing some board or other to recognize that they couldn't keep me here for ever, they either had to charge and sentence me, or let me go. When I got out, however, I discovered that the Czechs had also made a *démarche* on my behalf.

After Olga Doskářová had been to see me in Bautzen, it was decided to approach Beneš and present him with the icon that he had been given by the Soviet government in 1933 and which I had bought on the black market at the end of the German occupation. It was a superb travelling triptych from the early sixteenth century, exquisitely painted and in very good condition, unrenovated. Evidently it had been seized by the Nazis after Beneš slipped out of Prague, and stored somewhere. But when it became clear that the war was ending, the Germans thrust certain things onto the market. They didn't know much about icons, but I remembered this one from a picture published in a Czech magazine and immediately bought it with the idea of giving it back to the president. Now was the time to do this.

Karl Schwarzenberg set out everything in writing and was given an audience with the president's wife. She said that she doubted whether the president could do anything for me, especially as I was not a Czech citizen, but they could talk to the Czech ambassador in Moscow, who at the time was my old friend Professor Horák. Olga told me that Horák delivered a written statement to Molotov's ministry to the effect that Dr Nikolay Andreyev had been loyal to Czechoslovakia throughout the German occupation. This was the most they could say to help me. We think that eventually this document found its way to the 'organs' and met up somewhere with my own papers, and this may have been a factor in deciding my fate.

Surprise, of course, is the name of the game in the 'organs', and on the morning of my release there were no indications of what was going to happen. Out of the blue I was called to the prison office, where an unknown major informed me that the Soviet authorities were freeing me and he started returning my documents. He gave me everything except my address-book and keys. When he got to my doctoral degree, he said: 'What language is that?'

'Latin.'

'Never heard of it.'

'It's a *dead* language.'

He raised his eyebrows as though I was having him on, and I hastened to explain what a dead language was. The fountain-pen he gave me was not my own, but one with its owner's initials in gold Gothic. Once outside, I sold it, as I was afraid that a German might recognize it and conclude I had bumped off a relation of his and pinched his pen.

My release took place without pomp. The NCOs who knew I was going were very good to me and gave me packets of tobacco which I was able to sell on the black market. I was also given my own money back, which included German cash that was still legal tender, so I went out into the world with some capital.

3

Berlin and Freedom

I made for Berlin. Its centre was a graveyard of buildings that I shall never forget. Life was beginning again underground and moving upwards. Small shops and businesses had opened in the cellars and basements, but they had hardly anything to sell. The city's real life was in the suburbs, which were less devastated, and this is where most of the Allied administrations were. It had not yet been divided into East and West. In 1947 military uniforms still predominated on the streets, but there were crowds of Germans from prisoner-of-war camps and tens of thousands of refugees returning home.

Nevertheless, as I discovered on my first day, there was a terrible shortage of men for Berlin's female population. If you were prepared to share the couch of a German lady, you were literally waited on hand and foot: she would do your washing and ironing for you and try to fatten you up, although this was very difficult as black market prices were high. There was a cult of men, especially young men. Of course, morals had been lax in Prague during the war, but for entirely different reasons: '*carpe diem*', because tonight you might be arrested by the Gestapo or killed by an Allied bomb. In Berlin the women wanted a man around, they wanted his sympathy, often his psychological support. Because I was not married myself, I had never realized before how important normal matrimony is to society. I now understood that it was vital and the results of disrupting it were worst of all for women.

From my base in the American camp for displaced persons at Dahlem, I reckoned there were three routes for improving my situation: a Czechoslovak route, a German route, and a western route.

First I went to the Czechoslovak military mission. Soviet officers had told me about it when I was being released. I had kept saying I wanted to go to Prague, but these officers were very doubtful that it would be possible. One of them even said: 'You've been inside for the last two years, you don't realize that Germany is a sealed jar, the only people who enter and leave it are troops.'

At the Czech mission I was greeted with open arms. There were Czechs here who knew the Kondakov Institute, me, and many of my friends. They were over the moon that I'd been let out, and immediately said: 'We really need you, we'll get you a job as an interpreter here straightaway, because our biggest problem is all the interpreting at Karlshorst,[3] we have to go over there at least twice a week, no-one there knows Czech, and we can barely speak Russian.' They promised me a salary and military rations, they stood me an excellent meal in their cafeteria, and a stiff drink. But I said I wasn't sure that they would be able to take me without a Czech passport: I was a Russian émigré and had done a spell in a Soviet prison. 'That doesn't matter,' they replied, 'we'll fix it.'

When I went back three days later, it turned out I'd been right. As soon as the Soviet commandant heard that I was a Russian émigré (he didn't know I'd also been in prison, of course), he objected. He said that the Soviet administration could not accept that, and even showed them his rule book, which specified that

3   Karlshorst was where the headquarters of the Soviet Military Administration in Germany was situated.

18.   Nikolay Andreyev in December 1947 in Berlin,
      several months after leaving prison.

Russian émigrés were not to be used in dealings with foreign missions. The people at the Czechoslovak mission were embarrassed by this, but there was nothing they could do about it.

However, they did do me a favour. They sent a message to Prague to say that I was out, they discovered that Olga Doskářová was working in their London embassy, and they quickly informed her where I was. She told me that *mama* had been taken back to Estonia and Pyotr Khmyrov was my enemy. This man had helped me move the Institute to its new premises but subsequently denounced me to the 'organs' and run around Prague telling everyone I'd been given seven years. Inadvertently I had also let him know I was out, which enraged him and he was saying that if I turned up in Prague he would see to it that the Czechs put me away for longer than the Soviets. Olga warned me, therefore, not to go back to Prague in any circumstances. Although the Institute formally existed, it was not functioning and I'd best keep my nose out. It was good advice. I had to find 'winter quarters' in Berlin.

I now tried the German 'route', which was *Das Slavische Seminar* at Berlin University. I had visited it once before the war, and then corresponded with Professor Vasmer, its head. Vasmer was a famous philologist, a St Petersburg German who had lectured at the University there before the revolution. He was married to a Russian, spoke Russian at home, his German was perfect, of course, and after the Bolshevik putsch he left for Germany. He was erudite and unfailingly kind towards his colleagues. I found the latter at the Humboldt University. *Das Slavische Seminar* had been destroyed by a bomb and lost a lot of its library.

Vasmer was a tall, gaunt man, typically German in appearance, and very absent-minded. Someone once joked that when Vasmer was talking to you his mind was actually wandering in the groves of historical forms of the Slavonic verbs. He rose politely as I entered, and said: 'Dr *Andreyev* from the *Kondakov Institute*?! But you died!'

The times were so strange that I asked him: 'When?'

'Let me see…in December 1945!'

'Where?'

'In Cracow.'

'The rumour is much exaggerated,' I replied. 'I've never been to Cracow!'

Truly a dialogue of madmen. But I am repeating it verbatim, I haven't added a jot. After this exchange, we sat down and without asking me where I had come from or what had happened to me Vasmer said he was pleased to see me because he urgently needed people who knew Russian, Russian literature and Russian history, and he would immediately appoint me to a lectureship in the provinces at Magdeburg University in the eastern sector. I opened my mouth to say my German wasn't good enough, but he cut me short: 'Your German is perfectly good enough, the main thing is that you know Russian and Russian literature.' I should mention that in the Hitler period Vasmer fled to Sweden and taught there for a while, in Stockholm I think.

'Professor,' I said, 'the Soviets won't appoint me, I'm a Russian émigré.'

'We shan't consult them! I'm the one who appoints the teaching staff, they don't understand anything about teaching!'

'But I did a stretch in one of their political prisons.'

'That's irrelevant. They let you out. It'll be fine.'

But I was right again. When he let drop that he was appointing me to Magdeburg, the Soviet authorities immediately told him it was impossible, and not because I had been arrested, but because I was a Russian émigré. He then lost his cool and told them they were obstructing him, that there was a shortage of teachers, some had left for the West, and the authorities were being stupid.

'So,' he told me, 'I shall appoint you in Berlin.'

But this didn't happen either, and for the same reason. However, the whole group of Slavists in Berlin were very well-disposed towards me and I was terribly touched when they all clubbed together and gave me some of their food coupons. I had none at all and they enabled me to buy bread, meat and German sausage. They even offered me a sack of coal.

Meanwhile, I left the American D.P. camp in interesting circumstances.

I was interviewed there by a Captain Dupont, who I had already been warned was a pretty nasty intelligence officer. First he rifled through my wallet, which I took great exception to, and insisted on swapping my Czechoslovak Protectorate stamps and money for a packet of cigarettes. Then he said: Your documents are in perfect order, so you must be from the SS.'

'What?! I don't have a drop of German blood in me, how could I have been in the SS?'

'You're from the SS all right. Let's see if you have a tattoo.'

SS-men had tattoos on their upper arm, so he told me to take my shirt off. This made me livid: 'Go to hell! I'm not doing anything so ridiculous, and if you come near me I'll hit you!'

The captain seemed bemused by this, and said: 'OK, if you think you're not from the SS, fine. But you say you want to go to Czechoslovakia. You keep visiting the Czechoslovak military mission and you speak Czech. So you must listen to what they say there and report it to me. If you go there quite often and put in a report each time, I'll give you a room and we'll pay you a hundred marks a week.'

This made me incandescent, but I did not say anything because I had trained myself not to argue with 'organs'. Instead I went straight to see Father Sergy.

When I arrived in Berlin, without my address book, I remembered that there was a Russian church in a house on Nachodstrasse, and I went to find it. This was not difficult, as there was a group of women beating church carpets outside and talking Russian. As soon as I'd greeted them, one of them said: 'You've just come out of a Soviet prison, haven't you? You'd better go and see our priest!' So I went round the corner to his house and the door was opened by a youthful-looking man with a thick mane of hair, a trimmed beard and an open face like Christ Pantocrator on nineteenth-century icons. He sat me down in his little study and said: 'Tell me about yourself…' I was off, trying to stick to the most important things, but when I paused he said: 'Koka,' – this was a name I hadn't been called since I was a boy – 'how is Ekaterina Aleksandrovna, and I haven't heard of your father for a long time…' I looked at him stupefied, but he smiled and said: 'You've got a poor memory, Koka. You used to visit us at the cotton factory in Tallinn, when my *papa* worked there, and I used to visit your family with him. My name then was Seryozha Polozhensky.' Of course I remembered him! He had gone away to Paris to train in the Russian Theological Institute. So he must have been ordained and sent here… It was a very pleasant reunion.

He immediately understood the problem at the American D.P. camp. 'They're all tarred with the same brush,' he said. 'They're all "gestapoes", whether Soviet or American. They all want to destroy people. Of course you can't stay there. But you need different documents. Let's try in the French sector.'

Father Sergy wrote a letter, sealed it, and told me to take it to a Colonel Bibikov at the French Administration. 'Bibikov's a Kievan,' he said, 'and knows what he's talking about.'

Colonel Bibikov listened to my story and said: 'Yes, I understand. Look at that lot.' He pointed to a heap of pamphlets, fliers and even books. 'They are all instructions on how to treat the victims of Hitler. But there isn't a single instruction about how to treat the victims of Stalin! So this is what we will do. Go back to Father Sergy and ask him to write another letter in French, in which he says that you are working for him. He could enrol you in the choir. Of course it would be a fiction, but we just need a document, then we can register you. If he writes that you are going to get a room in the Russian church house at Tegel, we can register you there and you'll get ration coupons. That'll be your first foothold. Using that, you can go to the police and ask them to change your extraordinary German document, which has "Third Reich" and "Protectorate" all over it, for another one that is issued to stateless persons but is up-to-date. Once you've got that, you should be able to stay in Berlin. Because at the moment you're like a moth on a fence: the least gust of wind could blow you away.'

I hurried back to Father Sergy, who said: 'Thanks for the advice, but I cannot enrol you in the choir. I probably have the biggest church choir in Berlin or Central Europe – about 170 people. In fact there are only four old ladies in it, and they can't sing in tune! One of these days the Germans are going to call my bluff about this choir. But you're a doctor of philosophy. You can become the church archivist. Our archive was destroyed by Allied bombers and I'm not going to start another, but I can still have an archivist, can't I? We can't pay you anything, but as a Russian Orthodox Christian you of course support our church and therefore will take upon yourself the onerous duties of archivist!' And he wrote the letter.

'*Voilà! Très bien*,' said Bibikov when he read it. He initialled it, and a few minutes later I left the French Administration with a piece of paper saying that I lived in the church house at Tegel, was entitled to Category 2 coupons, and worked as the archivist of the Russian Orthodox Church in Nachodstrasse. Elated, I flew round to the German magistracy, was given my coupons on the spot and even some food products, then went over to the church house. Here I learned that three days before Father Sergy had made arrangements for me to be given a semi-basement room with a window at street level. It was clean, recently whitewashed, and had a stove.

Thus I gave Dupont the slip and started a new life in one of the two houses attached to the Russian cemetery church at Tegel, a charming building in the pseudo-Russian style of the reign of Alexander III. The territory was officially Soviet and the priest here was a great pragmatist whose home, in the smaller house, wanted for nothing from Soviet sources. The bigger house came under French jurisdiction. For some reason the French permitted a large number of elderly Russian émigrés to live here. There was a former lady opera-singer, engineers, Tsarist officers – a motley educated society.

Most of my activity, however, was in the centre of Berlin. I had a group of students at Vasmer's, I gave private lessons, and Horst-Yablonovsky helped me publish reviews and a large article on Russian icon-painting in German. I was extremely grateful to him. The article acted as a kind of visiting card: it told everyone that I was out, had shaken the dust from my feet, and found the energy to plunge back into academic work. It did me a lot of good amongst German Slavists and my many Russian friends.

My accommodation and heating were free, electricity was cheap, but I was still short of money. From time to time, therefore, I acted as a delivery man on the black market, for which I was paid ten per cent commission. My professional colleagues were horrified at this, but I saw it as helping people get what they needed and developing the real economy. Even so I was dependent on help from friends, who invited me for meals at least three times a week. There were also ladies of various nationalities who cosseted me and tried to ensnare me. But I was not intending to fall into Hymen's clutches that way. Psychologically, financially and professionally I wasn't ready for it. The period between leaving prison and early 1948 was one in which I was constantly adapting to new circumstances. I felt I was seeking something. What it was I didn't know, nor was I sure I would find it, but that was my underlying feeling.

Then suddenly Smith College in the USA inquired about me as a teacher and Slavist. I was sent a voluminous questionnaire which, since I did not know any English, was completed with the assistance of a Russian lady who worked with the English military administration. She gave me some useful tips. The main one was that when filling in an American questionnaire you must answer most of the questions in the affirmative and superlative. For instance, if they asked whether I could sing solo, or run a choir, I had to answer 'Yes'. I was shocked by this, because it wasn't true; but she said that no-one would mind that, once I was in America the situation would be different, but when I was being selected or given a visa the officials would not hesitate for a moment because I fitted all the boxes on the questionnaire. Consequently I gave the impression of being a universal genius. They also asked me an enormous amount about my domestic arrangements. The Russian lady said it was quite a good thing I wasn't married, because this always raised hopes at the women's colleges that a new teacher would arrive and wed one of them! In that case, I said, it would be better not to go...

The questionnaire was completed and sent off, but things turned out differently. The British, in the shape of Cambridge University, got there first.

One fine day I was summoned to what Father Sergy called 'the British Gestapo', i.e. their political police. He was rather concerned.

'What have you done for goodness' sake?'

'I don't know. Maybe it's something to do with the black market...'

'That's all we needed! First the Soviets put you away for political reasons, now the British are going to jail you for criminal offences. But don't worry: the Russian Orthodox Church will pray for you even if you are jailed as a criminal!'

So I went off to my appointment filled with fear. It was a sombre building and as I approached it my heart sank even further: standing outside were bulldog-like policemen with square jaws, square shoulders, white straps, guns, and a look that said they would sink their teeth in your leg at the drop of a hat and never let go.

I was shown into a hall full of people. 'Right, my dear Nikolay Yefremovich,' I said to myself, 'you'll be sitting here till nightfall!'

I took a seat and got out the newspaper I had prudently brought with me, when my name was called. I looked at my watch: exactly 10.15 as they had said. I was ushered into a booth, where there was a young man in civvies.

'Do you speak English?' he asked me in German.

'Unfortunately, no.'

'Right, we'll speak German. Do you want to leave Berlin?'

Such a point-blank question surprised and even scared me, so I said: 'It depends in which direction.'

'Well, to start with let's say westwards, into the British sector.'

'Where, exactly?'

'Let's assume Hanover.'

'What would I want to do in Hanover? I've got a flat here, I work here...'

Suddenly the young man looked at me intently and said: 'Do you know why you've been called here?'

'No, I don't.'

'Cambridge University is interested in you.'

It was utterly unexpected. I said: 'Thank you very much, but what do they want?'

'They want us to get you out of Berlin – first of all into the British sector, where your documents will be sorted out, and then to England, to Cambridge University. Would that suit you?'

'Good God,' I thought to myself, 'what on earth will I do at Cambridge University if I can't speak English? Probably I'll be some kind of porter...'

Then something flashed through my mind – I am always remembering famous sayings, whether appropriate to the occasion or not. I remembered Marx's words 'the proletariat has nothing to lose but its chains'. But I didn't have any chains, I could go wherever I liked! So I said: 'Yes, it suits me down to the ground.'

'Excellent. Here' – he pointed to a thick file in front of him – 'are the papers on you. I know everything about you, but we have to fill out a questionnaire. To save time, you sign it and I'll fill it in. You'll have to take it for granted that I am acting in your interests.'

'Thank you,' I said, and signed it.

It was a typical questionnaire of our times: two pages; where have you come from and why; wherefore, wherefore were you born; why do you exist; whence did you spring; and so forth.

'That's it, then,' he said. 'But before you go, let's agree that you will tell nobody about this. Except the priest whose house you are living in.'

'Sergy Polozhensky?'

'Yes, tell him what is going to happen. But nobody else. We are assuming that on (he named a day of the week) we shall be ready to fly you out of Berlin. At eleven o'clock that morning a German taxi will draw up at Trautenaustrasse 9, where you will be living. You will get into the taxi and it will take you to the airfield from which you will fly to West Germany. If the flight is changed or anything else happens, you, or rather the priest, will receive a letter on the morning of the same day containing another date.'

He was a serious, polite young man, and wished me 'bon voyage' and a pleasant time in Cambridge. When I got back to Father Sergy, I told him everything in strictest confidence. He said: 'Mm, I've heard of such things, but apparently they sometimes turn out differently: a taxi drives up and takes you to Karlshorst, to the Soviets, and they clap you in jail! Let's pray to God that in this instance you've been told the truth.'

I hinted to my lady friends that I was leaving, but I put the date back by at least a week. It caused a sensation, and what I had feared: 'Stay with me for ever!' But it was too late. My German girlfriend said to me: '*Du hast mich glücklich gemacht*' – 'You made me happy'. A simple yet serious statement, for which I was grateful. I was glad that I had been able to bring happiness to someone, if only a little.

Everything went like clockwork. We were watching from a window when the taxi arrived at eleven. Before that Father Sergy had blessed me and said a prayer for the journey, and I thought of my mother in Estonia. Father Sergy had always said: 'Your mother matters most to you, everything else is less important.' He was right, of course, but how could I help my mother from such a long way away, without knowing exactly where she was, and with no contacts there? I was very grateful to Father Sergy for all that he had done. He said to me: 'You have been through many ordeals. Go forth with faith and everything else will come right.'

We went down to the taxi together and it took me to Tempelhof, where the driver and I got out and he said there was nothing to pay. He accompanied me into the airport lounge and pointed me in the direction of a sign that said HANNOVER.

A British transport plane was waiting outside.

Afterword

Afterword

On the journey to England Nikolay Andreyev learnt the English phrase "Kiss me quick" from a British officer on the aeroplane who spoke to him in German. This was the only English he knew on arrival at a military aerodrome in East Anglia.[1] When his German occupation marks were exchanged, it turned out that he had 10d, in addition to a clean shirt and book about Ivan the Terrible in the small briefcase which he had retained from Soviet jail.[2] He recalled that this was all the subject of a number of jokes at Customs but he remained impassive as he was unable to understand them.

He was met and welcomed by Professor Elizabeth Hill, head of the department of Slavonic Studies at Cambridge University who took him to her house where he met her companion, Doris Mudie. Doris offered to wash his dirty shirt. Later he was taken to his lodgings in Park Parade and told that there would be a Slavonic Society meeting that evening in Corpus Christi. My father made his way there and being unable either to ask the way or to understand the reply, he located the society meeting from the level of noise emanating from a corner of the college. There he met his future students, many of whom had already acquired a knowledge of Russian from working alongside their Soviet counterparts in the armed forces. At his first lecture, he congratulated the audience on their knowledge of colloquial Russian and warned them that if they ever used some of the more colourful expressions again in their studies he would be forced to fail them!

My father was amazed by Britain in 1948. First of all, there were milk bottles on all the doorsteps in the morning and no one stole them. My father said that during the war there had not been a special milk ration for children in the Protectorate so he never drank milk and gave his ration to those with large families. In post-war Berlin, the idea of leaving milk on doorsteps unattended was unthinkable. He was also very surprised that when he asked his landlady for a key she replied that there was no need for one because she never locked the door. At that time, too, bicycles could be left unlocked and no one took them. The respect for law and order behind such attitudes seemed remarkable. It was also clear that the black market engendered completely different attitudes in Britain. Here it had been unpatriotic to deal in black market produce. Within the confines of the Third Reich, and within the Protectorate of Bohemia and Moravia, however, the black market had been a way in which one could circumvent Nazi restrictions and was a patriotic gesture.

Other attitudes, however, seemed more parochial. Professor Hill warned him not to talk of the fact that he had been in a Soviet prison. "People will think

---

1   An account of Nikolay Andreyev's arrival in the UK can be found in 'Your destination is Cambridge', *The Cambridge Review*, vol. C, No 2251 (29 June 1979), pp.176-181.

2   R. Vipper, *Ivan Grozny* (Moscow, 1944).

that you have been a common criminal, they don't understand about political prisoners." For Nikolay Andreyev, for whom the trauma of imprisonment was still very recent, this seemed to emphasize that he did not belong in England where such bitter memories could be belittled in this way. Moreover, almost no one at Cambridge knew or cared much about Russia or Russian culture. My father said that when he arrived in England in 1948, those with left-wing views idolized the Soviet Union, whereas conservatives by and large thought that Russia was backward and dangerous and got what she deserved. One exception to this rule was Sir Ellis Minns, President of Pembroke College. He had spent two long periods in Russia, before the Revolution, and spoke beautiful, expressive and slightly old-fashioned Russian and was an expert on Scythian antiquities. He was an honorary fellow of the Kondakov Institute and had visited Prague before the war. He was extremely helpful and my father always had great respect for his scholarship and was very grateful for his kindness and hospitality.

At weekends and in vacations, Nikolay Andreyev spent as much time as possible in London working in the British Library or visiting Russian friends. The émigré community in London was small by comparison with cities in Europe or America but there were a number of interesting people. Boris Ivanovich Elkin was an international lawyer and a friend of Paul Milyukov, the historian and politician. A highly intelligent man, he was always stimulating company. So too was Semyon Lyudvigovich Frank, a Russian idealist philosopher who had settled in London and whose son Victor was an old friend.[3] With Gleb Obolensky, Nikolay Andreyev produced a Russian newspaper, *Rossiyanin,* in which Andreyev wrote an amusing serial modelled on Gogol's *Dead Souls,* with Gogol's hero Chichikov appearing as a Russian émigré and a Displaced Person.[4]

He also met some people he had known in Prague. Olga Doskářová worked for a time in the Czech embassy in London but had to return home after the Communist seizure of power. He also met Dedio, who had been the Gestapo officer in Prague, at a conference in Germany. They exchanged greetings but when Dedio asked him where he now was and Nikolay Andreyev explained that he was now teaching at Cambridge, a look came into Dedio's eyes which seemed to say that he had been wrong in Prague, when Nikolay Andreyev had been denounced as a British spy. Dedio had thought that was not the case but obviously Andreyev had been a spy all along!

---

3   N. Andreyev, 'Bluzhdaiushchaia Sud'ba' in *Pamiati Viktora Franka* (London, 1974), pp.22-42.

4   I. Belobrovtseva, 'Pokhozhdeniia Chichikova kak prototekst i intertekst; N. Gogol', M. Bulgakov, N. Andreyev' in A. Wozniak and L. Puszak (eds.), *Literatura emigracyjna rosjan, ukrainjcow i bialorusinow* (Lublin, 2001), pp.75-85.

He enjoyed the company of his students, many of whom had done National Service and were slightly older. As well as undergraduates reading for a degree, there were those who were on the rapid courses sponsored by the War Office and designed to produce interpreters for the Cold War.[5] This large number of people engaged in learning Russian meant that such activities as putting on plays in Russian could thrive. Students often helped him when he needed to explain things to his landlady but no one was able to persuade her to give him anything other than tomato soup for supper which he was served every evening for all the six years that he rented rooms in Park Parade. He would never eat tomato soup after that. In 1954, he married one of his students, Gill Huddleston, and they had three children and a very happy family life. He said that my mother made him come to terms with Britain. He felt that he understood Central European society whereas he was never really at home here. Undoubtedly, the fact that to begin with he taught entirely in Russian and learnt English fairly slowly never helped. His English improved in the 1960s when National Service finished and standards of Russian in schools dropped. At that point my father said that first year undergraduates no longer understood him when they first arrived in Cambridge and he had to teach in English.

Although my father's personal life in Britain was very happy, his own verdict on his career was that it had been a failure. Although he was an excellent teacher, and many of those who became the next generation of Slavists in Britain were his pupils, he always regretted that he was never able to exercise his talents and interests in the way he would have wished.[6] Much of this was due to the personality of Professor Hill. Her extraordinary memoirs give little inkling of what it was like to work with her.[7] After his death, she apologized to my mother for not acting justly towards him. My father was astounded when she told him the reasons why she had invited him to Cambridge. She had been told that Nikolay Andreyev had been let out of prison and was the kind of scholar who could enhance the department at Cambridge. Instead of looking at his work, however, she told him that she had cast his horoscope and decided that it fitted

5   G. Elliot and H. Shukman, *Secret Classrooms: An Unknown Story of The Cold War* (London, 2002).

6   The publications: 'To Honor Nikolay Andreyev: Essays on the Occasion of his Seventieth Birthday' in *Canadian-American Slavic Studies*, vol. 13, 1-2 (1979) and W. Harrison and A. Pyman (eds.), *Poetry, Prose and Public Opinion: Aspects of Russia 1850-1970: essays presented in memory of Dr N.E. Andreyev* (Letchworth, 1984) are testimony to the esteem and affection in which he was held by both colleagues and pupils.

7   Jean Stafford Smith (ed.), *In the Mind's Eye: The Memoirs of Dame Elizabeth Hill* (Lewes, 1999).

252 A Moth on the Fence

with the horoscopes of the other members of the department and proceeded with the invitation.

His teaching load in the early days was heavy and could encompass a very wide variety of subjects. His more specialist courses included the history of Kievan and Muscovite Russian, nineteenth century political and social thought as well as seminars on Tolstoy and Dostoevsky for more advanced students. For some time he was on an annual renewable contract and his position at Cambridge was only confirmed when Professor Hill was on leave and Dr Robert Auty, standing in for her, allowed the position to become more permanent. Professor Hill was not a scholar but she was a good organizer and astute enough to see that Nikolay Andreyev was an asset to the department. It was very much to her advantage that for a long time he taught in Russian as had he known more English he would have had a clearer idea of what was happening. When he applied for a Chair of Russian at London University, Professor Hill was on the Board of Electors and she made sure that he did not get the post. He was bitterly disappointed and this was exacerbated by the fact that the position was left unfilled for a number of years. After Professor Hill's retirement, he was not elected to be her successor on the grounds that he was too old. His election to a Readership at Cambridge was also delayed on financial grounds and this affected his pension. All in all, his attitude to the Cambridge establishment was very sceptical. He felt that he was always held in low esteem because he was not an Englishman, not one of them, even though Charles University was older than Cambridge and despite his scholarly achievements. All of this was in his mind when he explained to me that he wanted us, my brothers and me, to speak Russian and to understand his culture, 'but I don't want you to be émigrés. I have been an émigré all my life and that has meant that I have been treated as second class everywhere.'

My father was generally an optimist. He was grateful to Cambridge for providing a haven and allowing many interesting possibilities. He was also conscious that financially he was more secure than he had ever been. He tried to look on the positive side but towards the end of his life, when the composition of his memoirs had meant that he had reviewed so many things, this bitterness about his career was apparent. He remained someone that Soviet scholars were always pleased to meet. He had been delighted when some of his research was published by the Soviet Academy of Sciences[8] The acknowledgement of his Soviet colleagues demonstrated not only the serious nature of his research but also that the history of Russian culture could only be understood if scholars were not divided by political attitudes. He also found meeting many of the dissidents who arrived in the UK from the 1970s onwards very stimulating.

---

8   N. Andreyev, 'Ob avtore pripisok v litevykh svodakh Groznogo', *Trudy Otdela Drevnerusskoi Literatury AN SSSR*, 18 (Leningrad, 1962), pp.117-148.

19.   Wedding of Nikolay and Gill Andreyev, July 1954.

Alexander Solzhenitsyn made a point of coming to see him on his first visit to Britain and asked him to write a history of Russia for Russian school children. Solzhenitsyn's view was that all existing histories were too old or politicized and something more objective was required. My father was pleased to be asked and saddened that age and infirmity prevented him from carrying out this task. He would also have been both pleased and amused that the publication of his memoirs has made him a subject worthy of historical study.[9] The memoirs show how comic and tragic elements in life become intertwined with the everyday and the banal. The subsequent fate of the memoirs would have produced a reflection on the ephemeral and paradoxical nature of success.

In November 1958, Nikolay Andreyev's mother Ekaterina Aleksandrovna Andreyeva arrived from Estonia. After my father's arrest he had not known what happened to her. She had continued to live in the Kondakov Institute for several months but then someone denounced her to the authorities and she was repatriated to Estonia. On arrival there, her first concern was to get a job as this was essential if she was to obtain ration cards and accommodation. She went to the Ministry of Education but was told that they did not employ people like her. As she left the Ministry in a state of considerable anxiety she met the main Inspector of Schools in Tallinn, whom she had known before she left Tallinn during the war, coming up the steps of the Ministry. He welcomed her with open arms saying that he was desperate for qualified teachers. He took her back into the Ministry and into the same office where minutes before she had been so rudely refused employment She continued to teach until her retirement in Tallinn and her state pension included the interwar and pre-Revolutionary years as copies of all official documents could now be found.

She and my father contacted one another again through an astonishing series of coincidences. Another mutual friend, Irina, had emigrated with her family to Australia and was looking for her brother, a musician, Roman Matsov, whom she eventually found by contacting the Estonian Conservatoire. She had learnt that he had survived the war after being told that one of his concerts had been reviewed in a Berlin newspaper. In a letter to her brother, she mentioned that her childhood friend Koka was alive and teaching at Cambridge University. She was unaware that Roman and his wife Asya were looking after my grandmother

9   P.N. Bazanov, 'Russkii uchenyi-emigrant N.E. Andreyev v Anglii', in O.B. Vasilevskaia (ed.), *Kul'turnoe nasledie rossiiskoi emigratsii v Velikobritanii (1917-1940-e gg.)* (Moscow, 2002), pp.158-65; I. Belobrovtseva, A. Rogachevskii, 'Estonskie gody N.E. Andreyeva: Materialy k bibliografii', *Diaspora: Novye materialy* (St Petersburg, 2002), vol. II, pp.687-702; V.G. Vovina, 'N.E. Andreyev – issledovatel' russkikh letopisei' in *Perekrestok kul'tur: Mezhdistsiplinarnye issledovaniia v oblasti gumanitarnykh nauk. Sbornik Statei.* (Moscow, 2004), pp.32-50.

20. Catherine

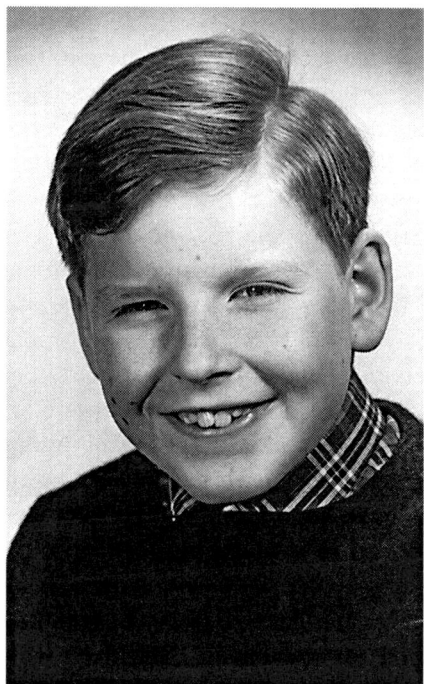
21. Jervoise

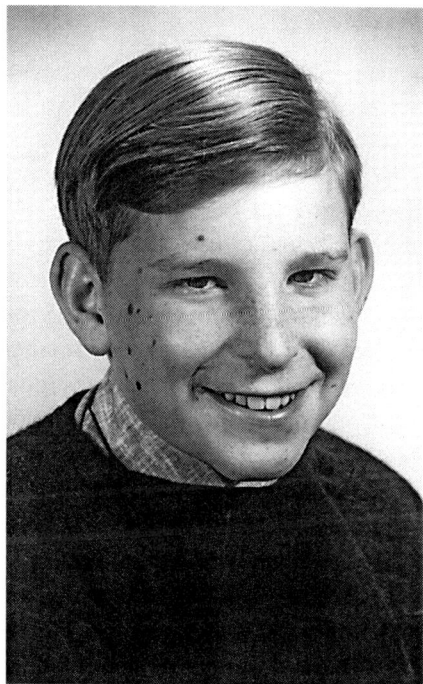
22. Michael

who by this stage was unwell and bedridden. Roman wrote to my father, giving him his mother's address and telephone number. This occurred some time after Khrushchev's secret speech in 1956 when restrictions began to be lifted. My father said that the letter was addressed in a very odd way but nevertheless got to him. When the letter arrived, my parents spent a whole day trying to telephone my grandmother. The telephonist had never heard of Estonia, there was no direct line and it had to be routed through Leningrad but eventually they got through. When contact was made, my grandmother burst into tears. My father asked her in that first conversation whether she wanted to come to live in England. To her question whether that was possible he replied: "Everything is possible."

The British processed the necessary papers for my grandmother to come after six weeks. The Soviet authorities took eighteen months to give permission for a bedridden old lady to join her son in England. The assumption was that the only reason she was allowed to leave was that it meant the state would no longer have to provide any medical care and her room would be useful. Before she left, she was asked to provide 36 photographs of herself. My parents surmised that one was sent to every exit of the Soviet Union so that no one else would use this opportunity to try and leave the country. In order to obtain the necessary papers, my grandmother had to put together her biography. She did so honestly but it was returned to her by her ex-pupils who were now in positions of authority in the Communist Party. They explained to her that if, for example, she said that her father had been a merchant then it was unlikely that she would be given permission to leave. Her pupils sat round the table in her room and rewrote her biography to fit the desired end. Her father in this account became a gardener as he had always loved gardening. Nearer the time for her departure, she was visited by the NKVD. Normally, anyone leaving the country would have been called into the police precinct but she was too ill for this to happen. When the NKVD car drew up, all the inhabitants of the block of flats were thrown into disarray. My grandmother later described the NKVD officers as very polite and well mannered young men, although my father reminded her not to be taken in by appearances. They gave her all kinds of information, including details of my English grandfather who had been Governor-General of the Sudan during the war. My grandmother knew that my father was married but not very much about my mother. The NKVD officers also gave her a toothbrush as hers was several years old and a rare commodity. They said it would be shaming to go to the West with such an old one. They also gave her some new underwear as hers was old and patched. She flew from the Baltic States to Brussels, and then to London and was brought to Cambridge in an ambulance. She lived with us for over two years and died on February 25 1961. Many years later, when my father died, my brother Jervoise asked about the date of my grandmother's death. When it transpired that both my father and grandmother had died on February 25 the coincidence seemed remarkable and served to emphasize the strength of the bond between mother and son.

Lightning Source UK Ltd.
Milton Keynes UK
UKOW03f2047220517
301735UK00002B/544/P